The American Civil War

The American Civil War

A popular illustrated history
of the years 1861-1865 as seen
by the artist-correspondents
who were there

by Earl Schenck Miers

A Ridge Press Book | Golden Press, New York

PREPARED AND PRODUCED BY
THE RIDGE PRESS, INC.
PRINTED IN THE UNITED STATES
OF AMERICA BY WESTERN PRINTING
AND LITHOGRAPHING COMPANY.
PUBLISHED BY GOLDEN PRESS,
ROCKEFELLER CENTER,
NEW YORK 20, NEW YORK

Editor-in-Chief: Jerry Mason
Editor: Adolph Suehsdorf
Art Director: Albert A. Squillace
Associate Editor: Edwina Hazard Glen
Associate Editor: Evelyn Claire Hannon
Art Associate: Leon Bolognese
Art Associate: Tony Frisina

PICTURE CREDITS FOR COLOR PORTFOLIO:

Chicago Historical Society: Pages 147, 169 bottom.

Library of Congress: Pages 145, 146, 152-7, 158 inset, 160-3, 166-8, 169 top, 172-6.

New-York Historical Society: Pages 148-9, 164, 170, 171 right.

The Official Records of the Union and Confederate Armies 1861-1865: Pages 150-1.

Prints Division, New York Public Library: Pages 158-9.

Rutgers University Library: Page 171 left.

*This book is dedicated,
with affection,
to my comrades-in-arms
with whom so many battles of the armchair
have been fought:*

PAUL M. ANGLE

LLOYD A. DUNLOP

CARL HAVERLIN

E. B. LONG

DAVID C. MEARNS

RALPH G. NEWMAN

*and to the ever-faithful staffs of
the Library of Congress,
the Library of the New York University Club,
and the Rutgers University Library*

CONTENTS

INTRODUCTION

1861
*"Northern Soldiers,
as Painted by the Artist
of the Mobile Advertiser."*

In Acton, Maine, on December 26, 1860, Ralph Farnham died at the age of one hundred and four years, five months, and nineteen days.

"Ain't there angels in the room?" Mr. Farnham asked his daughter.

"Father, do you think there are?"

"Oh, yes," Mr. Farnham said. "The room is full of them. They have come to assist me home."

And all America hoped that the angels had been sent to lead across the Dark Valley its last survivor of the Battle of Bunker Hill. Not many weeks before, Massachusetts' Governor Nathaniel P. Banks and his wife had visited Ralph Farnham and the old fellow had never been "so embarrassed" as when Mrs. Banks kissed him. He could not understand that even in his one-hundred-and-fourth year he remained a symbol of youth—a symbol of that courageous struggle when the nation had won its independence.

On the very evening when death closed the eyes of Ralph Farnham, Major Robert Anderson moved his small Federal garrison from Fort Moultrie, on the land side of Charleston, to Fort Sumter, guardian of the city's harbor, and the act had been committed that ultimately would divide the nation into warring factions. Thus in a small news item from Acton, Maine, and in a bulletin of devastating impact from Charleston, South Carolina, the country's proud past met its trembling future.

When another Christmas arrived, homes both North and South already were draped in mourning for their honored dead. Many battles had been fought—in Virginia at Big Bethel, Rich Mountain, Manassas, Cheat Mountain, and Drainesville, among others; in Missouri at Wilson's Creek, Lexington, Booneville, and Belmont; in South Carolina at Port Royal. Pritchard's Mills, Maryland—Santa Rosa, Florida—Alamosa, New Mexico—West Liberty and Piketown, Kentucky—week by week, across the map of America, place names were popping into the news as stories were told of raiders in the night burning homes and killing people believed to hold the wrong shade of sympathy. Like a prairie-grass fire, the war was racing on the wind. In New York, an enterprising George Leary was planning to build a hotel to accommodate tourists certain to flock to the first great battleground of the war at Bull Run, and in St. Louis a Mrs. Willow went to jail for selling poisoned pies to soldiers at Camp Benton.

Hate and fear, faith and loyalty, principle and passion, in all levels of American life, were caught up in the great conflict. Men of equal honor fought to save the Union and fought to secure southern independence. Others, perhaps just as creditable, fought simply to win and have

1862

*"Jeff Davis's New Coachman (his Old
One having come over to McDowell) driving
him in the Direction of the Last Ditch."*

the bad business ended. But always a deeper element was involved, for the war contained a mystery, and its basic battleground in the end would be a tormented American conscience. "Can treaties be more faithfully enforced between aliens than laws can among friends?" Lincoln had asked in his First Inaugural. "Suppose you go to war, you cannot fight always; and when, after much loss on both sides, and no gain on either, you cease fighting, the identical old questions as to terms of intercourse are again upon you . . ." But the war changed Lincoln as it changed America. Four years later, re-elected to the presidency, he probed the mystery of a war that still continued:

"Neither party expected for the war the magnitude and duration which it has already attained. . . . Each looked for an easier triumph, and a result less fundamental and astounding. Both read the same Bible, and pray to the same God; and each invokes His aid against the other. It may seem strange that any men should dare to ask a just God's assistance in wringing their bread from the sweat of other men's faces; but let us judge not, that we be not judged. The prayers of both could not be answered—that of neither has been answered fully."

So in the end the war revealed its secret. It was a war being contested finally for an ideal of freedom, and it would have only one indisputable achievement when it was over—slavery would be dead as a legal institution in America.

From 1861 to 1865, then, the epic story that the American people revealed to the world was of the struggle of a nation's conscience. The revolution that was accomplished—in large measure, without either the comprehension or consent of its participants—became one of the best documented stories in human history. A nation, expending its blood to emerge in a new dimension, became fascinated by the image of its own torment. Battle artists for *Harper's, Frank Leslie's,* and the New York *Illustrated News,* among others, were everywhere. And if, as Louis M. Starr has observed in his pioneering study of reporters in the war, "The woodcutter's awl and chisel, the artist's impressionistic pencil, tended to clothe the war in romantic pageantry," the result was adored by the people nonetheless, and the psychological effect was to sustain the struggle to its last acts of sacrifice and violence.

Exaggerations were common and, to the soldiers in the field, often laughable. The Cincinnati *Gazette's* sneering remark that, "Those who draw their conceptions of the appearance of the rebel soldiery from *Harper's Weekly* would

14

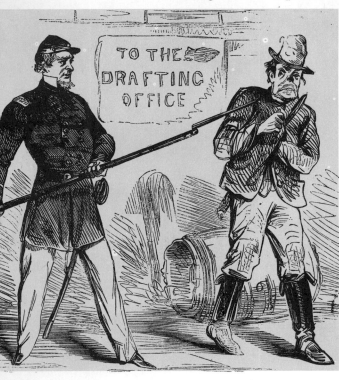

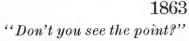

1864
Lincoln reacts to McClellan,
his political opponent.

hardly recognize one on sight," might be ascribed to a certain professional bias, but even more impartial observers — Starr quotes the executive committee of the New-York Historical Society in 1864 among them—cautioned the public that the works of the battle artists "are not always reliable." Cavalryman Francis W. Tupper, writing home from Vicksburg, lumped journalists and artists in the same class; one reason why "Vicksburg and other places come to be captured so often" was because the members of the Bohemian Brigade would send "any report they hear without ascertaining whether it is true or not." Yet studying a sketch in *Frank Leslie's* of the way "Secesh ladies make their appearance at our office to get an order on the commissary for rations," Cavalryman Tupper was compelled to admit that the representation was "a facsimile of the scene."

The obvious conclusion to be drawn was that the reproductions in the nation's illustrated weeklies were as good or bad as the professional scruples of the men who drew them. The moody Winslow Homer was always an impressionist and Thomas Nast inescapably a political satirist. Theodore Russell Davis, who represented *Harper's Weekly* on the Peninsula and before Vicksburg and who marched with Sherman to the sea, in the estimation of General John A. Logan had

seen more of the war at first hand than any man living. An indication of Davis's craftsmanship was his assignment in 1879 to design the porcelain service for the White House. Lean Alfred R. Waud, who switched from the New York *Illustrated News* to *Harper's Weekly* after First Manassas, was a faithful reporter in wash drawing and prose. *Frank Leslie's* Henri Lovie was no less a faithful observer of what he delineated; he once estimated that he traveled a thousand miles on horseback in a three-month period to find the materials that his quick pen had sketched. Still another artist for *Frank Leslie's* who was a pre-eminently accurate chronicler of army life and the battlefield was Edwin Forbes, who possessed a rare gift for capturing the homesickness of soldiers in camp and the dreariness of most scenes of war.

Winslow Homer, at twenty-six, was the high-priced member of the artist corps, and *Harper's* paid him as much as $60 for a two-page spread. The others, often working for no better than space rates, could only justify the risks they took and the hardships they encountered by the satisfaction they derived from their labors. Pluck and ingenuity they possessed, heaven knows. Prime examples were Davis, the *Harper's* man, helping himself to the new uniform of a dead Confederate in full view of the enemy, and

1865

*"Give me your hand, Comrade!
We have each lost a Leg for
the good cause; but, thank God,
we never lost heart."*

Arthur Lumley of the New York *Illustrated News* going aloft 1,000 feet in one of Dr. Lowe's newfangled gas-filled balloons to sketch war from a fresh approach. They were, in the main, a vastly talented crew. In later years Eugene Benson, a *Leslie's* man, was frequently exhibited in the Royal Academy, and Henry Mosler, a *Harper's* artist, won the cross of France's Legion of Honor.

There was little of the war that they failed to observe and to sketch, and if, on occasion, the details of their battle scenes sometimes impressed the veteran as ludicrous, their drawings still comprised the image of war that the majority of people saw and believed. A great deal of what they did delineate was thoroughly realistic—and perhaps as accurately as any group they documented the grand emotion of an enormous civil war that very often was as much a conflict of personal spirit and conscience as it was of charging bayonets and roaring cannon.

It is the war in this human dimension that this book seeks to recapture—the war of the eye sustaining the heart and of perception supporting the mind. For the sake of continuity, the book has been focused upon the war issues of *Harper's Weekly*. But a large amount of material has been drawn from other illustrated newspapers of the time. In addition, a number of splendid draw-

ings have been taken from *The London Illustrated Times, The Confederate Soldier in the Civil War,* edited by Ben La Bree (Louisville: 1895) and *The Soldier in the Civil War,* edited in two volumes by Paul F. Mottelay and T. Campbell-Copeland (New York: 1885). Special acknowledgement for the illustrations reproduced in the section in full color is made to the Library of Congress, the New York Public Library, the New-York Historical Society, the Chicago Historical Society, and the Rutgers University Library.

In the compilation of a work of this scope and complexity, an author is constantly aware of the devoted services of others who add pleasure and competence to the completed effort. Individuals to whom I would like to express special appreciation include: Adolph Suehsdorf, who makes an art of the editor's craft; Al Squillace, who brought good-humored skill to the production problems that this volume entailed; Lloyd A. Dunlop of the Library of Congress, who researched its collection of prints for me; and my close friend and good wife, Starling W. Miers, who was, once again, a capable amanuensis.

Earl Schenck Miers

EDISON, NEW JERSEY

THE APPLE CUT

THE D[...]

HUSKING CORN

THE B[...]

"This is essentially a People's contest... whose leading object is to elevate the condition of men—to lift artificial weights from all shoulders—to clear the paths of laudable pursuit for all—to afford all, an unfettered start, and a fair chance, in the race of life."

Abraham Lincoln

MESSAGE TO CONGRESS, JULY 4, 1861

SIX CRITICAL WEEKS

MAJOR ANDERSON LEADS FEDERAL SOLDIERS IN PRAYER AFTER SEIZING SUMTER.

Where palmettos grow
Christmas arouses gay thoughts
—but of war, not peace

December, 1860–April, 1861

In December, 1860, John Haskell was a student at South Carolina College in Columbia. His head was filled with war talk; the state "had gone wild on the subject of secession." College boys prayed for confirmation of Lincoln's election, for that news "would sweep the South from the Union over the opposition of those who did not favor secession and were regarded almost as traitors."

Swiftly, once it was certain that "Black Republicanism" had triumphed, South Carolina moved to fulfill a dream now two generations old. On December 17, in the Baptist Church in Columbia, South Carolina's secession convention met and old James L. Petigru, a testy Unionist, quipped: "It looks like a church, but is now a lunatic asylum; go right there and you will find one hundred and sixty-four maniacs within."

A smallpox epidemic forced an adjournment next day to Charleston. In this proud, historic city excited people thronged streets and open squares on December 20 when in St. Andrew's Hall the ordinance of secession was put to a vote: ayes 169, nays 0. Charleston became joyously delirious. Church bells tolled. All business was suspended. Cheering men and women embraced, danced, and toasted their new freedom.

Yet beneath the holiday atmosphere ugly tensions gripped Charleston. Old men marched and drilled, expecting a Negro uprising. Fretful eyes looked across the harbor toward antiquated Fort Moultrie, held by a small Federal garrison.

Major Robert Anderson, in command at Moultrie, knew he could not defend this fort, with cracked walls and sand hills heaped by sea breezes upon its shore front. Unexpectedly, on Christmas night, he occupied Fort Sumter, which could only be approached by water and controlled the sea lanes into Charleston. With daylight, people awoke to the realization that they had been tricked while they slumbered! This was war!

Frantically, crabby, bumbling President Buchanan tried to patch up some kind of compromise with an aroused South until he was out of office, when Mr. Lincoln could reap the wild harvest of the abolitionist seeds he had sown. While the country heaved around him, "Old Buck" hedged and dickered and feared for his life.

In the North, "Our Bob" Anderson became almost a folk hero. Songs celebrated his audacity. Even burlesque shows honored him with tableaux.

THE FLAG OF THE CONFEDERACY.

BUCHANAN'S DREAM—TO PASS THE CRISIS TO LINCOLN.

An old friend asked Jefferson Davis what he saw in the future, and the recently elected President of the Confederacy replied: "A war, long and bloody." The Charleston Mercury *reported Davis's arrival before cheering crowds in Montgomery, Alabama. Gone was the time for compromise, he told them, resolutely. Henceforth, opponents of the South must "smell Southern powder and feel Southern steel."*

Quickly, after Anderson moved into Sumter, Mississippi, Florida, Alabama, Georgia, Louisiana, and Texas followed South Carolina out of the Union. On February 4, delegates from these states poured into Montgomery, Alabama, set on seven hills like ancient Rome. Within a fortnight a provisional government for the Confederate States was organized, a constitution adopted that acknowledged the right of property in slaves, and Jefferson Davis inaugurated as President. Except for Sumter, Pickens in Pensacola Bay, and two small installations off the Florida coast, all Federal forts in these states had been seized, along with every arsenal, customhouse, and lighthouse. Without bloodshed the South had achieved a revolution and made a nation!

Abraham Lincoln once was described by his law partner as "the most secretive, reticent, shut-mouthed man that ever lived," and now, journeying from Springfield to Washington, he was reluctant to comment on the swiftly moving events in Montgomery. Many who read of the little actress Maggie Mitchell dancing on the Stars and Stripes at Davis's inaugural were disturbed by Mr. Lincoln's evasiveness and wondered if the President-elect wasn't another bungler after the cut of Buchanan. But twice Mr. Lincoln revealed depths of inner resolution. In Indianapolis, he asked: "By what principle of original right is it that one-fiftieth or one-ninetieth of a great nation, by calling themselves a State, have the right to break up and ruin that nation as a matter of original right?" And in Trenton, he told the New Jersey Assembly: "It may be necessary to put the foot down firmly."

A martial spirit swept the South. In the heady excitement of organizing a hundred military companies, like the "Southern Rejectors of Old Abe" or the "Cherokee Lincoln Killers," no one cared what Lincoln said. The New York *Tribune* found everyone in Charleston "spilin' for a muss," venting their spleen one day on Anderson and his garrison still in Sumter and the next on North Carolina and Virginia for staying out of the Confederacy. In mid-February the dapper little New Orleans Creole, General Pierre Gustave Toutant Beauregard, arrived to take over command of the city's defenses. A soldier of purpose, attended by a Spanish barber and valet, Beauregard captured Charlestonian hearts. "We are all delighted with him," Governor Pickens wrote Davis.

A divided nation, wavering between peace and the sword, waited for some clue as to whither Lincoln would turn. Growing disappointment in the President-elect mounted when an outrageous newspaper report pictured him sneaking through hostile Baltimore in the dead of night disguised in a Scotch-plaid cap and long military cloak. On March 4, Buchanan's weary ordeal ended when at noon he called at Willard's to escort Mr. Lincoln to the Capitol. Pennsylvania Avenue, rooftops, and street intersections were lined with soldiers on guard against a myriad of threatened assassins. Where the wing of the Capitol flanked the inaugural stand, riflemen stood poised and ready at each window.

As unruffled as the new black suit he wore, Mr. Lincoln spoke temperately. He ended on a passionate belief: "We are not enemies, but friends."

"The mystic chords of memory," Lincoln continued, "stretching from every battlefield, and patriot's grave, to every living heart and hearthstone . . . will yet swell the chorus of Union, when again touched, as surely they will be, by the better angels of our nature."

Kentucky-born Major Robert Anderson, who was sympathetic toward slavery, had been selected for command at Fort Sumter as a "safe" man by bold pro-secessionists in Buchanan's Cabinet. But Anderson's devotion to duty came first. His guides in life, a relative said, were the Ten Commandments, the U.S. Constitution, and Army Regulations.

An unpleasant surprise awaited Lincoln. Anderson reported that supplies were running low at Sumter and within the next few days the fort either must be provisioned or abandoned. To render the needed relief, Anderson claimed, would require a force of 20,000 "good and well-disciplined men." The President took the problem to his Cabinet, but Postmaster-General Montgomery Blair alone believed that reinforcing Sumter was worth the risk. He was reminded, Lincoln told his secretaries, of the children of Israel on the shore of the Red Sea. "Stand still and see the salvation of the Lord," advised Moses. He likewise should wait, Mr. Lincoln thought.

Among those who made the mistake of underestimating the President as a kind of Simple Susan was Secretary of State William H. Seward, still baffled over how this "prairie politician" had beaten him to the presidency. Dickering off-the-record with Confederate peace commissioners in Washington, Seward promised that Sumter would not be relieved, reflecting his own opinion that there was no point in starting a war to "regain a useless and unnecessary position."

Patiently the President continued to await "the salvation of the Lord." A scheme to let Sumter go, while saving face by seizing Fort Pickens in Pensacola Bay, was carefully considered and rejected. As the weeks slipped by, without any evidence to support Seward's suave promises that Sumter would be surrendered, Southern suspicions deepened. On April Fool's Day a restive

Beauregard wrote to Davis: "Batteries here ready to open Wednesday or Thursday. What instructions?"

Within Sumter, counting on his fingers the days until starvation would become a reality, Anderson was the unhappiest man in America. Rumors that he and his garrison were to be deserted came through Confederate sources. Stung to the quick, Anderson told Washington: "After thirty years of service I do not wish it said that I have treasonably abandoned a post and turned over to unauthorized persons public property intrusted to my charge." But Mr. Lincoln had reached a decision. On April 10, informed that a Federal fleet for the relief of Sumter was at sea, the Montgomery government instructed Beauregard to "at once demand [Sumter's] evacuation, and if this is refused, proceed in such a manner as you may determine, to reduce it."

Next day, fed up with the "gross perfidy" of Mr. Lincoln's Administration, the Confederate commissioners quit Washington. Like gentlemen arranging a duel, Beauregard's emissaries rowed out to offer Anderson his choice of surrender or a "useless effusion of blood." Charleston reverberated with the roll of drums, the tramp of soldiers over cobbled streets, the rattle of ambulances going to their posts, the throaty orders of the ancients in the Home Guard awaiting Negro insurrection. At four-thirty on the morning of April 12, the city heard the dull roar of a mortar. War had come!

As the secession crisis quickened, General Beauregard had resigned as superintendent of West Point, roundly denouncing those bureaucrats in Washington who refused to pay his expenses back to New Orleans so that he could oppose the national government. Wherever he went adoring crowds followed. He was called the "little Napoleon in Gray."

The burning fuse of the shell marked its course among the stars. The shell descended with increasing velocity and burst within the fort—a perfect hit. To save ammunition, Anderson waited until daylight to return fire and then lobbed only an occasional shot into the city. Mercilessly, Rebel guns pounded the island fort that had become a national symbol—of honor to the North, of insult to the South.

Early newspaper bulletins, read by stunned crowds in the cities of the North, emphasized the accuracy of southern marksmanship: "Two of Fort Sumter's guns have been silenced....It is reported that a Breach has been made in the southeast wall." Charlestonians tumbled from houses that rocked under the concussion of the big guns ringing the city. Along the Battery (upper right), with its handsome bronze lantern towering twenty-five feet overhead, a holiday spirit reigned after the "tears and prayers" of long weeks of waiting for this moment of release, in the words of the Mercury, from "hostile hirelings of Abolition hate and Northern tyranny." Within Sumter (lower right; above), gunners worried down a taste of salt pork and, to save manpower, fired only the casemate guns.

Mary Boykin Chesnut, whose husband had been one of Beauregard's emissaries warning Anderson of the attack, awoke to the crash of the guns. "I sprang out of bed," she said, "and on my knees, prostrate, I prayed as I never prayed before." Awed spectators thronged the rooftops in Charleston. "We could distinctly see the flames amidst the smoke," Emma Holmes recalled. "All the barracks were on fire."

Within Sumter an angry gunner in Captain Doubleday's command saw Charlestonians viewing the grim spectacle. So they wanted a taste of war? The bitter Yankee aimed two 42-pounders at the onlookers. The first shot struck about fifty yards short, and bounding over the heads of the astonished spectators crashed into the Moultrie House, an hotel. By the second shot, the gawpers were scampering for cover.

Yet small was the triumph of these moments for Anderson and his beleaguered handful of troops as the day wore on. Across Charleston Harbor breezes rising to gale force dimmed the hope that Federal warships, standing off the bar, could bring reinforcements. Through the night, though the guns of Sumter fell silent, the Confederate batteries kept up their savage rain of shells, and with daylight red-hot shot, dropping into the fort, started numerous fires. Soon even the powder magazine was enveloped by flames.

But these lively times along the Palmetto Coast were only part of the drama Sumter produced. Most of the dispatches foreshadowing the ultimate fall of the fort did not reach the North till Saturday morning. The calmest man in Washington, said the President's secretaries, was Mr. Lincoln, whose "inner consciousness was abroad in the wide realm of possibilities, busily searching out the dim and difficult path towards things to be." The State of Connecticut, rallying to the national emergency, designated the following day as "Battle Sunday." In Baltimore, two sympathizers in Southern cockades were assaulted and mobbed. Angry Philadelphians, rope in hand, sought out the editor of a secessionist weekly, but

he already was in flight to Richmond. In New York City, irate crowds marched down Nassau and Ann Streets, looking for James Gordon Bennett, whose *Herald* so long had advocated concession. "Come out, you yellow-bellied secessionist!" roared Mr. Bennett's disgruntled readers. In Chicago, a newspaperman reported succinctly: "Everybody was up to war point."

Early in the afternoon of April 13, Anderson decided that his only choice was to surrender. For thirty-four hours he had defended Sumter against overwhelming odds. Now the fort's quarters were entirely burned, its main gates destroyed, its gorge walls shattered, its magazine surrounded by fire, and the door sealed from the effects of the heat. Though the bombardment had produced no casualties, one Union soldier was killed and several were injured when a gun exploded while Anderson was saluting the flag after the surrender.

Bells ringing within Charleston gave news of the victory. Like sea gulls, boats darted from all directions across the bay as excited hordes tried to see for themselves the damage to the fort. Almost as though carried on the wind, the glad tidings of Sumter's capitulation spread through the South. People ran trembling along southern streets, embracing total strangers. Meanwhile, in New York old Horace Greeley, more owlish than ever, watched as two laboring men read a report that Anderson had been forced to haul down the flag. Tears slid down their cheeks and Greeley had his comment upon the events that had shaken the nation:

"Sumter is lost, but freedom is saved!"

GIRDING FOR WAR

*In unruly Baltimore
and in a tavern's dusty hallway,
the war quickly grows ugly*

DRUMMING OUT ALBANY VOLUNTEERS WHO REFUSED TO TAKE THE OATH.

THE EIGHTH MASSACHUSETTS REGIMENT IN THE ROTUNDA OF THE CAPITOL, WASHINGTON.

April, 1860–May, 1861

Giddy-headed, North and South rushed to war. "It was a wild time—a continuous day of fevered enthusiasm," a Georgian remembered. "Men, women and children participated in the exaltation of patriotic spirit." The comment easily could have applied to any southern crossroads and especially in Virginia, North Carolina, and Tennessee, which joined the Confederacy after Sumter. Stirred by blaring bands, owners of plantations and sharecroppers became comrades-in-arms as they organized companies of "Lincoln Killers." Only weeks before they had said that if Black Republicanism won the South must expect a wave of Negro uprisings. Now, spoiling for a fight, they marched off, leaving the home front in the care of these same Negroes.

But the North responded as illogically, for war had little real meaning. Few, indeed, were those who ever had seen a soldier in uniform. Many borrowed from overseas the image of themselves as warriors. Along almost any northern street they could be seen waddling by in the baggy yellow trousers of Algerian Zouaves. The New York 39th in the plumed hats of the Italian Bersaglieri became the Garibaldi Guards; the New York 79th in sporrans and kilts were Highlanders. Time brought bitter wisdom. With the realization that they were involved in an affair that was no mere Dixie knife-fight, a great many —like the poor devils on the left—preferred the shame of wearing a white feather to service at the front, under fire.

The cobbled streets of northern cities echoed now to the tramp of marching feet. The Battery in New York City was ablaze with the Zouave uniforms of firemen who turned to soldiering (above), and Broadway (right) responded with gay cheers as the New York 7th passed under a banner declaring "Jeff Davis, Jeff Davis beware of the day, when the 7th shall meet thee in battle array." Dubuque, Iowa (lower right) cheered regiments aboard river steamers.

The vast majority of northern citizens was stoically resolved to restore the Union at any cost. In Salisbury, Connecticut, George Coffin offered the government one hundred tons of iron to be molded into cannon balls; a report from Cincinnati declared that "merchants have stopped shipping goods to the South"; New York City read that Commodore Vanderbilt had placed his steamships at the disposal of the government; and Lincoln's lifelong political rival, Stephen A. Douglas, stumped the Midwest in behalf of the national policy, shouting: "Let no man attempt to sunder what Divine Providence has rendered indivisible!"

Washington, wrote the President's secretary, John G. Nicolay, became "a city under siege." Stores were closed and streets echoed to the footfalls of "hurrying patrols." Governmental clerks —with "the taint of treason" in their hearts— resigned by the hundreds and hurried back to their southern homes. Although on the surface Lincoln appeared calm and cheerful, no one rec-

ognized more keenly than Nicolay that intense anxiety haunted the President. One day, overcome with worry, he cried: "I begin to believe that there is no North."

Communications were slow and the President despaired needlessly. The 75,000 state troops that he wanted to serve the national army for many months were on the move. Had he called for three times the number, as Stephen Douglas had advised, the North would have given them with equal willingness.

Halltown, Virginia (right), was the rendezvous on the afternoon of April 18, 1861, for Southern troops sent to capture the Federal armory at Harpers Ferry, where stalked the ghost of old John Brown. Only a handful of Union soldiers protected the place, and Richmond depended on the workmen at the armory—Virginians all— to remain "true to their soil." Pickets gave warning of the Rebel approach through the night. Suddenly a mighty explosion shook the earth and soon the surrounding mountains were alight with "the steady glare of ascending flames" (below). Many machineshops and a rifleworks were captured intact, however, causing the fretful artist of these sketches to ask his readers: "Brethren, what has forced this fatal necessity upon us?" Clearly the North must quicken its war effort.

On the day after flames destroyed the armory at Harpers Ferry, troops of the Massachusetts 6th reached pro-secessionist Baltimore. Arriving at the Philadelphia and Baltimore Railroad station, the Bay State soldiers were forced to transfer in cars drawn by horses to the Baltimore and Ohio station in order to reach Washington. This route covered more than a mile and crossed the heart of a city where the anger had mounted to the boiling point at this "invasion" of its sovereign soil.

The Yankees, already alerted to approaching danger by the insults hurled by Baltimoreans the day before at Pennsylvania troops passing by the same route through the city, tried to give no offense. The band was ordered to play "safe" tunes—and, most of all, not to render the rousing strains of "Dixie." Yet, prudently, the quartermaster issued twenty rounds of ball cartridges to each man.

Amid hostile, jeering crowds, the Massachusetts soldiers began their journey between the railroad depots. All went well until, near Commerce Street, the brake failed on a car. Then, remembered Frederic Emory, an eyewitness, the mob "began to attack the occupants with stones. Windows were broken, and a few of the soldiers were hurt, but not seriously." The driver lost his head and backed the car away, giving the mob a sense of forcing a retreat.

Across the bridge on Pratt Street the unruly Baltimoreans threw up a barricade, "Paris fashion." The tracks and pavement were torn up for a distance of perhaps fifty yards. Colonel Edward F. Jones, leading his Massachusetts boys on foot in a double column, gave the order to force a passage through a crowd emboldened by a waving Confederate flag and screams for Jeff Davis. John W. Hanson, chaplain-historian of the regiment, attested to the scene of bloodshed that followed as the troops passed along Pratt Street:

"...pistols and guns were fired at them from the windows and doors of stores and houses; and our boys, getting a little accustomed to the strange circumstances in which they were placed, loaded their guns as they marched...and, whenever they saw a hostile demonstration they took as good aim as they could, and fired." It was far from a one-sided battle, by Emory's account: "Some of the rioters fought like madmen." A soldier, taking dead aim at a rioter, had his gun fail to go off, when, Emory said, "the rioters rushed forward, seized the gun, wrested it by an almost superhuman effort from the soldier's grasp, and plunged the bayonet through the man's shoulder...."

Again and again the soldiers fired as Colonel Jones gave the command to his soldiers to advance on the "double quick."

Grudgingly, the Baltimore rioters gave ground. Twelve of their number were dead. And so also were four soldiers: Whitney and Ladd, mechanics of Lowell; Taylor, a decorative painter, and Needham, a plasterer, both of Boston.

In a depressed mood Lincoln spoke next day to the wounded soldiers of the Massachusetts 6th. Later the President grumbled to Nicolay that all talk of the New York 7th being on its way to defend Washington was simply "a myth." So, too, was the report that Rhode Island troops were en route to the capital. "You are the only real thing," Lincoln told Nicolay.

Then, on April 25, the New York 7th reached Washington and marched up Pennsylvania Avenue. The city was swept with holiday gaiety as the smartly clad New Yorkers stepped briskly along with flags floating, bands playing, people cheering, and youngsters shouting and waving small banners. Nicolay wrote: "For the first time, the combined spirit and power of Liberty entered the nation's capital." Lincoln's anxious waiting had ended. There *was* a North.

What filled the days of the President as the nation organized for war? In the week following the arrival of the New York 7th his activities included addressing the Frontier Guard on April 26: "I have desired as sincerely as any man—I

Confederate Cabinet (left to right): Attorney-General Benjamin, Navy Secretary Mallory, Treasury Secretary Menninger, Vice-President Stephens, War Secretary Walker, President Davis, Postmaster-General Reagen, Secretary of State Toombs.

sometimes think more than any other man—that our present difficulties might be settled without the shedding of blood." On April 27, a grim aftermath of the Baltimore riot, he suspended the writ of habeas corpus along the line of troop movements between Philadelphia and Washington. On the twenty-eighth he visited the quarters of the New York 7th in the House Chamber of the Capitol. On the twenty-ninth he had his picture taken with the citizen-soldiers of the Cassius M. Clay Battalion. On the thirtieth he gave an audience to three Potawatomi Indians. At a band concert on the White House lawn on May 1 he spoke briefly, and on the following day he was

Federal Cabinet (left to right): Post-master-General Blair, Interior Secretary Smith, Treasury Secretary Chase, President Lincoln, Secretary of State Seward, War Secretary Cameron, Attorney-General Bates, Navy Secretary Welles.

engaged in ceremonies which saw the flag raised over the Patent Office.

Affairs large and small also occupied Jefferson Davis in Montgomery, a pleasant city of hills and wide, sandy streets. Its two hotels were crowded to the bursting point, and those who had to stay in Montgomery Hall bore proof that it retained the stench of cattlemen who had used it for years. Slave auctions attracted many buyers who were killing time till they could see the President. Everyone had an opinion of what Davis should or should not do. An eyewitness described Montgomery as Washington on a smaller scale where "every knot of men had its griev-ances" and where "state secrets were openly discussed in this Curbstone Congress."

The Confederate President possessed a number of grievances of his own, among them the fact that in quitting Harpers Ferry the Union soldiers had destroyed "public buildings" which, under the United States Constitution, had been provided "for the common defense." To Davis a good legalistic argument was as precious as life's breath, and years afterward he berated the Washington government for condoning this destruction of property that belonged to each state equally with the others. "How unreasonable, how blind with rage" the government in Washington had become, Davis told his callers in Montgomery, who must have listened politely and nodded and sometimes wondered to what extremes the President would carry a point.

Meanwhile, Lincoln and his Cabinet believed that the only regret they owed the nation over the affair at Harpers Ferry was for the fact that more of its installations had not burned. They hoped for better luck at Norfolk.

The U.S. frigate Cumberland *catches the* Merrimack *at anchor off the Gosport Navy Yard in Norfolk on the night of April 20, 1861 (above). Fires started about midnight destroy two immense ship houses. One contained the entire frame of a 74-gun vessel.*

When American naval men spoke of the vessel that above all others was a joy to the eye the *Merrimack* was the ship they mentioned. Sturdy live-oak frames gave her beauty, and everyone who had been aboard her bragged that she was "fast and handy" under sail. Commissioned at Boston late in 1855, the *Merrimack* had sailed to Europe, through the West Indies, and around the Horn to the Pacific as an object lesson to the world of America's growing prowess as a builder of ships.

On April 20—the day after Virginia seceded —a Federal fleet under Commodore McCauley steamed through Hampton Roads determined that this prize, among others, should not fall into Confederate hands. Later the Union's Secretary of the Navy, Gideon Welles, would write a tight-lipped report about a "faithful" but

"feeble" officer who had proved "incompetent for the crisis," which was as good a face as any navy man could put on a contest that had been lost to a land-lubberly railroad president.

Yet William Mahone, boss of the Norfolk and Petersburg Railroad, was a devoted Virginian with the flexibility of mind essential to running a small railroad in that age. As McCauley brought his vessels up the Elizabeth River, a ruse to make the navy men believe they would be overwhelmed by Confederate forces if they lingered long, filled Mahone's inspired brain. He ordered trains shuttled in and out of the Norfolk station to give the impression that a vast army was arriving. Under his lead, bands of civilians whooped and shouted in a wild reception to this imaginary horde of arriving warriors.

How well Mahone's trick succeeded would be revealed in the final report of the hasty affair at Norfolk. True, three old ships-of-the-line, two frigates, two sloops-of-war, and a brig were sunk or partially wrecked. True, two ship houses were burned. True, the sea valves were opened on the *Merrimack* and flames raced up her masts as she settled in the mud of the Elizabeth River.

But alert Confederate troops rushed into the Gosport Navy Yard that the Federals abandoned too prudently. In succeeding weeks reports filtering into Washington would make uneasy reading for Lincoln and his Cabinet. Not only had the fire been extinguished on the *Merrimack*, but, raised and rechristened the *Virginia*, the pride of the Union Navy was now in dry dock to undergo extensive repairs. So the *Merrimack* endured to fight again—really to rewrite naval history around the world, as events proved.

Life in the South became a mixture of new patterns blended with the old. Across the river from Montgomery, the slaves hoed a cotton field (left) and the President lived in a "White House" rented for $5,000 a year (right). A Negro drummed up recruits for the army (lower left) and doubtless took no heed of the slave auction he passed.

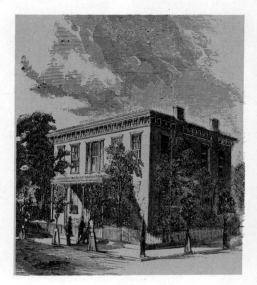

John Hay, who also served Lincoln as a secretary, described a visit to the bivouac occupied by the "magnificent men" in the New York 11th who served under twenty-four-year-old Colonel Elmer Ellsworth: "They played over the sward like kittens, lithe and agile in their strength." A story that Ellsworth's boys had been "terrifying all the maiden antiques" in Washington was attributed by Hay to the "restless brain" of "the press-gang." Ellsworth's soldiers had enlisted in a war to the finish; as the idols of Washington these New York firemen turned warriors for the Union had, as one might well expect, their envious detractors.

When on May 9 a fire broke out in the vicinity of fashionable Willard's Hotel, the men of the New York 11th showed their reputation was deserved. The *Times* reported rapturously how Ellsworth's soldiers raced to the scene, "formed pyramids on each other's shoulders," climbed into windows and scaled lightning rods and within two hours had the blaze under complete control. An unforgettable moment of the day came when two firefighters, lacking a ladder, held a comrade from the eaves by his legs while he played water into the burning building.

In order to defend the national capital, a strip of land in Virginia was needed, and so on May 24 the occupation of Alexandria was ordered. Colonel Ellsworth's Fire Zouaves went down the Potomac on a steamer, anticipating a hard fight for the city, but the Confederate infantry left by

The New York 11th—the Fire Zouaves—were led by Colonel Elmer Ellsworth (center), who had studied law in Lincoln's Springfield office and who became an idol in Washington. Fire breaking out next to Willard's Hotel (left) gave the Zouaves a chance to demonstrate their heroism. The fatal shot (right) that produced the North's first martyr.

train as the Federals entered. Not so easily subdued was the proprietor of the Marshall House—*Harper's Weekly* would call it only "a second-rate tavern"—who flew the Confederate flag in open defiance of the occupying forces.

There was a limit to what Ellsworth's high-spirited nature could endure. With a bounding stride he went up the stairs of the Marshall House, climbed a ladder to the roof, and cut down the flag. The proprietor, snatching his shotgun, dashed into the hall. "I have a trophy," cried Ellsworth—his last words, for the first shot from the double-barrelled gun killed him instantly.

The "murder" of the youthful Ellsworth stunned the North. Scores of poems eulogized his bold act. Washington ministers read to hushed congregations his last letter home: "My darling and ever-loved parents, good-by. God bless, protect, and care for you." No one in the nation felt more keenly than Lincoln the death of Ellsworth. "A boy only," the President commented, writing the young colonel's parents a letter of condolence. "So much of promised usefulness to one's country, and of bright hopes for one's self and friends, have rarely been so suddenly dashed, as in his fall."

Four soldiers, twelve citizens dead on the streets of Baltimore, now a Washington idol struck down in a dim tavern hallway. Grimly, people realized that war was something more than a lark.

CLASH OF ARMS

*Boys, marching off to
battle, stopped to pick berries.
Then they "saw the elephant"*

June–July, 1861

While farm-lads-turned-soldier drilled and waited, loafed and sported, gambled and danced, talked about the eye-opening attractions in Mr. Sinn's Variety Theater or the remarkable doings of the Light sisters whose mother acted as the madam of the establishment, generals and politicians argued over how to finish this war in three months—as promised. Washington, ringed with "the watch-fires of a hundred circling camps," cast worried eyes upon Manassas Junction only thirty miles to the southwest. Here the Confederates had concentrated troops for sound reason—to threaten the national capital while screening Richmond.

Through hot June the impatience mounted to get the war over, with Horace Greeley's New York *Tribune* screaming once a day: "Forward to Richmond!... The Rebel Congress must not be allowed to meet there on the 20th of July!" Lincoln had to live with the political reality. Either he made a military move or lost the confidence of the public. Old Winfield Scott tried to resist the demand for a quick action into Virginia, arguing that the Federal army wasn't ready for a battle and, anyhow, the way to win this war was by a massive advance down the Mississippi River in the fall. The politicians threw up their hands in despair and Lincoln overruled his general-in-chief. Scott did the best he could under the circumstances, calling on a trusted and experienced officer, Brigadier General Irvin McDowell, to present a plan for a campaign into Virginia.

McDowell argued sensibly. No Federal movement could be kept secret; therefore, any plan must accept the fact that at the first sign of danger the Confederates would attempt to reinforce their 25,000 troops at Manassas Junction. To prevent this reinforcement, McDowell said, the Rebel force under General Joseph E. Johnston, at Harpers Ferry, must be driven off. Federals under sixty-nine-year-old Robert Patterson were sent to handle Johnston, but after crossing the Potomac, Patterson lost both his nerve and energy and when mid-July arrived, nine miles separated him from Johnston. For McDowell, who would order the Army of the Potomac forward on July 16, Patterson's hesitancy would have the fatal effect of permitting Johnston to move wherever he wished.

Nor was that the sum of the factors working against McDowell. Washington still was overrun with Confederate spies, and in a residence near the White House, on the morning McDowell moved, a lady breakfasted with a governmental clerk who had brought her the Federal plan. Soon the clerk was speeding to Manassas Junction where Beauregard, the cocky little hero of Sumter, commanded. One thing was certain now. McDowell's arrival would be no surprise.

WRITING A LETTER HOME.

"THE DAUGHTER OF THE REGIMENT."

ALWAYS AN EVENT—THE PAPER ARRIVES.

WASHDAY, CAMP STYLE, HELPED KILL TIME.

GAY ZOUAVES RESPOND TO A FIDDLER.

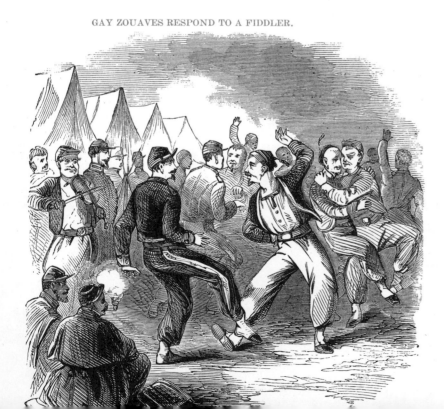

AT DRILL IN CAMP—TROOPS RALLYING BY FOURS.

Meanwhile, in the mountains of western Virginia, Federal forces under George B. McClellan and William Starke Rosecrans were carrying on a campaign that, if vigorously pursued, had the promise of gaining the mountain passes and roads of the watershed of the Allegheny Mountains. The "hill people" of western Virginia did not own slaves and were lively allies who informed the Federals of Rebel movements. In a theater of the war that Washington still ignored, a great Northern victory could be in the making. Above are pictured skirmishes at Buckhannon and Bealington or Laurel Hill in early July that brought on a decisive triumph for the Union at Rich Mountain and Carrick's Ford on July 11-13, 1861. Casualties generally were small, but the fighting was vicious, and the pen of Winslow Homer caught (right) the spirit of battle where men died "till the buzzards are gorged with their spoil."

Washington had only a vague notion of what was happening in western Virginia, so obsessed was it with the belief that if the Federal army could smash through the Confederate lines at Manassas, all that was needed to end the war would be to race to Richmond and hang Jeff Davis to a sour-apple tree. In a holiday mood, as though civil war were like a baseball game, congressmen and senators hired carriages so that they could follow the army and witness the "show." They cluttered the roads over which soldiers and artillery caissons should be passing. They unpacked the luncheons they had brought and picnicked along the roadside.

Raw recruits shambled along behind their commanders, caught up in the same spirit. To William Tecumseh Sherman, in later years, the march to the first great battle of the war demonstrated nothing so much as "the general laxity of discipline; for all my personal efforts, I could not prevent the men from straggling for water, blackberries, or anything on the way they fan-

WAS STILL A COUNTRY TOWN WITH OPEN SEWERS—AND MOSQUITOES!

cied." A lieutenant with the 5th Maine remembered: "For miles the road was strewed with blankets, haversacks, coats thrown aside by the almost exhausted soldiers."

The Federal columns pressed on, while some men collapsed by the roadside with sunstroke, and others were "wind-broken" or bleeding at nose, mouth, ears. After three days of marching, the Union forces reached a little stream that local residents called Bull Run. Here advance Rebel pickets fired a few shots, killed four or five Yan-

kees, then retired. Thereafter the Federals maneuvered much more cautiously until on the morning of July 21, 1861, they collided head on with Beauregard's army. Each commander tried to wheel his army around the right flank of the other, without success. But battles rarely develop as planned, and in the end the only adjectives that would describe the affair at Manassas (northern accounts called it Bull Run) were brutal, confused, a seesaw of panic for North and South.

Still only a colonel, and a reluctant recruit in the war, Sherman never forgot: "When for the first time in my life I saw cannonballs strike men and crash through the trees and saplings above and around us, and realized the always sickening confusion as one approaches a fight from the rear . . . the terrible scare of a poor Negro caught between our lines . . . the crossing of Bull Run, and the fear lest we should be fired on by our own men . . . and the first scenes of a field strewed with dead men and horses. Yet, at that period of the battle, we were the victors and felt jubilant." Like a wave, the Rebels rolled back.

Exultantly, the Federals pushed on, be-
lieving they had won. Then, unexpected-
ly, they were running—routed, disordered.

Suddenly for farm boys, North and South, who
had "seen the elephant"—that is, fought in a
battle—war lost its glamor. And for Beauregard,
faced with a possible rout, the morning likewise
was grim. In the first place, McDowell struck
two hours before the little "Napoleon in Gray"
had planned to launch his attack, a thoroughly
disconcerting circumstance. The Union boys,
rolling up the hill by Henry House, seemed to
be carrying the field, but in that desperate moment—or so legend persists—the Confederates
rallied when General Bee cried to his men:
"Look at Jackson's brigade! It stands there like
a stone wall." Beauregard confessed that at the
time the disorder appeared "irretrievable," but
then "happily the thought occurred" to him
that if the colors were placed in front of the men
they might rally to them. Beauregard, riding forward beside General Joseph E. Johnston, was
delighted with the result: "With the colors of the
4th Alabama by our side, the line that had fought
all morning, and had fled, routed and disordered,
now advanced again into position as steadily as
veterans."

Sherman was convinced that the Rebels were
broken. Too late, as the Confederates surged
back, he realized the truth: "We were beaten."
And beaten more badly than Sherman could
guess: "I then realized that the whole army was
'in retreat,' and that my own men were individu-
ally making back for the stone bridge." Like
scared rabbits, he might have added. At any rate,
Sherman managed to get his four regiments in
parallel lines in a field; there was promise here
of the future general who one day would be the
best remembered man in history on the field of
Bull Run. At the time, a slow, mizzling rain
added to his gloom.

Federal troops, wagons, batteries cluttered the roads. And congressmen and senators. The scene, William Howard Russell reported to the London *Times*, almost defied description: "Infantry soldiers on mules and draft horses, with the harness clinging to their heels, as much frightened as their riders; Negro servants on their masters' chargers; ambulances crowded with unwounded soldiers; wagons swarming with men who threw out the contents in the road to make room, grinding through a shouting, screaming mass of men on foot, who were literally yelling with rage at every halt." Lincoln's warm friend from Illinois, Senator Lyman Trumbull, tried to be philosophical at what he had witnessed and failed: "God's ways are inscrutable. I am dreadfully disappointed and mortified." A Union private blamed the debacle on the officers who had allowed the baggage wagons to come to the front: "The stampede and confusion began among them first"; but another private, testifying before a congressional committee, said with perhaps a great deal more logic: "There was a panic which nobody can explain."

Satisfied with winning the honors for the day, the Confederates failed to follow up the disor-ganized Federal columns reeling back upon Washington, so that in the end the North contended mostly with a bitter humiliation. The casualty figures gave the South some edge: of 28,452 effectives engaged, the Union had lost 481 killed, 1,011 wounded and 1,216 missing, whereas the Confederates, with 32,232 effectives engaged, had lost 387 killed, 1,582 wounded, and 12 missing.

When news of the defeat reached Washington, Lincoln and the Cabinet met with General Scott. All available troops were rushed to McDowell's support, Baltimore alerted, and telegrams sent to nearby northern recruiting stations to hurry their organized regiments to the capital. The first eyewitnesses to the disaster at Manassas began arriving in Washington about midnight, and reclining on a lounge in the Cabinet room of the White House the President listened to their excited, often exaggerated stories. At daybreak he was still listening. By noon the failure of the Confederates to pursue the Federal columns could be confirmed, and Lincoln—and Washington—began to take heart. Indeed, the War Department soon was sending the President news that the Union's loss was much less than at first believed. Lincoln went next day to visit the forts

The Union's Irvin McDowell (left), and the Confederacy's Pierre Gustave Toutant Beauregard (center) and Joseph E. Johnston, who directed the war's first great battle at Manassas Junction (Bull Run), a seesaw between victory and rout.

and camps across the river in Arlington Heights. With good cheer and confidence he addressed the regiments. The North would endure.

Edward A. Pollard, editor of the Richmond *Examiner*, realized in later years that victory at Manassas actually had amounted to a disaster for the South. Pollard remembered how, after the battle, Jefferson Davis had assured "intimate friends" that recognition of the Confederacy by the powers of Europe was now certain. Southern newspapers and speechmakers, in love with a cliché, cheerfully and complacently insisted at every opportunity that "one Southerner [was] equal to five Yankees."

The editors of *De Bow's Review,* losing their heads completely, called Manassas one of the decisive battles in world history. More damaging to the morale of the Confederacy, in Pollard's estimation, was how "the politicians actually commenced plotting for the presidential succession," which was then more than six years distant. Hunter reputedly resigned from the Cabinet, unwilling to have the errors of the present administration "damage" his own chance of one day becoming President, and, the editor declared, "there was actually a controversy between

different states as to the location of the capital of a government . . . which they could not understand was yet imperiled by war." To Pollard, in retrospect, the small victory at Manassas was "the greatest misfortune that could have befallen the Confederacy."

Harper's Weekly sneered openly at journals like the New York *Tribune*, which, "at this critical moment," berated General Scott and Secretary Seward. Such periodicals, the editors believed, "ought to be banished from every honest man's home, as the most efficient, if not the hired instruments of the rebels." *Harper's Weekly* thought it understood perfectly what the North must learn in the wake of Manassas: "Montesquieu tells us that the only difficulty with republican governments is that they require so much virtue in their citizens. That is just the point. If our people have enough virtue—that is to say, courage, perseverance, loyalty to themselves and to truth, fidelity to their principles, and honesty of purpose—they can carry on this war just as well as any despot could. If they have not, the war will end, some day, in the sacrifice of honor and nationality, and the United States will sink lower than Mexico."

THE MANY FACES OF WAR

PRESIDENT LINCOLN WELCOMES PRINCE NAPOLEON (FIFTH FROM LEFT) AT FORMAL RECEPTION IN THE WHITE HOUSE.

*With an army still to
build, the North suddenly faces a
war with angry John Bull*

August–December, 1861

Puzzled by their quarrelsome American cousins, the editors of the London *Times* inquired: "Are they in earnest, or are they playing at war?" Anthony Trollope, visiting in America, assured his countrymen that both northerners and southerners acted from a "strong and unanimous impulse"; and Trollope added: "Each may have been guided by a just and noble feeling; though each was brought to its present condition by bad government and dishonest statesmen."

Another visitor to America at the time was Prince Napoleon, who sometimes was known as "Plon Plon" and who impressed a French wit as "a good copy of the first Emperor dipped in German grease." The Prince's aide-de-camp, Camille Ferri Pisani, described their first call at the White House: "The Prince, arriving with Baron Mercier, found no one—neither butler nor doorman—at the main entrance to show him in, or at least to open the door." While admiring simplicity, Pisani believed that such behavior passed understanding. "If the Republic," he wrote, "does not give the President enough to live on and to maintain a staff of servants, let her lodge him in a more modest dwelling where a single steward would be sufficient!"

The President received each month for his services a salary warrant for $2,083.33—in Pisani's phrase, "enough to live on." If that August 3, when the Prince called, the President seemed preoccupied, his mood in part may have been explained by a meeting of the Cabinet to consider a memorandum from General McClellan concerning the vast military problems that now confronted the North. Also the explosive situation in Missouri, which could become worse at any moment, was very much on Mr. Lincoln's mind. But perhaps the Prince was mollified when that evening—and in the proper attire—the President honored his royal visitor with a formal reception and a dinner for forty guests at the White House.

The war remained a young giant who had not yet fully awakened and who, though resting his

A FAVORITE RENDEZVOUS: THE BAR OF THE SPOTTSWOOD IN RICHMOND.

Confederate raiders under General John Magruder rode into Hampton one August night and put a torch to the town. An embittered Associated Press *reported that nothing remained beyond charred chimneys after this "dastardly work."*

BRIGADIER FRANZ SIGEL

head in Virginia, certainly was wriggling his toes in Missouri.

With the Confederate capital now in Richmond, the North's military thinking did not ignore the fact that Richmond was situated in a state whose rivers were open to Union warships. But McClellan moved at his own pace—a snail's pace, it far too often seemed to the general's critics—and the best anyone could say for the lagging Federal situation in Virginia that quiescent summer of 1861 was that it was rich with future promise.

Missouri was another story entirely. With the outbreak of hostilities, Governor Claiborne F. Jackson had revealed he was as southern as fried chicken by calling Lincoln's appeal for troops "illegal, unconstitutional and revolutionary . . . inhuman and diabolical." Clearly, Jackson intended to offer no assistance to the President's "unholy crusade," but Missouri also contained a strong pro-Union element, especially among the numerous Germans in St. Louis who went off so proudly to "fight mit Sigel"—Franz Sigel, a German-born brigadier general who was idolized by mid-westerners of the same ethnic origin. The situation that developed within Missouri could be described as a war within a war.

The Union boys had struck the first blow by seizing the arsenal in St. Louis. Later, in mid-June at Booneville, pro-secessionists and pro-

Union forces had fought a bitter, inconclusive battle. Jackson's Rebels retreated toward Arkansas, and Union forces that included that "damn Dutchman" Sigel and his pig-headed Germans pursued them doggedly. Another battle at Carthage left the issue undecided.

In camp near Maysville, Arkansas, the Rebels licked their wounds and attempted to knock together an army of frontiersmen, who could not have read a drill manual if they had possessed one. Their weapons included shotguns, old-fashioned flintlocks, now and then a percussion musket; and their horses fed on prairie grass. Regimental drills were impossible, and since officers were recruited among country lawyers an order to a soldier usually drew the casual reply: "Jedge, when I git to it — what's the hell-fired hurry?" A drum and a fife sounded all calls. Officers and men ate at the same mess, and only a fool would have tried to tell these backwoodsmen, who were hunters by necessity, how to handle a gun or a Bowie knife (which, in their idiom, was invariably an "Arkansas toothpick"). By professional standards, the Missouri Rebels might seem a ridiculous lot, but their strength was in the characteristics that produced a frontiersman — bravery, intelligence, shrewdness, cunning, wariness, a quick wit when faced with an emergency. How well these men could fight, the Union boys soon discovered.

On the home front the war reflected many moods, many passions as a Massachusetts editor of suspected anti-Lincoln sentiments discovered when he was tarred and feathered (left). In the South, families that still held a place in their hearts for the Union were prudent if they moved North, bag and baggage (above). Meanwhile, spirited recruiting for the Confederate army appealed to the small fry in a town like Woodstock, Virginia (below).

In mid-August at Wilson's Creek the opposing forces once more clashed in a brisk battle which, when it ended, still settled very little. The names of other Missouri towns appeared in the news—Brunswick, Bird's Point—denoting places where fierce skirmishes were fought in this hit-and-run warfare, but none by itself had any real significance. John C. Frémont, already famous for his western explorations as "The Pathfinder" and as the Republican presidential candidate in 1856, was commander of all Federal forces in Missouri. As the month ended, Frémont, unable to understand that a commanding general must serve as an instrument of government, issued a proclamation that invoked martial law, seized the property of Missourians in rebellion against the national government, and freed the slaves they held.

Lincoln, ever sensitive to how he must walk a political tightrope if he would retain the loyalty of the border states, was not to be swept from his purpose by the approving cries of antislavery radicals for Frémont's order. Tactfully, he suggested that the general modify his proclamation to eliminate the confiscation of slaves, but Frémont in a stubborn mood refused to change his order or "shade it." Lincoln did the job for him, while antislavery men like Senator Sumner of Massachusetts ranted over what a shame it was to have Lincoln's power "and not use it godlike."

Lincoln was not intimidated, believing that he understood the way to handle the border states better than Frémont or Sumner. "I do not say," he wrote Senator Browning of Illinois, "Congress might not with propriety pass a law, on the point, just such as General Frémont proclaimed. I do not say I might not as a member of Congress vote for it. What I object to, is, that I as President, shall expressly or impliedly seize

What were some of the many faces the war now assumed? In Baltimore, pro-secessionist ladies (left) taunted occupying Union troops by wearing the Rebel flag on their bosoms. In Phillipi, Virginia (center), hungry soldiers won a battle over hostile pigs. In Davenport, Iowa (right), 1,200 volunteers passed under the "Triumphal Arch" amid cheers.

and exercise the permanent functions of the government." The lawyer in Lincoln was perhaps his greatest virtue. He could not compromise on a principle. His old partner in Springfield, William Herndon, had warned another Senator from Massachusetts, Henry Wilson, that such would be the case: ". . . on justice, right, liberty, the Government, the Constitution, and the Union, then you may all stand aside; he will rule then, and no man can move him—no set of men can do it. There is no fail here. This is Lincoln, and you mark my prediction. You and I must keep the people right; God will keep Lincoln right."

Irresistibly, the war ground on, touching more and more of the country. In the Gulf of Mexico on September 17, Union forces occupied Ship Island, Mississippi. An Episcopal bishop now fighting for the Confederacy—Leonidas Polk—disrupted the myth of Kentucky's neutrality by occupying Columbus, impelling an obscure Union general named Ulysses Grant to checkmate this move by occupying Paducah at the mouth of the Tennessee River. In western Virginia a still-obscure general in the Confederate military hierarchy, Robert E. Lee, was fighting arrogant subordinates, bad weather, and green soldiers, and losing rather than winning a reputation. Many in Richmond began to wonder if Lee possessed the talent for command.

In Missouri other place names appeared in the news that September: Bennett's Mills, one Union soldier killed, eight wounded; Dallas, two Union soldiers killed; Dry Wood, four Union soldiers killed, nine wounded. Then at Lexington, from the twelfth to the twentieth, the Missouri Rebels under Sterling Price, a renegade Republican turned secessionist, clashed with 2,800 Federals under Colonel James Mulligan—and thrashed them soundly.

Illinois troops supported the Missouri Unionists under Colonel Mulligan in eight days of savage battle at Lexington. But Price's frontiersmen (foreground), for all their lack of discipline, fought the Federals to a standstill and Mulligan at last retreated, leaving behind forty-two dead, 108 wounded and 1,624 missing—a terrific pasting, statistically. Confederate losses (at a loose estimate) were only twenty-five killed and seventy-five wounded. The war for Missouri went on.

The war added a new word for slave to the American language, an invention of the always pliable mind of Major General Benjamin F. Butler, commanding at Fortress Monroe, opposite Norfolk. As "contrabands" of war, slaves could be seized and put to work, and as such Butler used them (left, top). Below, a sad moment—a sign of changing times—was General Scott's last meeting with the Cabinet.

In Washington during these months, the dazzling figure was General George B. McClellan, who had won the small Union victory in western Virginia in the days immediately preceding the disaster at Bull Run. A man of remarkable administrative ability, McClellan could offer a great deal as commander of that enormous fighting force which in time would become the Army of the Potomac. But McClellan's private correspondence revealed all too clearly that he saw himself as the man who, all alone, must save the Union.

Old Winfield Scott, who had served the country in the days of Lundy's Lane and was its only lieutenant general since George Washington, was forty years McClellan's senior, but Little Mac, in his exciting role as the "Napoleon in Blue," was only irked by his venerable superior. Scott, in McClellan's estimate, was "the great obstacle." Like the President, McClellan said, Scott "cannot or will not see the true state of affairs." Later, at a meeting in Scott's office, what McClellan obviously expected happened: "the general raised a row with me." Writing to his wife, McClellan exploded: "I am weary of all this." And surely his wife would understand why both Lincoln and the old general drove him to despair when he told her: "Their reply to everything is, 'Impossible! Impossible!' They think nothing is possible which is against their wishes."

Lincoln was up against it. An intellectually honest man, he had to admit that he comprehended very little—really nothing—about how to run an army, though he was borrowing books on the subject from the Library of Congress in order to teach himself the rudiments of being the nation's commander-in-chief. And poor old Scott, now older than the capital itself, was far too fond of his canvasback duck and Madeira wine. He was simply overweight and dropsical, defeated at long last by his own appetite. So the aggressive McClellan stepped into a sort of vacuum, believing the "letter after letter" he received and the "conversation after conversation" he held in which he was called upon to save the nation through allusions "to the presidency, dictatorship, etc."

In the pitch-black of a rainy morning early in November, McClellan won his triumph. Scott was characteristically polite to a successor who had arisen at four o'clock to escort him to the depot. Any elation that McClellan had experienced at becoming at last the "major-general commanding the army" faded when he looked at Scott: "...it may be that at some distant day I, too, shall totter away from Washington, a worn-out soldier, with naught to do but make my peace with God. The sight this morning was a lesson to me which I hope not soon to forget."

But McClellan did. He would never see himself so clearly again.

Yet, as an administrator, "Little Mac" accomplished much that was praiseworthy. What the general found in the capital, as one reporter wrote, was "rather a mob than an army." There was no army to command, McClellan complained, but "a mere collection of regiments cowering on the banks of the Potomac." The creation of a Provost Marshal department put an end to the rampant desertions and straggling, and by prohibiting whiskey in camp the drunkenness was reduced.

Less than 1,000 cavalrymen, nine field batteries of rather nondescript character, and about 50,000 infantrymen comprised the fighting force that McClellan took over. A West Pointer who had studied military problems during the Crimean War, McClellan began to whip these apple-green troops into disciplined soldiers. A change was gradually effected, and no one approved more wholeheartedly as order was imposed on army life than the soldiers themselves. Their respect for McClellan grew into positive affection. This camaraderie in no small part would help to forge the Army of the Potomac into an organization that equaled a city like Albany or Indianapolis picking up and moving from battle to battle.

Reporter George Townsend described a day in camp with Ord's brigade. Tents were pitched in a fine grove of oaks, and the men—talking and singing—gathered around open-air fires. Brass Napoleons unlimbered in the front, pointing to the south and west. Along the roadside muskets were neatly stacked. Men wrapped in warm blankets dozed by the sputtering fagots, and when Townsend asked for a pillow, the colonel answered that he once had put a man on double duty for resting his head on a snowball. Townsend awakened to watch a soldier calmly shaving with a saber honed to a fine razor's edge.

Weeks went by as generals argued over strategy and tactics and the boys in blue marched, drilled, camped, and expressed their nighttime loneliness and homesickness in such sentimental ballads as "The Girl I Left Behind Me" or "Listen to the Mocking Bird." Moods brightened with the daylight, and many were the parodies among the soldiers' collection of songs, such as the defiant words that Yankees sang to the tune of "Dixie":

Away down South in the land of traitors,
Rebel hearts and Union haters,
Look away, look away, look away to the
traitor's land...

And forbidding whiskey in camp did not stop all toping by any means, so that the Yankee was

equally as appreciative as the Rebel at this comic song of Southern origin:

> Tom Jennings who never could drinking avoid
> Tho' vows he was always a-making.
> But after each bout he was always annoyed
> With a nervousness and a head aching.
> Going out to a party one evening last week,
> His wife said to him as a warning,
> "Be careful dear Thomas and mind what you take,
> And think of your head in the morning."

Doubtless Thomas failed to take warning, and so ran through the list of camp punishments: a turn in the guardhouse, digging latrines, digging stumps, burying dead horses. Old Winfield Scott had been much more imaginative with heavy drinkers during the Black Hawk War, having them dig the graves they would occupy if they failed to conquer the habit.

The gamblers flourished in war as in peace. Except on eve of battle, when the boys threw away their cards and told God in their prayers that they were not bad fellows at heart, games of poker, faro, and dice were never difficult to locate. Sports and games filled many leisurely hours in camp, and the popular pastimes included wrestling, boxing, leapfrog, cricket, races, baseball, and football.

The Maryland 1st plays a spirited game of soccer before the evening parade (left) at Camp Johnson near Winchester, Virginia. Like all soldiers, this unidentified regiment (above), took a profound interest in the activities of the camp kitchen.

Gradually, a new pattern of war was emerging, and with time both North and South learned how to live with this native martial product. In this new style of war balloons were sent aloft to spy on the enemy, hundreds of miles of wire were strung for telegraph communication, the "Bohemian Brigade" (as newspaper war correspondents were called) could be found everywhere snooping out military information, and photographers lugged wagonloads of equipment over roads already clogged with marching men. Nor was that all. Civilian entertainers roamed the camps, politicians bargained for future votes with barrels of whiskey, nurses and doctors appeared with peculiar ideas of humanity amidst man's inhumanity, and sutlers and cotton speculators vied with opportunistic officers of all ranks for a fast buck.

Life in the Army of the Potomac (above) found men frolicking when evening parade ended, while others solemnly stood picket-guard. Provisioning this army (right), wrote Colonel Henry S. Olcott, produced a "Carnival of Fraud" and in Washington "Contractors, bloated with the profits on shoddy, rode in emblazoned carriages, which, a little while before, they would have been glad to drive as hirelings; and vulgar faces and grimy fingers were made more vulgar with the glare of diamonds."

Provisioning and equipping the Union armies brought grafter with patriot to Washington. An expert in rooting out these sharpsters was a special investigator for the War Department, Colonel Henry S. Olcott, who declared: "Intrigue held the key to the kitchen-stairs of the White House, shaped legislation, sat cheek by jowl with Congressmen, and seduced commissioned officers from the strict path of duty." A sailor who went to sea in a ship constructed from green timbers and equipped with a junk-shop engine greased with "sperm" oil derived from mossbunkers (menhaden) and the fat of dead horses had a fair notion why Olcott complained. And so also did the soldier "given guns that would not shoot, powder that would only half explode, shoes of which the soles were filled with shavings, hats that dissolved often in a month's showers, and clothing made of old cloth, ground up and fabricated over again." In New York City a rich importer, Solomon Kohnstann, working in league with neighborhood saloon keepers, was doing a land-office business in forging military rent-vouchers until Olcott caught up with him.

Graft, extortion, and dishonesty were hardly an invention of the North. Shortages in the South provided a carnival for the profiteer, and a week's provisions that in 1860 had sold for $6.55 were costing by early 1863 at least ten times that figure. John B. Jones, a clerk in the Confederate War Department, by 1863 was paying $15 for coarse shoes worth $1.50, and $4 for a yard of coarse woolen goods that had cost a mere forty cents before the war. When the quartermaster general appealed for shirts for the soldiers, Jones commented cynically: "The people will not trust him to convey the clothing to their sons and brothers, and so the army must suffer on."

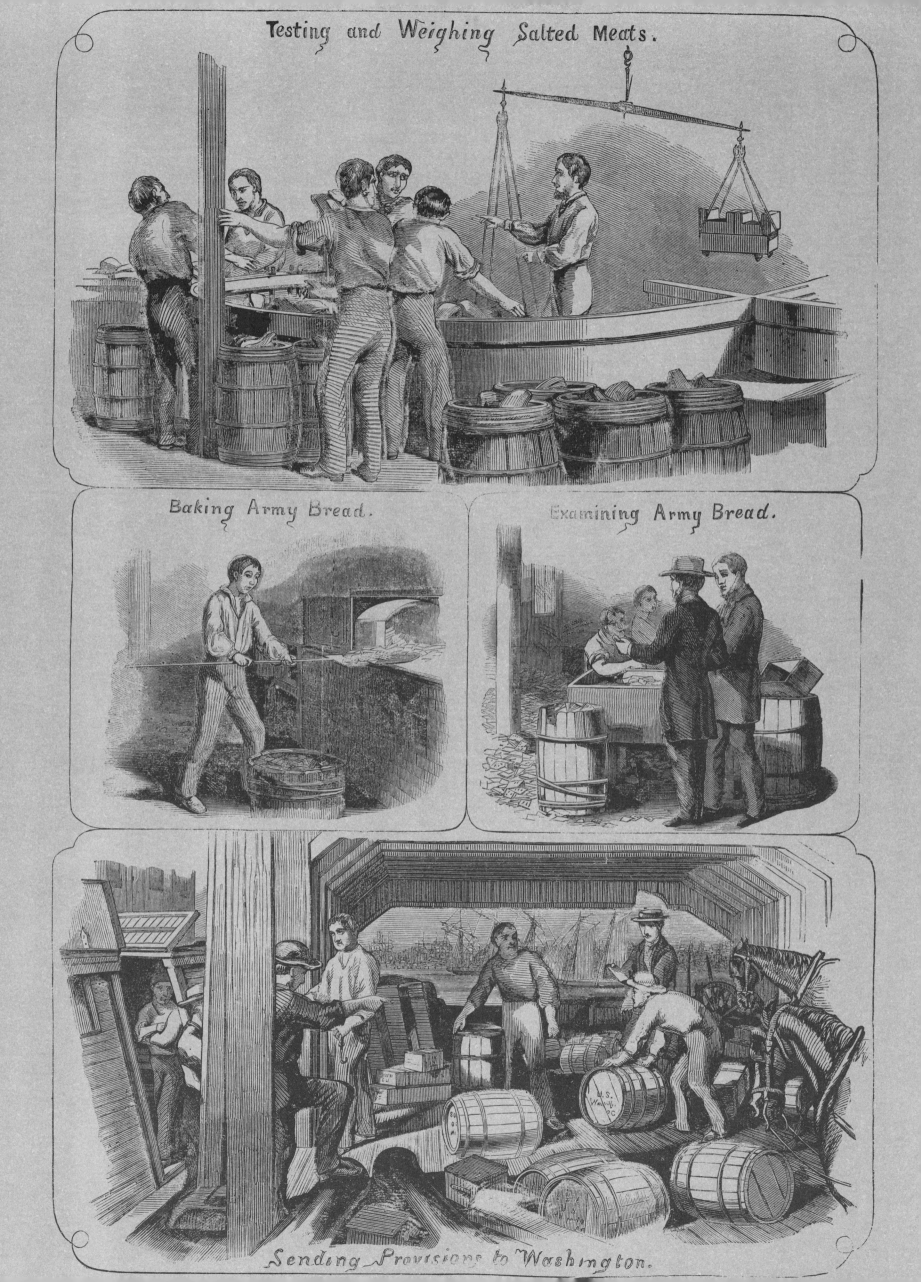

Testing and Weighing Salted Meats.

Baking Army Bread.

Examining Army Bread.

Sending Provisions to Washington.

Disagreeable though Richmond and Washington found the visage of the bloated contractor, both capitals in December, 1861, were preoccupied with the greatest diplomatic crisis of the war. As agents of the Confederacy, James M. Mason, bound for England, and John Slidell, en route to France, sailed from Havana in late November aboard a British contract mailpacket, the *Trent*. A Federal warship, the *San Jacinto,* commanded by Captain Charles Wilkes, intercepted the *Trent*. Acting without orders, Captain Wilkes removed Mason and Slidell and carried them to an American port.

England raged at this insult to its sovereignty, and in Parliament, clubs, and newspapers the subject obsessed Britishers. The time had come, Matthew Arnold declared, for Americans to be taught a lesson, and with reason Lincoln's diplomats in London feared that since "the mob and *The Times* have the mastery" nothing less than war would satisfy Britain.

Anthony Trollope was in Boston when Wilkes arrived with Mason and Slidell. He was aghast at how Americans lost their heads and treated Wilkes as a hero: "His health was drunk with great applause, and thanks were voted to him by one of the Houses of Congress." A true Britisher, Trollope could not disguise a rising scorn for these Bostonians: "I have my common sense to guide me. Two men living in one street, quarrel and shy brickbats at each other, and make the whole street very uncomfortable. Not only is no one to interfere with them, but they are to have the privilege of deciding that their brickbats have the right of way, rather than the ordinary intercourse of the neighborhood! If that be national law, national law must be changed. It might do for some centuries back, but it cannot do now."

In London, Lincoln's minister to England, Charles Francis Adams, not only was concerned by the war talk he heard on all sides, but also was disturbed (as he later admitted in a letter to his fellow minister in Russia) at his government's loss of "dignity" through openly flaunting the rights of neutrals. "It is not for us to abandon them under the transient impulse given by the capture of a couple of unworthy traitors," Adams wrote Cassius M. Clay. But for a time Washington diplomacy demanded that the "cardinal principles" of American statesmanship be abandoned. Adams had to live with that fact. Increasingly, the press in Britain expressed the view that England and France should join in breaking the blockade of southern ports. The war would then come to a quick

The cast of characters in a diplomatic drama (left to right): Captain Charles Wilkes of the San Jacinto; James Murray Mason of Virginia, who had served in the U. S. Congress; and John Slidell of Louisiana whose brother-in-law was General P. G. T. Beauregard, the hero of the attack on Fort Sumter.

end, prophesied the Wakefield *Journal and Examiner,* for the South would be able to carry on the conflict "vigorously and effectively" with European economic assistance.

Buckingham Palace was far more conciliatory than either Parliament or the press. In mid-December reports from the Palace admitted that for several days Prince Albert had been seriously ill. The Queen, concerned with this growing worry, was understood at the American legation to be opposed to war with the North, and Benjamin Moran, a secretary at the legation, noted in his diary "that she and Prince Albert greatly modified the demands, and the tone of the despatch to our Gov't. on the Trent affair." On December 15 the Prince Consort died of typhoid fever and England became a nation absorbed in mourning. A few days later, after sensible second thoughts, Seward "cheerfully liberated" the two Confederate agents and the diplomatic crisis ended.

In Washington that unfailing gadabout, Trollope, attended one of the "field-days in the Senate" after Mason and Slidell were released. He was, of course, elated that the British position had been sustained, and yet he admitted: "It is, I think, manifest that our own pretensions as to the right of search must be modified after this." The South was depressed over the fact that, in the comment of War Clerk J. B. Jones, "Seward has cowered before the roar of the British Lion," and Jefferson Davis confessed that he had little expected the Lincoln government to capitulate. Awaiting the settlement of the *Trent* affair, Britain had held up sending arms, blankets, and shoes to the Confederacy, not knowing whether she might need them for a war of her own. The New Year approached gloomily in official Richmond.

Londoners rejoiced at the diplomatic victory, and Benjamin Moran said that when in most theaters the news was announced between acts "the audiences rose like one & cheered tremendously." The strain had been enormous on Charles Francis Adams, who had received crank letters threatening to blow up the Embassy, who had once told Moran "in so many words" that President Lincoln was "unfit for his place," and who had expected at Christmas to be homeward bound by the middle of January. It was no surprise to Moran when at last the "load of lead" was lifted from their hearts "Mr. & Mrs. Adams heartily congratulated each other." In contrast, there were those in the North who agreed with *Harper's* editors they had had to swallow "a bitter pill."

STAR ASCENDING

*Lost in the struggle
for military power, an obscure man
forces his opportunities*

November, 1861—February, 1862

From earliest childhood Hiram Ulysses Grant was known by his middle name. A youth who was a natural horseman and grew dizzy if forced to take a backward step, he was entered in West Point as "U. S. Grant"; friends called him Uncle Sam. He fought bravely in the Mexican War, married, and then served in California where his loneliness for his family was symbolized by the locket containing a strand of his wife's hair that he wore beneath his shirt. Perhaps, as some said, his drinking became excessive. Perhaps, as unkind critics remarked, he resigned from the army to avoid a court-martial. Perhaps, as many biographers insist, his later adventures in farming, real estate, and the leather business were a series of failures. With Grant it is always wise to remember Twain's comment that Wagner's music was better than it sounded. Grant, both the man and the general, was always better than he appeared.

Grant's early commands came under a group of generals best known, in turn, for their showiness (John C. Frémont), their bluster (John Pope), and their ambition (Henry Halleck), and if they shared any trait in common it was an apparent unwillingness ever to let Grant fight. When with Polk in Columbus, Kentucky, an alert Grant seized Paducah to hold the Rebels in checkmate, Frémont took a dim view of Grant's success, charging fretfully that Grant had acted without specific orders.

Well, so he had—and would again. Unassuming, stumpy, informal, unmilitary in gait and appearance, Grant might seem less like a general than anyone in the Union army, but many made the same mistake with Grant as they did with Lincoln. Underestimating Grant's strength and intelligence, like underestimating the innate greatness of Lincoln, was a game usually of one winner—Grant or Lincoln—and of several losers. In November, 1861, Grant remained an obscure general stuck in the mud of Cairo, Illinois, and four months later he was on the cover of *Harper's Weekly* as the North's first bonafide hero. Needless to say, not one of his superiors was overjoyed.

For Frémont an uncomfortable month of the war was November, 1861. First, Lincoln was repudiating his proclamation emancipating the slaves of Missouri, and then the rag-tag army of Rebel frontiersmen was raising hell around Lexington. Frémont wanted Polk's forces held in Columbus, and he ordered Grant to make a demonstration for this purpose. That a battle might result was evidently the last thing in Frémont's thoughts.

Friends complained that artists tended to give the public a wrong impression of Sam Grant (right), making this stump of a man appear to be a "burly beef-contractor."

HARPER'S WEEKLY.

A JOURNAL OF CIVILIZATION

Vol. VI.—No. 271.]   NEW YORK, SATURDAY, MARCH 8, 1862.   [SINGLE COPIES SIX CENTS.
$2 50 PER YEAR IN ADVANCE.

Entered according to Act of Congress, in the Year 1862, by Harper & Brothers, in the Clerk's Office of the District Court for the Southern District of New York.

At Belmont, Missouri, Grant revealed for the first time that, no matter what his superiors believed, he knew how to handle a battle. He struck the Rebels hard. Disorganized, they fled from their camp.

A few shanties perched atop the river mud—such was Belmont, Missouri, in 1861 when Grant brought his 3,000 raw recruits down river in five steamers. A Confederate force of about equal strength under General Gideon J. Pillow waited to give him a warm reception. Writing to his father, Grant put the resulting battle in its best light, telling how from tree to tree his boys fought their way into Belmont, charged the place and captured the Rebel camp, which was true to the extent that after four hours of bitter fighting Pillow abandoned the camp in disorder.

Grant simply omitted most of the significant events that followed, by far the best part of the story. Polk's guns on the bluffs of Columbus made Belmont untenable. The inexperienced Yankees, certain they had won a major victory that might end the war, ignored Grant's orders in a jubilant spree of pillaging. Polk's guns poured a withering fire on the celebrants, and Pillow, picking up three fresh regiments, placed his forces between the camp and Grant's river boats, thus springing a trap on the unsuspecting Federals.

Grant was hip-deep in potential disaster, and knew it. His raw troops panicked. On all sides he heard pleas to surrender. But Grant was more than a fair-weather warrior. Resolutely, he said: "We must cut our way out as we cut our way in." Grant rallied his boys and gave Pillow a fight he wouldn't soon forget, judging by the letter home of one Confederate observer: "The scene was grand, but it was terrible, and when I closed my eyes about four o'clock next morning, I could see regiments charging and retreating—men falling and yelling—horses and men torn and mangled—and myriads of horrid spectacles. It was a bloody enjoyment, but we do not know the loss on either side yet."

The ratio of casualties at Belmont was almost two to one in Grant's favor: 498 to 966. He had pinned down Polk and brought his boys back to Cairo in fine style, reason enough to write his

father afterward that he felt "truly proud to command such men." The North had a comer in Grant although Frémont never realized that fact. But Frémont's days in Missouri were numbered and Lincoln replaced him in command in St. Louis with Henry W. Halleck, an ambitious fellow who was known among army intimates as "Old Brains."

Lincoln had ideas of his own about how the war in the west should be run. Always sentimental toward the strong Unionist sympathies that dominated east Tennessee, the President pressed hard for an action aimed at Knoxville and Chattanooga. Any such movement, of course, ran the risk of Confederate forces in Missouri and western Tennessee falling upon the rear of a Federal army advancing to their south and east. Moreover, there was really one too many Federal commanders in the west: stiff-necked Don Carlos Buell in charge of the Department of the Ohio and Halleck in charge of the Department of the Missouri.

Buell argued soundly. It was nonsense to move into east Tennessee unless the action was co-ordinated with an operation in western Kentucky and western Tennessee. Halleck was inclined to do nothing, and he was in no mood to listen to an upstart subordinate who arrived in St. Louis with a plan for breaking the Rebel line on the Tennessee River. Grant never quite forgave the manner in which "Old Brains" used him: "I was cut short as if my plan was preposterous."

Meanwhile, in Washington, McClellan recovered from typhoid fever and suddenly Buell received orders to move into east Tennessee without waiting for help from Halleck. Buell swallowed his better judgment and chose the right man to command the expedition: Virginia-born George H. Thomas, who was loyal to the Union in every bone. A Confederate army under General Felix Zollicoffer, then near Somerset on the Cumberland, was Thomas's quarry. The forces collided at Mill Springs on January 19, 1862, and Thomas won a resounding victory.

George H. Thomas, destined for enduring fame as "The Rock of Chickamauga," proved his mettle at Mill Springs, Kentucky. So untrained were the troops and officers who fought across meadows and through woodlots that the Confederate general, Felix Zollicoffer, rode into the Union army's lines and was shot dead.

Halleck was no fool. Unless he moved fast, Thomas's success at Mill Springs made Buell the front-runner in the unannounced contest for supreme command in the west. Now Halleck not only remembered that Grant had called at St. Louis with a plan to break the Rebel hold on the Tennessee, but with the pliability of mind that "Old Brains" possessed, he decided to adopt Grant's plan as his own. What Grant had tried to tell him, the commander of the gunboat fleet, Andrew Foote, confirmed. No reason in the world existed why a combined land and naval operation could not be launched against Confederate forts on the Tennessee and the Cumberland. Orders for Grant to move without delay against Fort Henry on the Tennessee were received on January 29.

Bad roads slowed down Grant's movement of troops and Foote's gunboats, unsupported, hammered the fort into virtual submission before the army arrived. Grant was more than willing to thank Foote for a ready-made victory; and

when he arose next morning his mind churned restlessly with ideas for taking Fort Donelson, ten miles east of Henry on the Cumberland River. On February 12, he started from Henry with 15,000 men. In balmy weather, Grant's troops moved off gaily, casting aside heavy blankets and overcoats. Suddenly rain alternating with snow blew in on freezing winter winds. Without shelter, and with campfires forbidden so as not to forewarn the enemy, the men suffered the torments of an arctic climate.

Confederate gunners in Fort Henry locked in a duel for life with Foote's Federal gunboats, often hidden from view by the smoke of battle. Foote's boats approached stoically, swerving neither to right nor left. Shells from the river tore apart sandbags and gabions, covering the guns and smothering those who stood serving them. Grant was handed his victory.

Raw Union troops, throwing away their overcoats, fought Rebels, ice, and sleet at Donelson in one of the cruelest battles of the entire war. The contest followed no military pattern. Frostbitten soldiers fought where—and how—they could and a Richmond reporter, preparing his readers for a disaster, spoke of the dead piled up in heaps while everywhere "their gore trickled in red lines along the snow."

A picket froze to death at his post. Hundreds suffered from frostbite. Snow drifts piled high and the temperature fell to twenty degrees below freezing.

Donelson was a formidable place, set on a bend of the Cumberland where hillside water batteries and bastioned earthworks afforded protection to a fortress sprawled over a hundred acres. Nature also was helping the Confederates at the moment, since to the north of Donelson the waters of Hickman Creek had overflowed to form an impassable barrier, and to the south high water in Indian Creek threatened the narrow road to Nashville by way of Dover and Charlotte.

Grant, cigar atilt, knew that he was in for a bitter struggle and it came Friday morning when 3,000 Rebels stormed out of the fort, supported by twelve batteries of artillery. The battle, reported the New York *Times,* "rolled over a hill, anon poured along a ravine, always in the woods," but no matter where the conflict raged it marked its track "in characters of blood." Shivering Yankees hid behind trees, logs, and rocks "and blazed away whenever a hostile head appeared." The Rebels succeeded once in cutting an opening on the road to Nashville. Then a confusion in orders recalled the Confederates into the fortress and Grant blocked the road. The battle, said the *Times,* sounded like a heavy tornado with the Rebels pouring torrents of canister, shell, and round shot into Grant's columns.

Saturday was "the Rubicon of Fort Donelson." The Richmond *Dispatch* contended that disaster resulted because Grant's superior numbers became too much for "our jaded soldiers." One of Grant's lieutenants offered another view —and a sounder one—declaring that the Confederate commander "threw away his army by fighting outside his works." Grimly, General Simon Bolivar Buckner asked for terms and received the answer that would make Grant famous: "No terms but immediate and unconditional surrender."

Buckner capitulated and 12,000 prisoners became not the least of the prize that Grant won at Donelson. *Harper's Weekly* not only devoted its cover to "The Hero of Donelson" (see page 77), but its editors believed that the fall of the fort was "probably the culminating point in the struggle," which was sheer nonsense. At least one result might have been prophesied with more accuracy. Neither Halleck nor McClellan had planned this campaign to convert the obscure Grant into the nation's darling. Quickly Halleck was reporting to Washington that he could obtain "no returns, no reports, no information of any kind" from Grant and also repeating ugly, if unconfirmed, rumors that "Grant has resumed his former bad habits." McClellan, not needing a second cue, was snapping back by telegraph: "Do not hesitate to arrest Grant if the good of the service requires it."

Doubtless Halleck would have been happy to oblige McClellan except for two difficulties. First, "it is hard to censure a successful general immediately after a victory." Second, he would have to find Grant to arrest him.

Grant was on his way to Nashville, believing that with the fall of Donelson "the way was opened to the National forces all over the Southwest without much resistance." As Grant had expected, Rebel forces under Albert Sidney Johnston did not linger long in Nashville, leaving the city on February 18. Six days later Federal forces under Buell occupied the city, but Grant pushed on to see the place for himself. The only ladies who received him warmly, reported the *Times,* were from the "lower walks." The others remained "as full of treason as of . . . loveliness." Grant knew how he would run the war if only he were commanding troops west of the Alleghenies. To an aggressive general a large and attractive assortment of plums awaited the plucking: Chattanooga and Corinth, Memphis and Vicksburg. It was a tantalizing prospect.

At the moment, Grant not only was not running the war in the west, but three weeks after Donelson he learned from Halleck that he had been relieved of his present command. For Grant, who described himself as "virtually in arrest," the action seemed unjustified. Lincoln asked Halleck for a report on "Grant's unauthorized visit to Nashville." Placed in command of all forces in the west, Halleck fell into a much more conciliatory mood, replying that Grant had gone to Nashville to communicate with Buell, a motive Halleck now described as "proper." He advised that the case be dropped; but Lincoln went a step further, and Grant not only was restored to command, but also received his stripes as a major general.

Neither Halleck nor McClellan had yet divined the truth about Grant—that he might be the best general in the North. Some would say later that Grant was "a born soldier." Perhaps. Or was the secret of Grant simply the fact, as a perceptive critic commented, that he was "a man of correct methods and a fixed will"? He was, by this estimate, a born soldier only in the sense that, under other circumstances, he might have been a born railroad president "or a born anything to which he had once in good earnest turned his hand."

In any case, for all that the tone-deaf general couldn't keep in step unless the bands played "Yankee Doodle"—the only tune he recognized—here was a rising star. He had made his own opportunity at Paducah and Belmont and had kept on coming. He was indeed, as another admirer said, "an uncommon common man."

A view of Nashville, Tennessee, a city of 20,000 set on the banks of the Cumberland. Buell occupied Nashville on February 24, 1862. After the fall of Fort Henry, gunboats sailed down the Tennessee to receive a warm welcome from Union supporters in Alabama.

ON THE HIGH SEAS

*Blockade runner and
Rebel raider make our civil war
a world-wide conflagration*

THE FRIGATE MERRIMACK ON FIRE IN THE NORFOLK NAVY YARD.

November, 1861–March, 1862

One of Lincoln's first acts after the war erupted at Sumter was to declare a blockade of the coastline of all seceding states. The Union's entire navy then consisted of ninety vessels, of which only twenty-nine were driven by steam. The Federal navy's complement of officers in 1861 numbered 1,300, its seamen 7,500, and its annual budget was $12,000,000. How well the national government organized for war, once it learned the martial trade, would be reflected in the comparative figures for 1865, when the navy's ships would number 670, its officers 6,700, its seamen 51,500, and its annual budget would amount to $123,000,000.

On the high seas, as on land, this brothers' quarrel was fought to the hilt. With blockade runner and armed raider, the South struck back, carrying the war to any ocean where Yankee merchantman or whaler could be found. The flag of the Confederacy was raised in battle even in the frozen wastes of the North Pacific and off the steaming coasts of eastern Africa, such were the global dimensions that this naval war took

on. In a single day off Hampton Roads, Virginia, the wooden navies of the world would be rendered obsolete through the ingenuity of the Confederates in reconditioning the *Merrimack* and the genius of John Ericsson (above), a Swedish marine engineer living in New York City. Famous as an inventor in Europe as well as America, Ericsson told Lincoln that "attachment to the Union alone impels me to offer my services at this fearful crisis—my life if need be." At first, of course, no one heeded him.

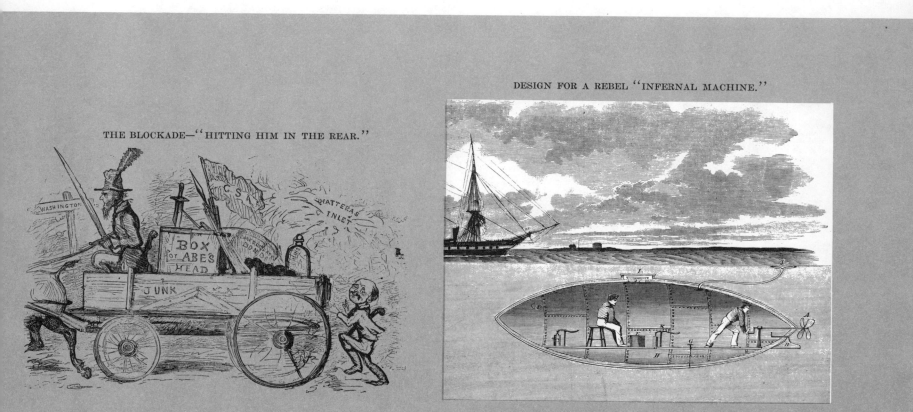

THE BLOCKADE—"HITTING HIM IN THE REAR."

DESIGN FOR A REBEL "INFERNAL MACHINE."

On August 1, 1861, the U. S. Frigate St. Lawrence caught the Rebel privateer Petrel (formerly the Aiken, a revenue cutter) off the Carolinas, and sank her quickly with a well-placed shell in the bow just at the waterline.

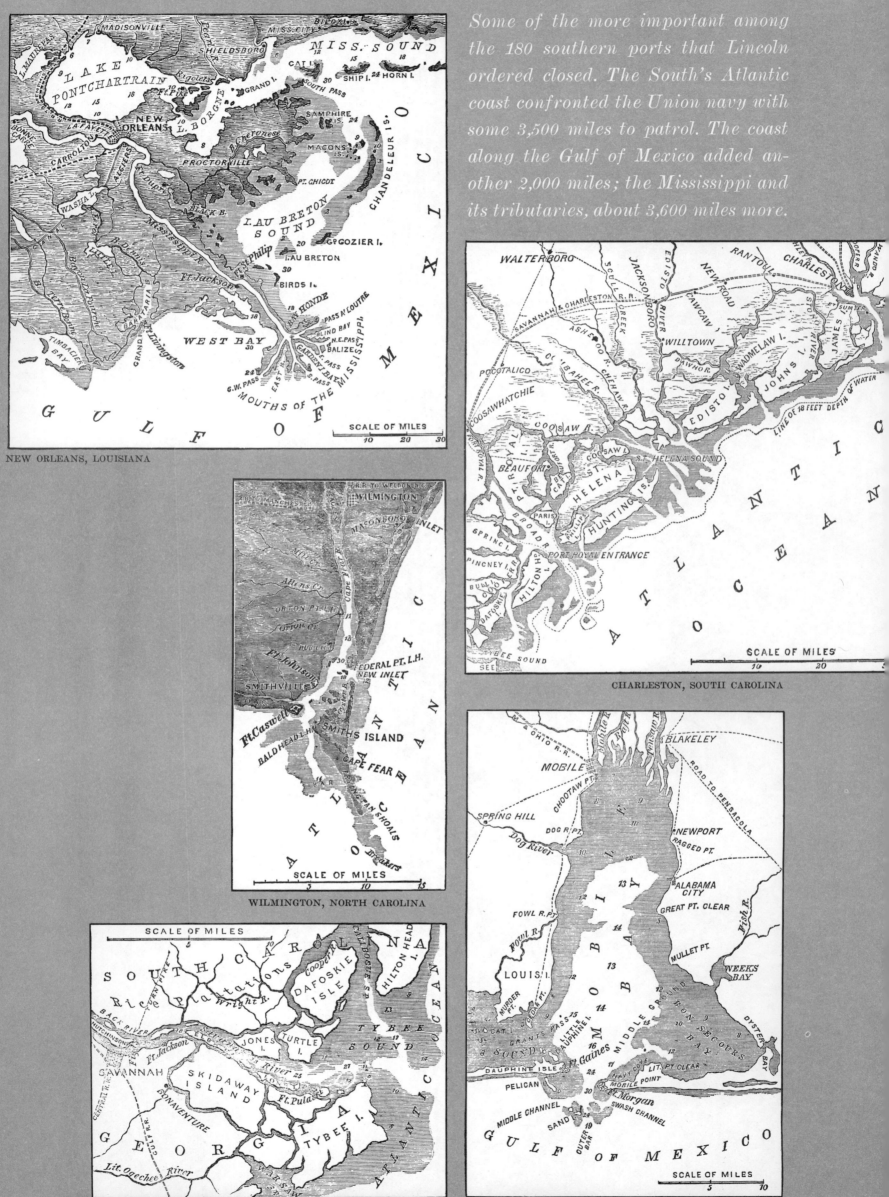

Some of the more important among the 180 southern ports that Lincoln ordered closed. The South's Atlantic coast confronted the Union navy with some 3,500 miles to patrol. The coast along the Gulf of Mexico added another 2,000 miles; the Mississippi and its tributaries, about 3,600 miles more.

NEW ORLEANS, LOUISIANA

CHARLESTON, SOUTH CAROLINA

WILMINGTON, NORTH CAROLINA

SAVANNAH, GEORGIA

MOBILE, ALABAMA

THE CAPTION IN HARPER'S WEEKLY: "A 'SMASH' FOR JEFF DAVIS."

"Talk about the Yankees worshiping the almighty dollar," recalled a Confederate officer who served in Wilmington, North Carolina. "You should have seen the adoration paid the Golden Calf... during the days of blockade-running. Everybody was engaged in it save the private soldiers and a few poor line and staff officers, who were not within the 'ring'."

When steamers arrived, men, women, and children rushed to the wharves "to buy, beg, or steal something." Nobody, contended the Confederate officer, was more excited than the average woman who was looking for gloves, parasols, hoop skirts, corsets, flannels, bonnets, silks, and calicoes. The lucky ones were those who were friendly with the cook and could "get a part of the stealings from the pantry or the drippings from the kitchen." The officer recoiled at how "well-dressed gentlemen" degraded themselves "by sponging and loafing," adding: "We have seen many a fellow, bearing a commission, for hours eyeing from a stand-point on the wharf a blockade-runner as a cat would a mouse, and then just about lunch-time drop aboard to enjoy the Champagne or porter, the Parmesan and English cheese." Wilmington in those times "swarmed with foreigners." Young toughs fought in the streets and prostitutes were commonplace. Yet profits from a single voyage ran as high as 700 per cent, which was fair recompense for the indignities suffered and the risks taken.

Blockade-runners carried their cotton and tobacco to four ports: Nassau, Bermuda, Havana, and Matamoras. A run from Wilmington to the Bahamas averaged three days, and the return voyage was planned so that the blockade-runner would reach the Carolina coast on a moonless night with the tide running high. Approaching port, the ship was blacked out, binnacle and fire-room hatch covered, steam blown off underwater. The routine of Union sailors on the patrol boats was as well known to the blockade-runner as to Secretary of the Navy Welles: breakfast at 8 a.m., dinner at noon, supper at 4:30 p.m. Southerners laughed at the poor Yankees on their old tubs, in good weather and bad, steaming in circles day after day. Upon occasion, however, a blockade-runner failed to reach port. Someone else did the laughing then.

Off Hatteras high winds and a heavy sea had badly buffeted the Federal warships and transports that approached Port Royal Inlet in early November, 1861. The *Governor* foundered at sea and seven of her crew were lost. The *Peerless,* a transport laden only with stores, went down. Three steamers—the *Belvidere, Osceola,* and *Union*—carrying stores but no troops, sank or failed to reach their destination. A large transport, the *Winfield Scott,* limped into the inlet on her last voyage. The following morning brought bright skies and a smooth sea. In good spirits the Federal armada steamed ahead, spoiling for a fight, while Acting Secretary of War Benjamin in Richmond dispatched an urgent message warning Governor Pickens of South Carolina:

"I have just received information, which I consider entirely reliable, that the enemy's expedition is intended for Port Royal."

Even though the Union had lost the element of surprise, nerves in official Richmond remained sorely frayed. An unhappy man in the Confederate capital those days was Robert E. Lee, who was suffering sharp criticism for his failure to stop a Federal invasion in western Virginia. "His bonnie face has only brought us ill luck," southerners grumbled. Lee was trying to secure steamer passage to spend a weekend with his family and thus forget the tensions of Richmond, when he was summoned to the President's office. A new military department of South Carolina, Georgia, and Florida had just been created, Jeff Davis announced. It was Robert E. Lee's to command.

If, as Lee wrote home, he believed that he had been sent on another "forlorn hope expedition," few could blame him. From Coosawhatchie, the railroad station nearest Port Royal, he sped by horseback to the scene of battle, hearing on all sides rumors of an impending Confederate disaster. For once the tale-bearers had

not exaggerated. The Federal navy was making proud history against Forts Beauregard and Walker as the warships of the main line slowly passed toward the sea, each throwing its shells with deadly aim into the earthworks. Ten vessels supplemented this destruction with an enfilading fire, until shortly after one o'clock the Rebels quit Fort Walker. As the Federal flag was run up, the wild cheers of Yankee seamen, bounding across the inlet, startled the defenders of Fort Beauregard. Grim face turned on grim face within the second fort. Clearly their hours also were briefly numbered.

The fall of Port Royal, exposing such vital seaports as Savannah and Charleston to invasion and attack, was a frightful blow. With scattered state troops and four old wooden vessels, Lee somehow was expected to defend the Confederacy's Atlantic Coast against the Union navy. Hopeless indeed seemed the task that confronted Lee, but he succeeded.

On November 7, 1861, Federal warships steamed into Port Royal Inlet, South Carolina (left), and unleashed a terrific bombardment upon the Rebel forts, Walker and Beauregard. Alarmed Richmond speeded Robert E. Lee to this point of trouble, and at long last the distinguished Virginian began his climb to immortality. But the war on the high seas was not one-sided, by any means. Among early Confederate raiders that sank unsuspecting northern merchantmen was the Sumter *(above), which has just opened fire upon the* Joseph Parks, *out of Boston. A crew boarded the* Joseph Parks, *and sent her, afire, to a watery grave.*

There was in Lee a boundless energy, a doggedness of purpose that emerged now. Faced with a 300-mile front to protect, he worked furiously at obstructing rivers, throwing up inner lines of defense, enlisting reinforcements. He tried to be everywhere and give personal supervision to every project. He boasted that he had grown "a beautiful white beard" and chuckled when on one occasion he overheard a teamster complaining: "Who *is* that durned old fool? He's always a-poking around my horses as if he meant to steal one of 'em."

Underneath, Lee felt the strain. "It is very hard to get anything done," he wrote his wife. "While all wish well and mean well, it is so difficult to get them to act energetically and promptly." Another letter told Mary Lee that the people of the South should be "taught to be less boastful, less selfish, and more devoted to right and justice to all the world." Again, to his daughter Annie, he was filled with bitterness for southerners willing "to nurse themselves and their dimes" while others assumed "the protection of themselves and families." Then fresh disaster struck the South with the invasion of Roanoke Island, convincing Lee anew that "our soldiers have not realized the necessity for the endurance and the labor they are called upon to undergo, and that it is better to sacrifice themselves than our cause."

A combined Federal naval and military expedition under the command of Acting Major General Ambrose E. Burnside steamed into Pamlico Sound on the morning of February 7, 1862. By the afternoon of the following day Burnside could reckon that he had done rather a neat job, having captured six forts, forty guns, 2,000 prisoners, and some 3,000 small arms. Apparently the Union boys had fought well. In the opinion of the New York *Tribune's* correspondent, "regulars were never more steady," and he described a vigorous charge by Hawkins's high-spirited Zouaves (the New York 9th) on one of the forts:

". . . They started on the run, yelling like devils, cheered by our forces on every side. Colonel Hawkins, who was leading two companies in the flank movement, joined his regiment on the way. On they went, with fixed bayonets, shouting 'Zou! Zou! Zou!' into the battery, cheered more loudly than ever. The rebels, taking fright as the Zouaves started, went out when they went in, leaving pretty much everything behind them, not even stopping to spike their guns, or take away their dead and wounded that had not been removed."

The Federal navy under Flag Officer Louis M. Goldsborough likewise was enjoying a good fight, according to the enthusiastic report of Commander Rowan:

"The *Commodore Perry* was in the advance, and made for the rebel steamer *Sea-Bird,* the flagship of the rebel navy . . . and run her down, cutting her through. The *Ceres* ran straight into the rebel steamer *Ellis* and run her down in like manner, boarding her at the same time. The *Underwriter* took the *Forrest* in the same style; while the *Delaware* took the *Fanny* in fine shape, she having received ten shots from our squadron, which made daylight through her in as many places. . . . The terrified rebels, as they for-sook their gunboats, fired them, and thus all but the *Ellis* were burned, including a new one on the stocks. Four were burned, one captured, and two made their escape—the *Raleigh* and *Beaufort.* They are in the canal which leads to Norfolk, but are not able to go through, on account of the locks having been destroyed; consequently they will be captured before this reaches you, as they can go only some few miles toward Norfolk."

Where next would the Union strike? Lee did not need a second guess. Savannah was the logical objective. Lee worked steadily on a line of defense at Fort Jackson, while Yankee gunboats pushed through creeks and marshes and shelled steamers on the Savannah River.

Lee resolutely wrote home that he'd "damage them yet."

Architects of Union victory at Roanoke Island: General Ambrose E. Burnside (left) and Flag Officer Louis M. Goldsborough. Six forts were captured and the Rebel fleet was rammed and sunk in the mud of Pamlico Sound. Lee, discouraged with the South's want of energy, could only hope it had learned a lesson. Meanwhile, he worked furiously to prepare Savannah for an attack that was almost certain to come next.

A Negro woman who lived in Norfolk appeared one day in the office of the Union's Secretary of the Navy. From the bosom of her dress she took the plans she had smuggled and Gideon Welles saw for the first time how the Confederates were reconditioning the *Merrimack*. The ship had been cut down to the waterline and a superstructure of oak and pine raised on her 160-foot berth deck. Armor plate, three inches thick, protected her slanting sides. In round figures, she could carry a crew of 350 and her ten guns fired 150-pound shot.

Welles's heart must have chilled. The North had only one hope of contending with this new sea monster, and at the moment that seemed an outside hope at best. As far as the Navy Department's Committee on Ironclads was concerned, John Ericsson might never have received a serious hearing for his ridiculous "cheesebox on a raft" except that a mutual friend brought a model of the *Monitor* to Washington to show the President. "All I can say," Lincoln commented, "is what the girl said when she put her foot in the stocking: 'It strikes me that there's something in it.'" Ericsson had asked for $275,000 and one hundred days in which to build his freak. Some old navy men called the whole thing preposterous. How could you tell anything about a ship when there were not even blueprints to study? But Ericsson—with Lincoln's support—had his chance. So workmen began to knock together the *Monitor,* covering her "crazy" revolving gun turret with armor plate eight inches thick while critics wanted to know what she expected to accomplish with only two guns. Supremely confident, Ericsson gave everyone the same answer. In a half hour, he stubbornly insisted, he would "split the rebel fleet at Norfolk into matches."

The problem was, would Ericsson ever get the chance to prove his point? The *Merrimack* hit suddenly, sounding a death knell to wooden navies around the world. Her iron plates made ping-pong balls of the Federal shells. That first afternoon she left the *Minnesota* grounded, the *Cumberland* grounded and burning.

The scene from the battery at Newport News, Virginia (opposite page), with the United States warships Congress *(left) and* Cumberland *(right), at anchor. On the afternoon of March 8, 1862, a Federal lookout shouted suddenly: "That Thing is coming down!" With dense columns of smoke pouring from her stacks and a black flag flying at her bow, the iron-plated* Merrimack *succeeded in the remaining hours of daylight to remake naval history around the world. The mighty frigate* Cumberland *was helpless against the ramming blows of the* Merrimack *(below). News of the disaster to the Federal fleet stunned official Washington. Lincoln called a special meeting of the Cabinet. No port in the North from Portland to Baltimore was safe against this new kind of warship. The war could end at once.*

With daylight, the *Merrimack* intended to return to her destruction of the Union navy and the pilot of the tug *Mystic* offered heartfelt advice to a Federal officer: "If I were you I would get just as far away from here as the good Lord would let me." Gloom fell upon the special Cabinet meeting that Lincoln called. The Secretary of War, Edwin M. Stanton, in "great agitation," paced the floor and filled the room with censure for "everything that had been done or was omitted to be done." Stanton "had no doubt" that at this very moment "the monster" was on her way to Washington. Looking out the window, he added grimly: "Not unlikely we shall have a shell or cannon-ball from one of her guns in the White House before we leave this room." Welles, who told the story, possibly exaggerated insofar as Stanton's tirade was directed principally at him. Welles held to his faith in "the untried *Monitor* experiment," and,

anyway, the *Merrimack* had too much draught to pass Kettle Bottom Shoals in the Potomac.

The *Merrimack* came back next morning to finish her job. Across her path suddenly appeared Ericsson's little *Monitor*. A crew of forty-eight against 350, two guns against ten—never had there been a battle more easily described. A pygmy versus a giant, that was the sum of it.

Aboard the *Monitor* seamen on wobbly legs, for they had been battered almost constantly by rough seas on the voyage to Virginia, manned the guns. The *Merrimack* at first ignored the little freak, for the southerners wanted to complete their destruction of the grounded *Minnesota*. But the *Monitor* would have none of that. On she came, looking to one reporter like "a raft, with an army ambulance amidship." She laid herself alongside the *Merrimack*.

Men told different stories about the battle,

depending on their point of vantage. As the *Merrimack* raked the *Monitor* with whole broadsides, the jubilant commander of the *Minnesota* believed they had no more effect than "so many pebble-stones thrown by a child." A reporter described the marvelous way the turret of the *Monitor* worked, spinning around, dropping a port cover, popping out an eleven-inch gun, pounding home its shot, and then in a twinkling having its gun disappear as the port cover slammed shut. The *Merrimack* tried to sink Ericsson's little seadog as she had the *Cumberland*—by ramming—and the *Monitor's* engineer recorded proudly: "Her bow passed over our deck, and our sharp upper-edged side cut through the light iron shoe upon her stem and well into her oak. She will not try that again. She gave us a tremendous thump, but did not injure us in the least."

Twenty-two times the *Merrimack* struck the

The Monitor *and the* Merrimack *locked in an immortal sea battle. In a single morning the giant was humbled by the pygmy. Wild with joy, northerners soon were smoking "El Monitor" cigars and the country's newest dance craze was "Ericsson's Gallope." With good reason, Welles wore a big smile.*

Monitor, and yet Ericsson's vessel kept coming on as full of fight as ever. Said an unhappy officer aboard the *Merrimack:* "I can do about as much damage to the *Monitor* by snapping my fingers at her." Toward noon, "sagging" at the stern as though "badly aleak," the *Merrimack* turned toward Norfolk, admitting her galling defeat. "Thousands have this day blessed you," a Federal officer wrote Ericsson.

BELEAGUERED SOUTH

The bold soldier boy

Failure at Shiloh,
the fall of New Orleans test
Johnny Reb's will to win

February–May, 1862

In Richmond on February 22, 1862, Jefferson Davis was formally inaugurated as President of the Confederate States of America. War Clerk Jones confided in his diary: "Such a day! The heavens weep incessantly. Capitol Square is black with umbrellas; and a shelter has been erected for the President to stand under." Yet the ceremonies proved agreeable and Davis, in Jones's opinion, read his inaugural well, "and seemed self-poised in the midst of disasters." Jones hoped that the South would learn from past errors: "We have attempted operations on too extensive a scale, thus diffusing our powers which should have been concentrated."

In Columbia, South Carolina, chatty Mary Boykin Chesnut, whose husband was a trusted advisor of Jefferson Davis, was equally gloomy in her musings that February: "Confederate affairs are in a blue way. Roanoke taken, Fort Henry on the Tennessee open to them, and we fear for the Mississippi River too. We have evacuated Romney—wherever that is. New armies and new fleets are swarming and threatening. . . . England's eye is scornful and scoffing as she turns it on our miseries. I have nervous chills every day. Bad news is killing me."

No less depressed was Robert Garlick Hill Kean, who labored in the War Office at Richmond: "Virginia must fight her own battles, defend as best she may her own soil and in so doing defend the whole eastern part of the Confederacy. . . . Noble, grand old State! I love her dearer in her days of tribulation than in her prosperity, and while life is spared me I will fight in her behalf so long as a foe is on her soil, or raises a hand against her. . . ."

The South, though troubled, was far from defeated, and perhaps no tendency among northerners led to false expectations of a victory the day after tomorrow than believing the slanders of their own propagandists. "The Yankees," sneered Edward A. Pollard, editor of the Richmond *Examiner*, "were pleasantly entertained with stories of our suffering. Their pictorials

were adorned with caricatures of 'secesh' in skeleton soldiers and gaunt cavalrymen with spurs strapped to their naked heels. Their perfumed fops and dainty ladies had the fashion of tittering at the rags of our prisoners. They had an overwhelming sense of the ludicrous in the idea of Southern women cutting up the carpets in their houses to serve for blankets and garments for our soldiers."

Pollard exaggerated, yet he advanced a sound argument. The people of the South were resolute, brave, and prudent. Though adversities mounted around them along the coast, the Tennessee, the Cumberland, they had fortitude and staying power. The early months of 1862 would bring new setbacks, new dangers, but no lessening of the determination of the southern people to carry on until independence had been won.

The war produced hundreds of songs. Soldier and civilian alike found release from tension and renewed will to carry on the struggle in such tunes as "Dixie," "The Bold Soldier Boy" (left), and the "Rogues' March" (below).

March added to the Confederate gloom. Toward mid-month a Federal force under Burnside captured New Bern, North Carolina, and about two weeks later in New Mexico's Apache Canyon in the battle of Pigeon's Ranch or Glorieta—often called "the Gettysburg of the Southwest"—Union troops ended dreams of the Confederacy someday extending its empire as far as southern California. On March 8, the day before the *Monitor* and *Merrimack* duelled at Hampton Roads, a more critical action ended in Arkansas at Pea Ridge (or Elkhorn Tavern). Union General Samuel Curtis, who won his only decisive battle of the war here (but with badly needed help from the stubborn Germans who fought "mit Sigel"), admitted he had paid for his victory: "Our loss is heavy. The enemy's can never

be ascertained, for their dead are scattered over a large field. Their wounded, too, may many of them be lost and perish. The force is scattered in all directions. . . ." Official figures at Pea Ridge would list, among 11,250 Federal effectives engaged, 203 killed, 908 wounded, and 201 missing. Among the 14,000 Confederate effectives involved, 600 had been killed and wounded and 200 were missing.

New Madrid, Missouri, fell to Federal troops under John Pope on March 14, and in Richmond, in the face of the increasing setbacks, Jefferson Davis reshuffled his Cabinet. But New Madrid was merely a prelude to more depressing news, and in early April, on a night when lightning flecked the sky and thunder rolled through the surrounding hills, Union gunboats converged on

Island No. 10, key to the control of the upper Mississippi. Within the Rebel fort bugles summoned the alarm, but the murky night shielded the boats except when their roaring guns flashed. Although Pope was pleased to take credit for the fall of Island No. 10, and for the bag of 7,000 prisoners, the victory actually had belonged to the naval forces.

Yet early April brought its worst battle along the yellow bluffs of the Tennessee. Grant's army was camped comfortably beneath the sweet scent of the peach blossoms around Shiloh Meetinghouse, awaiting the arrival of the army under Don Carlos Buell. A Confederate army under Albert Sidney Johnston was at nearby Corinth, but no one in the Union high command was fool enough to expect an attack.

North Carolina, New Mexico, Arkansas, Missouri—each was the scene of disaster for the Confederacy during March, 1862. The final advance of the Federal force at Pea Ridge (left) on March 8 gave Samuel Curtis his single claim to fame during the war, and the Union now had wrested control of mountainous Arkansas. Six days later the capture of New Madrid, Missouri, opened the way in early April for Union gunboats to bombard into submission (above) the Confederate defenders of Island No. 10, key to holding the upper Mississippi River.

The Confederate high command at Shiloh (left): standing (from left to right), Beauregard, Breckinridge, Johnston, Bragg, Hardee; seated, Polk. Leading his army into a flaming surprise attack, Johnston was mortally wounded (right). As Federal troops scattered and cowered against the bluffs of the Tennessee, the Rebel forces smashed forward in what promised to become a crushing victory (below, left). Scenes of disaster such as this awaited Grant when he finally reached a battle already hours old. His middle name, some said, was "Surprise."

When the Rebel army under Albert Sidney Johnston struck unexpectedly at Shiloh in the Sabbath dawn of April 6, it caught Union troops still in bed, or washing and dressing, or preparing breakfast. With screaming yells, Confederates raced through the camp, firing as they came, catching laggards with their bayonets. Shells hurtling from the woods tore the tents into shreds. Some Yankees died while asleep. Thus began Bloody Shiloh, one of the most tragic battles of the war. Four horses that day would be shot from beneath William Tecumseh Sherman. Blood would thicken brooks crossing the battleground, and with reason a reporter who surveyed the dreadful carnage of the battlefield informed readers of the Cincinnati *Times* that he hoped never again to behold such sights: "Men with their entrails protruding, others with bullets in their breasts or shoulders, and one poor wretch I found whose eyes had been shot entirely away."

Grant, suffering a painfully swollen ankle as a result of a fall from a horse, heard the distant sounds of battle from his headquarters in the Cherry House. When he could reach Shiloh, panic surrounded him. Half-crippled and in pain, Grant rose suddenly to superb heights of command. He rallied stragglers, ordered up reserves, dispatched couriers to hurry Buell's advancing army, found ammunition for regiments that had fired their last rounds, and brought back fighting spirit to discouraged troops. At nightfall, when others advised a retreat, Grant put his foot down. "We can hold them off till to-morrow," he said. "Then they'll be exhausted and we'll go at them with fresh troops!" Grant's generalship, in the opinion of Major General J. F. C. Fuller, a fine British military student, could only be called "wonderful." But the country was staggered at the cost of Shiloh, for all that Grant next day smashed his way to victory. The Union's dead were 1,754; its wounded, 8,408; its missing, 2,885. Confederate forces suffered as badly: killed, 1,723; wounded, 8,012; missing, 959. Some said nastily that the North had suffered near defeat only because Grant was a drunken incompetent. Stung by the abusive criticism, the North's best general decided to resign.

Those who fought at Shiloh never forgot it. Like a haunting nightmare, it lived on, reminding boys of how in a day they had lost all sense of their youth. Yet an Iowan remembered that, in the midst of its horrors, "little birds were singing in the green trees over our heads!" A Kentuckian beseeched: "Hold on, Bill, don't shoot there any more! That's father!"

Simultaneously attacked by a Confederate fire-raft and the ram Manassas, *the Federal flagship* Hartford *runs the gantlet of Forts Jackson and St. Philip. With shot and shell "whistling like locomotive demons around, above, before, and in the rear," the* Hartford *fought her way into the Mississippi while "Rebeldom"—and the proud city of New Orleans—"began to quake."*

A gifted southern author, George Washington Cable, said New Orleans was never the same after "the awful day of Shiloh." The body of Albert Sidney Johnston, brought home from that fearful field of carnage, was carried up St. Charles Street behind muffled drums. Saddened residents watched this last tribute to their "great chevalier." They remembered the sons and brothers and fathers who once had marched down this same street to trumpets blaring "Listen to the Mockingbird" and who now slumbered beneath the peach blossoms at Shiloh.

Ended forever for New Orleans were days when every boy in town, watching jaunty regiments in the garb of Hussars and Zouaves at drill, became an expert in the manual of arms; when the shouts of *"un, deux, trois, quatre"* proclaimed that French-speaking Creoles were parading by the steamboat landing; when the owners of any kind of sea-going craft, from towboat to sidewheeler, were discovering profit with patriotism. Irresistibly a change came. The blockade "closed in like a prison-gate" and the ships tied up at the docks, their boilers cold and their machinery rusting. The trade of the city found merchant outmaneuvering merchant in the game of extortion, and Cable recalled a little old wholesaler in groceries who spent his days getting tipsy rather than "speculate on the food of a distressed city." Then Shiloh wrote its death roll on the hearts of those who lived within "the Paris of America." No eye really ever sparkled thereafter, no lips again sang with true gaiety. The war pressing down, and drawing ominously closer, became a mood holding New Orleans together in common dread and grief.

Through the rising sea mists on the morning of April 13, a Federal fleet swept down on Forts Jackson and St. Philip, guarding the sea lanes into New Orleans. Aboard the Federal flagship *Hartford* was remarkable David G. Farragut, who had joined the navy at the age of nine, and fought his first sea battle during the War of 1812 at the age of thirteen. Farragut was now in his early sixties. A young gunner aboard the *Hartford,* Bartholomew Diggins, described him as of "square build, about 160 pounds; hair medium, between light and dark; clear hazel eyes, heavy eyebrows; very bald, which he tried to cover by combing the side hair across the top of his head." He was, always, a proud man—proud of his country, his ships, his personal code. He was a man who read his Bible and planned his battles; a man who would not give his crew a shot of whiskey before an action. "No, sir!" Farragut always retorted. "I never found that I needed rum to do my duty." Hot coffee they could have. Hot coffee was good for any man.

Harper's Weekly pictured the "awful scene" as the Confederate ram *Manassas,* with a fire raft, opened battle against the *Hartford:* "The flames caught our rigging and side, and for a moment it seemed we must fall a prey to the ravages of fire ... we gave the Ram a dose of rifle shell. She, however, came up for us again, but some other vessel tackled her and she hauled off. During this stage of affairs we grounded ... but our men worked like beavers, and the engineers soon got the ship astern and afloat.... The river and its banks were one sheet of flame, and the messengers of death were moving with lightning speed in all directions. Steadily we plied shell and grape, interspersed with shrapnel...."

At the end of the first day Fort Jackson was in flames. Its batteries were not seriously damaged, since the river was at flood tide and the shells buried themselves in the muddy ground. Farragut, however, had come for a fight to the finish. Chains protected the sides of his ships. Sandbags were banked around the boilers. Fire brigades with tubs of water placed around the deck awaited emergencies. A battle was won by planning and quick thinking, in Farragut's rule book, and on April 25, with alarm bells ringing in the city, he passed all the hazards and steamed around Slaughter House Bend.

To David Porter, the scene at the docks as the fleet steamed down on New Orleans was almost

beyond description. "Crowds of maniacs," he declared, rushed everywhere with "the men smashing in the rice tierces and the women scraping up all that could be gathered." In later years, George Washington Cable recoiled at the memory: "What a gathering! The riffraff of the wharves, the town, the gutters. Such women— such wrecks of women!" To many it appeared as though history had not known such a scene since the fall of Babylon, and Cable, with a superb recollection of significant detail, remembered amid the screams of rage on the levee "one old tar on the *Hartford,* standing with lanyard in hand beside a great pivot-gun, so plain to view that you could see him smile, [who] silently patted its big black breech and blandly grinned."

cer passed her house, was exiled to Ship Island. William B. Mumford, head of a gambling ring in New Orleans, who tore down the United States flag from the Mint, was hanged at the scene of his offense, for Butler liked style in his disciplinary measures. Nor was he hesitant to deal with the "she-adders of New Orleans," to use his own phrase. Broadsides throughout the South soon aroused its citizens to fight on at any risk and any sacrifice rather than to submit to a "Beast" Butler:

BUTLER'S PROCLAMATION.

His outrageous insult to the
Women of New Orleans!

Southern Men, avenge
their wrongs!!!

Headquarters, Department of the Gulf,
New Orleans, May 15, 1862.

General Orders, No. 28.

As the Officers and Soldiers of the United States have been subject to repeated insults from the women calling themselves ladies of New Orleans, in return for the most scrupulous non-interference and courtesy on our part, it is ordered that hereafter when any Female shall, by word, gesture, or movement, insult or show contempt for any officer or soldier of the United States, she shall be regarded and held liable to be treated as a woman of the town plying her avocation.

By Command of Maj.-Gen. Butler,
George C. Strong,
A.A.G. Chief of Stables.
By Lincoln's direction, the order was rescinded.

In balding, pudgy, strong-willed Benjamin F. Butler the city received a military administrator who met charges of severity by reminding New Orleans's citizens that they should learn to count their blessings. After all, they had not been roasted like the inhabitants of Algiers during the French campaign. A Mrs. Phillips, who laughed when the funeral train of a Union offi-

"Ah, me!" wrote George Washington Cable, remembering Farragut's ships at anchor off New Orleans. "I see them now as they come slowly around Slaughterhouse Point into full view, silent, grim, and terrible; black with men, heavy with deadly portent; the long-banished Stars and Stripes flying against the frowning sky."

Off the West Coast of Africa in August of 1860, the United States steamer *Mohican* intercepted a little vessel, the *Erie,* which had been beating hard to north with all sail set. Aboard the *Erie,* were 897 Negroes, about half of whom were children. "Nastiness and wretchedness reigned supreme," reported the New York *Times,* which had no sympathy to waste on her captain, Nathaniel Gordon of Maine. Yet though for forty years the law had made slave trading a form of piracy punishable by death, the Federal government had hesitated to execute anyone for doing on the high seas "that which"—or so *Harper's Weekly* contended—"in half the Union, is done daily without censure." Enormous pressure was placed upon the Lincoln Administration to pardon Gordon, and Ralph Waldo Emerson, in Washington to deliver a lecture, was far from satisfied with the attitude of Secretary of State Seward who "twisted his cigar, and . . . twisted his nose also," and to Mr. Emerson seemed singularly devoid of "the new spirit." Lincoln studied the case carefully, again the lawyer of the Illinois Eighth Circuit, exhibiting "a fidelity and conscientiousness" that Mr. Emerson greatly admired. Clearly, the President understood the nation's "new spirit" for on February 21, 1862, the New York *Times* reported with great satisfaction that Gordon, who was not sober and wore a senseless smile, had fallen "the length of the rope . . . still regardless of pain or pleasure."

Other evidence of the country's "new spirit" was reflected in the excited report Secretary of the Treasury Chase received from young Edward Lillie Pierce, a treasury agent who had been sent to the islands off the coast of South Carolina to save all that he could of 2,500,000 pounds of ginned long-staple Sea Island cotton that had fallen into the Union's hands with the capture of Port Royal. Pierce was far more interested in saving the slaves "for useful citizenship," begging Chase to send him doctors, nurses, teach-

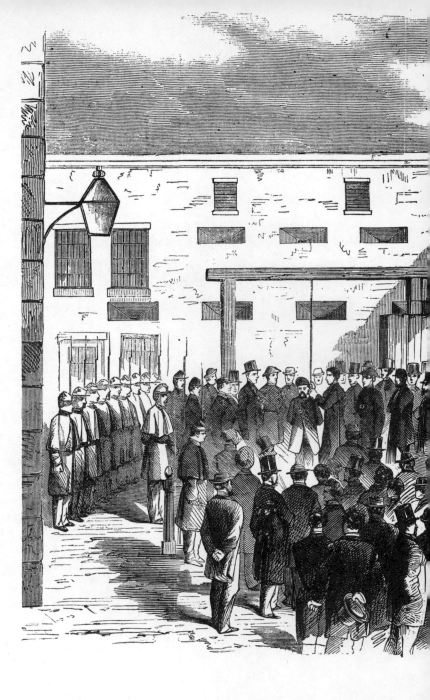

ers, and social service workers so that Pierce could begin preparing the Island Negroes for freedom. Though the Secretary had no funds for social experiments, he permitted Pierce to appeal for voluntary subscriptions and groups in Boston, New York, and Philadelphia responded handsomely. Seventy-four men and nineteen women were sent to educate the Negroes, with results that exhilarated Pierce. "The children learn without urging by their parents, and as rapidly as white persons of the same age, often more so," he wrote Chase. Pierce did not deny that there were tremendous problems to overcome, arising principally from a system that treated children as belonging more to the plantation than to their family, yet his enthusiasm for the future of the Negro broke through time and again. He, too, spoke of freedom in a new dimension.

Nathaniel Gordon, slave trader of Maine, became the first and only American to die for this crime when with "no twitchings, no convulsions, no throes, no agonies" he was hanged in New York City on February 21, 1862 (left). The Gordon case received Lincoln's personal attention, since great pressure was exerted to save the life of the slave-runner. With the capture of the islands off the coast of South Carolina, the Federal government faced up to the problems of feeding and clothing hundreds of Negro slaves (below). Voluntary assistance made possible a social experiment in educating these slaves to responsible citizenship.

LEE SAVES RICHMOND

Suddenly called back
to Richmond, Lee begins his march
into history and legend

March–July, 1862

Lee pushed ahead, preparing Savannah for an expected attack, but he was caught in a backwash of the main stream of the war. In letters home, he tried to appear cheerful, but underneath there was always a note of uneasiness. He hoped, he wrote Mary, that the South had learned the real lesson in the *Trent* affair: "We must make up our minds to fight our battles and win our independence alone. No one will help us." In the news—from Forts Henry and Donelson—appeared the name of Grant, yet for Lee the war in the west was too impersonal to grasp. All of Lee's energies were consumed in preaching the gospel of work, sacrifice, and danger to a people more enchanted by the azaleas and japonicas now in bloom. If Lee owed a vote of gratitude to anyone, it was to Union General Thomas W. Sherman, who prodded at Savannah in a manner approaching downright sluggishness. Then Lee was called back to Richmond.

Lee returned to a capital swept by gloom and under martial law, for every stranger was believed to be a Yankee spy. Now only eight months after winning a victory at Manassas, the Confederate commander there, Joseph E. Johnston, so feared an attack on his right flank as Federal strength mounted, that he proposed to withdraw to the line of the Rappahannock. Lee received a new assignment, and whereas his responsibility for supervising all military operations under presidential authority carried an impressive ring, at least one critic wondered if Lee was anything more than "an orderly sergeant." Lee,

writing home, offered a characteristic comment: "I will not complain, but do my best."

Waves of despair washed over Richmond. Once Johnston had withdrawn behind the Rappahannock, he was again impelled to act prudently, withdrawing across the Rapidan. Meanwhile, with Burnside occupying New Bern, North Carolina, Lee had to face the possibility of a new disaster if the Yankees pushed inland to Goldsboro and cut the main railroad line connecting Richmond with the coastal states to the south. Lee acted promptly, borrowing two brigades of infantry and two companies of artillery from Johnston's army, combining them with such regiments as he dared to nibble from the force at Norfolk, and rushing these troops to the defense of North Carolina. Frankly, in the most charitable view, Lee was robbing Peter to pay Paul. But in the circumstances he had no other choice.

Late March brought grimmer news. A convoy of twenty steamers, moving down Chesapeake Bay, were disembarking Federal troops across the inlet from Hampton Roads. Lee was confronted with a guessing game. Were these reinforcements for a campaign in North Carolina? Or was McClellan moving his Army of the Potomac, with a march up the Peninsula to Richmond as his objective? In that event, what chance had the Federals of also mounting an assault on Richmond from the north? Could Lee risk bringing Johnston's army to the defense of the Peninsula? Lee thought hard and long.

General Joseph E. Johnston was never an easy man to handle since, resigning as Quartermaster General of the United States Army at the outbreak of war, he believed that he should have ranked first among southern generals. He was placed fourth by Jefferson Davis and his dignity never recovered. Lee also had to contend with Johnston's injured vanity and it was certainly to the credit of the "orderly sergeant" that he did so with considerable tact.

By early April reports from Alexandria left no doubt. McClellan's objective was to use the strip of land between the York and James rivers as a highway into Richmond. Lee no longer hesitated—Johnston was needed on the Peninsula—and at Lee's advice Davis ordered Johnston to bring two divisions to Richmond while a third division, under General Richard Ewell, was left on the Rappahannock to watch the Yankees and, should opportunity offer, co-operate with Stonewall Jackson in a Shenandoah Valley campaign.

Joe Johnston, reaching Richmond in a huff, made an inspection of the Peninsula and returned to the Confederate capital in a bigger

huff. He couldn't possibly defend the lower Peninsula, Johnston said. His advice was to bring all the available troops from Virginia, the Carolinas, and Georgia to a line in front of Richmond, thus forcing McClellan to attack as far as possible from his base of supplies. Lee had an uncomfortable fortnight. Obviously, Johnston believed that in time McClellan on the Peninsula would be aided by a Union force from the north under McDowell in a pincer movement against Richmond. Lee wanted nothing less, but intended that this deviltry should not develop. Thus he set

Jackson in motion in the Valley to threaten Washington and pin down McDowell's troops in defense of the national capital. Few plans in the war ever have worked more perfectly. McClellan berated Washington for failing to send him McDowell's forces, but the government, worried sick by Jackson's successful blows in the Valley, stood by its decision to guard the capital at whatever cost to McClellan's outraged dignity.

But if Lincoln and his friends in Washington had the jitters, so too did Johnston, who simply wouldn't fight on the lower Peninsula.

THE RICHMOND TO WHICH LEE RETURNED IN THE CRITICAL DAYS OF EARLY MARCH, 1862.

Lee ordered the James River obstructed, the fortifications guarding the Confederate capital strengthened, precautions that saved Richmond when a Federal gunboat flotilla was turned back by guns at Fort Darling. The balloon view (left) shows the gunboats Galena *and* Monitor *in the lead, Richmond in background above the river obstructions. At right, McClellan arrives in Yorktown to take command of Union forces moving down the Peninsula between the James and the York rivers.*

Lee's distress mounted as slowly, irresistibly the Federals began to push their way up the Peninsula, not because McClellan exerted any great aggressiveness, but more because Joe Johnston could not be prodded into offering better than a token defense. Early May brought gloomy news to Richmond: Yorktown had fallen to the Federals virtually by default and Union gunboats had steamed up the York River to West Point, thirty-seven miles from the Confederate capital. Next day the two armies fought in the rain at Williamsburg and the Confederates had to quit the place, leaving their wounded on the field.

Early May also brought Lincoln to Fortress Monroe to judge the situation for himself. Discovering that Norfolk remained unoccupied and the threat of the *Merrimack* ignored, Lincoln angrily slammed his hat on the ground. The result, the Secretary of the Treasury wrote his daughter, was "a brilliant week's campaign of the President." With Federal troops finally in Norfolk, Chase added exuberantly: "The whole coast is now virtually ours." But McClellan, cautious by nature and alarmed by reports from Alan Pinkerton's agents that set the strength of

the Rebels at more than double the actual figure, was not inclined to change character because Lincoln had spent a week at Fortress Monroe.

Meanwhile, Johnston's peevishness with Jefferson Davis deepened, and he asked to be relieved of "a merely geographical command." In a situation that called for a mountain of tact, Lee soothed Johnston's wounded feelings, but "Old Joe" still continued to fall back until by mid-May he was across the Chickahominy and McClellan's soldiers, going aloft in balloons, could look down onto the spires of Richmond.

Davis called a meeting of the Cabinet and invited Lee to attend. Already War Department papers were being shipped to Lynchburg and Columbia, South Carolina, for safety. Should the capital be abandoned? Lee answered: "Richmond must not be given up—it shall not be given up." Postmaster-General Reagen remembered: "As he spoke the tears ran down his cheeks. . . . I never saw him show equally deep emotion." Then Richmond's fortifications beat back the advance of Federal gunboats like the *Monitor* and the *Galena*. Hearts lifted and Congress resolved to defend the city "at all hazards."

Rebel works seen from Gen.! Porter's Division.

Scenes as McClellan's Federals occupied Yorktown, Virginia, across fields enshrined in American history. (Here Washington's decisive victory over Lord Cornwallis and his Redcoats virtually ended the Revolution.) On the next day the Federals were in Williamsburg, a Rebel's roost that had spawned such patriots of the past as Thomas Jefferson, Patrick Henry, Richard Henry Lee, Richard Bland, George Wythe, among many other illustrious men.

The enemy's m

Berdan's Sharpshooters picking off the enemy's gunners.

Reconnoissance in force by Genl Gorman

...r Yorktown

"It would have been easy for me to have sacrificed 10,000 lives in taking Yorktown," McClellan wrote home, "and I presume the world would have thought it more brilliant. I am content ... Had I reached the field three hours earlier I could have gained far greater results and have saved a thousand lives. It is, perhaps, as well as it is, for officers and men feel that I saved the day." Lincoln may have expected more, but what did he know?

Religious services in Camp of 61st N.Y. Volunteers.

With May almost over, northern newspapers declared that by June 15, as an outside date, Richmond must fall. Lee felt edgy, depressed by rain and sullen skies and wishing there was a place for him with the army in the field. On the last day of May, the Federal army was spread along the east bank of the Chickahominy River from Mechanicsville to Bottom Bridge, and two corps, thrown across the stream, had entrenched on a line from Seven Pines to Fair Oaks Station. But the rain, flooding the Chickahominy, imperiled the bridges on which the Federals depended. The situation was ready-made for hitting those two exposed corps and their shaky routes of reinforcement or retreat.

Johnston did. Lee hurried to field headquarters, hoping he could help, but all he seemed to manage was an argument with Johnston about whether the firing to the southwest was musketry (as Lee believed) or simply an artillery exchange. Johnston rode off, leaving Lee to join Jefferson Davis, another fretful visitor to the scene of action. Around the President and his "orderly sergeant" swirled the Battle of Seven Pines. Confused masses of men, North and South, collided in a savage contest; Johnston had not guessed right about the firing to the southwest. Musket fire, poured point-blank into charging columns, wrought a bitter toll. The heavy guns of the artillery toppled trees as though they were matchsticks, and beneath the clouds of smoke hanging everywhere over the field the dead were piled upon the dead.

What did it all mean? For one thing, Seven Pines demonstrated that, put to the test, the Federals could fight magnificently. By throwing a corps across "almost ruined bridges," by holding on until the coming of darkness and by delaying the fighting on the extreme right as long as possible, the left wing of McClellan's army was saved from destruction. For the South the change that Seven Pines brought came unexpectedly as Jefferson Davis and Lee watched litter-bearers bringing a wounded Johnston up the

road, for, in excruciating pain and perhaps mortally wounded, the general could not bear the jostling of an ambulance. Through the darkness, Davis rode into Richmond, lost in his own reveries. Then, coming to a decision, he spoke quietly to the soldier at his side:

"General Lee, in the morning you will take command of the army."

So Lee—a failure in western Virginia, a planner of coastal defenses, a headquarters general without real combat experience—suddenly was thrust forward as the man who must save the Confederacy. He must have known that his subordinates viewed him as a commander on trial,

but Lee accepted the reality of that situation with good humor and did the thing always characteristic of him. He rolled up his sleeves and went to work. If, in a military sense, Seven Pines had decided nothing, Lee still suspected that the right wing of McClellan's army, north of the Chickahominy, was "in the air." Lee needed to be sure before he acted, and he knew the one man he could depend upon to ascertain the truth.

So Jeb Stuart also was brought forward onto the stage of history—carefree Jeb, not yet in his thirtieth year, whom a Union general called "the best cavalry leader ever foaled."

Through the woods surrounding Williamsburg, McClellan's army marches toward Richmond. The general's private letters revealed that he was at war on a dual front. He was "heartily tired" of leading a life with "always some little absurd thing being done by those gentry in Washington." By May 20 he reported that "we are gradually drawing near the rascals." He expected a fight in front of Richmond: "It will be a decisive battle."

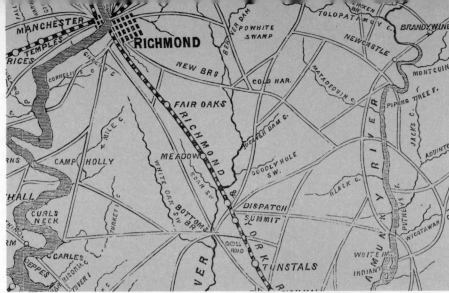

SCENE OF THE BATTLE OF SEVEN PINES.

General Jeb Stuart's audacious "ride around McClellan's army" followed, confirming Lee's hunch. Meanwhile, Lee had summoned Jackson to bring his main army to the Peninsula and in mid-June, "red with the dust of three Virginia counties," Jackson was in Richmond. Lee believed that he had McClellan caught over the Chickahominy like a cow hung over a fence. He planned carefully to strike a surprise that would shatter the Federals.

Jackson fumbled, failing to give support to the opening of the Battles of the Seven Days. The Yankees struck back savagely and when night closed in, the slopes of Beaver Dam Creek were soaked with Confederate blood. Through darkness Lee marched Dan Hill's boys along the Upper Cold Harbor road to meet with Jackson. Thus, dawn breaking over the scenes of yesterday's disaster revealed the trap Lee had sprung on McClellan at Gaines' Mills. By swinging to the east, Jackson would flank the Federal position on Beaver Dam Creek and McClellan's

Daniel E. Sickles, Tammany Hall warrior become general, leads a charge on Rebel lines at Fair Oaks Station. From drummer boy to troops of the line, the Federals proved their fighting caliber when they saved the left wing of McClellan's army under Johnston's quick blow on May 31.

base of supplies at White House would become untenable.

Lee won handily that day. To Confederate General E. M. Law "men fell like leaves in the autumn wind," and the New York *Tribune* prepared the North for a calamity: "A motley mob started pell-mell for the bridges...every minute a man struck down; wagons and ambulances and cannon blockading the way . . . and the sun just disappearing, large and blood-red." Staggered, McClellan blamed Washington.

Lee's timing was faulty as the Battles of the Seven Days opened. Confederate troops were driven from Mechanicsville under the pounding of Union batteries (left). Still, Lee kept his head, brought up reserves through the night, and at Gaines' Mill turned a seeming defeat into a crushing victory. His hope was to force McClellan back on his base at White House (below) and to capture or destroy his entire army. What Lee never dreamed was the possibility that McClellan would move his army from the York to the protection of Federal gunboats on the James. When Lee awoke, White House was in flames.

To the North's astonishment, Lee saved Richmond. And now, to the South's astonishment, McClellan saved his army. After Gaines' Mills, Lee, though counting his loss in dead and wounded at 8,000 against Federal losses in killed, wounded, and missing of 6,837, told Jefferson Davis that he was "profoundly grateful to Almighty God" for his victory. Then, next morning came distressing news when a Confederate officer, climbing a tree, reported that the Federals were moving southward. Thus McClellan, who would not sacrifice an army to win a victory, was beginning what Lee never had expected—a move of base from the York River to the James River.

Frustration piled upon frustration for Lee, who had reckoned on nothing less than the annihilation of McClellan's army. The critical day for the Federal army was Sunday, when it had to plunge into White Oak Swamp. On this day, when Jackson seemed capable of delivering a crippling blow, that old Calvinist appeared more concerned with resting and writing his wife about how much money she should give to their local church. That night McClellan passed through White Oak Swamp and occupied Mal-

With a brilliant forced march, McClellan escaped to the James and entrenched on Malvern Hill. Lee had lost the initiative and further assaults failed to budge the Federals. "It was not war," avowed Rebel Dan Hill, sadly. "It was murder."

vern Hill within reach of Harrison's Landing and the protection of Yankee gunboats on the James River.

July 1 faced Lee with a difficult decision. Not until late in the afternoon did he feel in position to strike the Federal left on Malvern Hill, and when the sun disappeared and rain fell heavily, he did not appear to comprehend his losses that day as clearly as General Dan Hill did: "It was not war—it was murder." In the dense fog of the next morning exhausted Rebels, who had slept on their arms through the night, reached for the bluecoats. But McClellan's boys were gone, and Lee had failed in destroying his army. Still, in an optimistic view, a southerner said: "The serpent has been killed, though it exhibits some motions."

MARYLAND, MY MARYLAND

CEDAR MOUNTAIN, FOUGHT ON AUGUST 9, 1862, WAS CALLED A BATTLE IN AN ANTEDILUVIAN WORLD.

*Lee settles a grudge,
and carries the scourge of war
onto the soil of the North*

August–September, 1862

Dug in at Harrison's Landing, McClellan's army of 90,000 still threatened Richmond, and Lee had to reckon with the possibility that, crossing the James, the Federals might swing around Petersburg and come at the capital through its "back" door. The Lincoln government, however, fretted over Washington's exposure to attack and, combining the forces of Irvin McDowell, N. P. Banks, and Franz Sigel organized an army of 43,000 to safeguard the national capital. At the head of these troops Lincoln placed the hero of Island No. 10—John Pope, a bustling gamecock who came out of the Midwest bursting with profanity and bluster.

Trained at West Point, a veteran of the Mexican War, an experimenter with artesian wells, Pope told his eastern troops: "I have come to you from an army . . . whose policy has been attack, not defense." Henceforth these soldiers must "look before and not behind," for, declared the loquacious Pope, "Success and glory are in the advance. Disaster and shame lurk in the rear." In an astonishing order to his generals, Pope authorized the arrest of "all disloyal and male citizens" within their lines. Those who refused to take an oath of allegiance were to be "conducted south" with a warning that if they were found again they would be "considered as spies and subjected to the extreme rigor of military law." If troops were fired upon by "bushwhackers," Pope ordered homes in the vicinity "razed to the grounds" and the assailants "shot without civil process." He directed the Army to live off the country and not waste "force and energy" protecting the private property of those "most hostile to the Government."

Lee was furious at Pope's orders which, in the Confederate view, instituted a campaign of "robbery and murder" against "unarmed citizens." Fired with anger, Lee warned the Lincoln Administration that if this was the way it wanted to fight, then "we shall be reluctantly forced to the last resort of accepting the war on the terms chosen by our enemies, until the voice of an outraged humanity shall compel a respect for the recognized usages of war." Pope became almost an obsession with Lee, who called him a "miscreant" that must be "suppressed."

While Lee's generals bickered—Toombs called Dan Hill a virtual coward and Longstreet put Powell Hill under arrest—Lee planned to teach Pope a lesson. His guess was that if Washington were threatened, McClellan would be withdrawn from the Peninsula. In early August Lee had a division under Stonewall Jackson racing north to find Pope.

Reinforced by Powell Hill's troops, Jackson commanded an army of about 24,000. A report that the Federals were advancing leisurely on Culpeper gave Old Jack a chance that suited his fighting style, a swift movement to destroy the first Federal corps arriving there. But Old Jack had his shortcomings. He liked to keep a plan secret, with the result that his own generals, uninformed of their objective, pushed ahead too slowly. At Cedar Mountain on August 9, it was the Federals under Banks who struck viciously. Jackson, glass in hand, stood on the mountain side, directing every operation. The battle, one witness said, was fought in "bog, barren, ditch, creek, forest, and mountain." Banks had attacked impetuously, without reserves and without sending for reinforcements. Out of 8,030 troops engaged, Banks listed 314 killed, 1,445 wounded, and 594 missing for a total loss of 2,353, whereas Jackson, with 16,868 men engaged, had only 231 killed, 1,107 wounded, and none missing.

For Lee, the great success at Cedar Mountain was its psychological impact upon Washington where jittery orders directed McClellan to speed to the assistance of Pope. Lee, wanting nothing less, moved with Longstreet's corps to bolster Jackson. Lee's intention was to strike Pope's eastern flank, isolating him from Washington and preventing a union with McClellan, but a surprise attack on Stuart's cavalry gave Pope a copy of the plan. He drew back quickly.

JOHN POPE

But two could play this game, and Jeb Stuart, capturing Pope's headquarters at Catlett's Station, brought Lee the information that McClellan would join Pope within five days. Already outnumbered 75,000 to 55,000, Lee knew that to stand on the defensive was simply to court an eventual defeat; and, anyway, in Lee's opinion, Pope's generalship was fumbling at best. In as bold a plan as the war produced, Lee divided his army, sending Jackson and Stuart's cavalry ahead to cut the Federal line of communication while he followed with the remaining troops.

Pope misread the movement by Jackson and Jeb Stuart, believing that Old Jack was returning to his favorite haunts in the Valley. Even after Pope discovered the Confederates on the railroad to his rear, he mistook the movement for a mere raid. Longstreet marched to join Jackson, giving Pope a chance to overwhelm some 30,000 Rebels while they were west of the

AT THE BATTLE OF SECOND MANASSAS, AUGUST 29-30, 1862,

Bull Run Mountains. Again, Pope failed to guess the truth, and at times, like a punch-drunk pugilist, seemed to be marching his army in a confused circle. Lee's gamble had paid off, and his subsequent victory at the Battle of Second Manassas, on August 29-30, 1862, was among the great military achievements of the war.

Jackson, entrenched behind a railroad cut with 20,000, held off Pope's 62,000 until Longstreet joined him, and had the attack been pressed vigorously the Rebels might have discovered the two-mile gap that separated the corps of Fitz-John Porter from the other Federal forces. A day later, still unaware that Longstreet's soldiers were on the field, Pope charged the Confederate left, opening his own weakened flank to a pulverizing assault by the troops of Longstreet. As Lee said afterward—a masterpiece of understatement—Pope "did not appear to be aware of his situation."

JAMES LONGSTREET

EE'S MASTERFUL PLAN SETTLED HIS GRUDGE WITH POPE.

There were those who argued that Lee could have done better. After all, if he had moved faster and caught Pope between the Rapidan and the Rappahannock, might not he have destroyed an entire Federal army? Or why had he not pursued Pope's disordered columns, smashing them to pieces and taking a poorly defended Washington in the bargain? Lee's answer, simply and sensibly, was that his men were tired and hungry and he didn't know that the national capital was poorly defended. Moreover, thrown by a frightened horse, Lee suffered from a pair of broken wrists.

As September came on and his injuries began to mend, Lee turned his gaze on Maryland. To carry the war out of Virginia—what could he wish more? And was it not common knowledge that there was a large pro-southern population

in Maryland? Captivated by both the military and the political situation, Lee planned an invasion of the North and on September 8 issued a proclamation "To the People of Maryland" in which he listed the constitutional violations the government in Washington had forced upon the Old Line State: ". . . your chief city has been usurped by strangers; your Legislature has been dissolved by the unlawful arrest of its members; freedom of the press and of speech have been suppressed; words have been declared offences by an arbitrary desire of the Federal Executive, and citizens ordered to be tried by military commission for what they may dare to speak."

Obviously, Lee was talking himself into the firm belief that he had only to enter Maryland and thousands would rally to his banner. Long before he reached Frederick sullen faces re-

Confederate troops, fording the Potomac (left), carry the war into Maryland where Lee expected southern sympathizers to rally to his banner. A cartoon in Harper's Weekly (above) lampooned Lee's proclamation to the people of Maryland, urging them to enjoy once more "their ancient freedom of thought and speech" by rising to arms.

vealed how far wrong he had been. One Marylander, recalling Lee's soldiers, described them as "the dirtiest men I ever saw, a most ragged, lean, and hungry set of wolves." A surgeon remembered: "A Union man from whom they wished to purchase forage, told them that their scrip depreciated the paper on which it was printed."

Lee swallowed this disappointment and again, unimpressed by the generalship opposing him (McClellan had been restored to full command), decided to divide his army. Thus Jackson was sent to capture Federal troops and provisions at Harpers Ferry, while Lee pressed on toward his own bold objective—"the long bridge of the Pennsylvania Railroad over the Susquehanna, a few miles west of Harrisburg"—thus cutting off communication with the west except by the cir-

cuitous route by way of the Great Lakes. After this he would turn his attention to Philadelphia, Baltimore, or Washington, "as may seem best for our interests." Lee could not have asked for any more accommodating factor in his plans than the leisurely pace at which McClellan pursued him into Maryland. And no one honestly could expect that a Federal skirmisher, resting in the grass, would place his hand on two cigars wrapped in a copy of Lee's secret order sending Jackson to Harpers Ferry.

McClellan read the secret order in an exuberant mood. "If I don't crush Lee now," he said, "you may call me whatever you please." Lee, of course, knew nothing of the discovery. Suddenly, as though inspired by a military sixth sense, McClellan appeared over the Catoctin Mountain, threatening to isolate Lee from Jackson.

Longstreet pleaded with Lee not to fight at South Mountain, but to fall back on Sharpsburg, and a savage day of fighting demonstrated that Longstreet was right. Another day would see McClellan storming and taking the mountain pass. Prudently, on the night of September 14, Lee drew back to Sharpsburg, moving his gray columns across the bridge over Antietam Creek and forming in line of battle along a range of hills between the town and the stream. Lee counted on McClellan to follow cautiously, and guessed right. While the Federal commander threw away a day, the Rebels cheered Jackson's great triumph at Harpers Ferry, where 12,000 men, seventy pieces of artillery, and 13,000 small arms had been captured. Jackson, reaching Sharpsburg on the night of the sixteenth, shook his head. "I thought I knew McClellan," he said, "but this movement of his puzzles me."

More puzzling to the historian would be why McClellan waited until September 17 to fight the "bloodiest day of the war" at Antietam. Or why, after the battle had raged furiously over the stone bridge, along a sunken road now enshrined in history as the "Bloody Lane," around a little white Dunkard church and across a cornfield, McClellan failed to use his reserves. Next day Lee waited for the Federals to resume the battle, but his fretfulness was wasted. All the fight had been knocked out of McClellan. The following morning, the Confederates recrossed the Potomac. "Thank God!" Lee said.

McClellan, pursuing Lee into Maryland, is warmly welcomed by citizens of Frederick (left). McClellan's troops storm the Rebel lines on South Mountain (above). A focal point of "the bloodiest day of the war"—the stone bridge over Antietam Creek (below). For the next generation fathers would tell sons of the grim events that occurred here.

Huddled in the homes and factories of Sharpsburg, women and children numbly lived through the battle of Antietam (above). Once artillerymen held their fire while women in their Mother Hubbards, with hair streaming in the wind and children strung out behind, scrambled to safety. "We sat in silence," a resident recalled. "There were no impatient words, few tears; only silence, and a drawing close together, as if for comfort. We were almost hopeless, yet clung to the thought that we were hoping."

Since July, on the advice of the Secretary of State, Lincoln had kept locked in his desk the draft of a preliminary Emancipation Proclamation. To issue this directive without a military success to support it, Seward had argued, would appear to be "the last measure of an exhausted government." It would be viewed, Seward insisted, as "the government stretching forth its hand to Ethiopia, instead of Ethiopia stretching forth her hand to the government." Lincoln had agreed and bided his time.

Now Antietam gave the President the "military success" for which he waited and five days later he issued a preliminary proclamation warning states, or parts of states, then at war with the Union, that if they did not cease their

rebellion by January 1, 1863, he would issue a second proclamation declaring slaves in those regions to be "forever free." As a document of military necessity, the Emancipation Proclamation, in both its first and final forms, may have been as weak-kneed as the South claimed. But as a tool of psychological warfare, at home and abroad, it performed miracles.

Very likely, even Lincoln did not comprehend fully that he had fashioned an instrument of revolution. Reactions ran the full range of emotion, from the Cockney woman who dashed through the streets of London shouting, "Lincoln's been and gone and done it," to Jefferson Davis assuring the Confederate Congress of his "profound contempt for the impotent rage" that

the Proclamation disclosed. *Harper's Weekly,* behind the Union to the finish, not only employed one of its more talented artist-propagandists, Thomas Nast, to wring the last drop of emotional appeal from the Proclamation (see next page), but was cheered to reflect that the war had produced "a remarkable change in the opinions of educated and liberal men." Since for years the North had been "moving heaven and earth" to recruit a labor force from Europe, *Harper's Weekly* contended that a group who tried to frighten the North with threats of competition from the emancipated Negro "insults the understanding of our laboring class." The threats continued, nonetheless. All at once the basic conflict had been identified.

Nast depicts "institutions" in America that must disappear as emancipation achieves its purpose: a female slave being whipped at the post (left), a slave on the auction block (above). Not until 1865, however, would this victory of which Nast dreamed be realized.

Emancipation gave Democrats and Copperheads an effective issue of political campaigning, and they used it as evidence that the war had been devised by Lincoln as an instrument for gaining despotic control over the nation. Now Lincoln was taking the next logical step in this direction by destroying white supremacy. State legislatures—New Jersey was a conspicuous example —received numerous petitions from communities decrying the support of a war whose ultimate objective was to put the Negro and the white man on an even footing.

Yet what *Harper's Weekly* called the "educated and liberal men" of the North rallied to the support of the doctrine that all men are created equal, and among them was Henry Clay Work, whose "Kingdom Comin'" became one of the popular songs of the war:

> Say, darkeys, hab you seen de massa,
> Wid de muffstash on his face,

> Go long de road some time dis mornin',
> Like he gwine to leab de place?
> He seen a smoke way up de ribber,
> Whar de Linkum gunboats lay;
> He took his hat, an' lef berry sudden,
> An' I spec he's run away!
> > De massa run? ha, ha!
> > De darkey stay? ho, ho!
> > It mus' be now de kingdom comin'
> > An' de year ob Jubilo!

The emotional war that confronted America— this war whose battlefields had been the gallows for Nathaniel Gordon, a spirited hymn for Julia Ward Howe that called on the North to die to make men free as Christ had died to make men holy—had become solidified. It belonged to everyone now. It was a war of heart and conscience, and what it meant was that slavery had not only divided the nation but, in no small measure, also had sundered Christian religion.

AN ALBUM

OFF FOR THE WAR.

A Portfolio of the People and the War

J*efferson Davis, President of the Confederate States of America.*
At right, a rare portrait of Abraham Lincoln as he appeared
at the time of his nomination for the presidency. Painted by Thomas
Hicks, it was signed June 14, 1860, at Springfield, Illinois.

Painted from Life
by Thomas Hicks, Springfield, Illinois.
June 14th 1860.

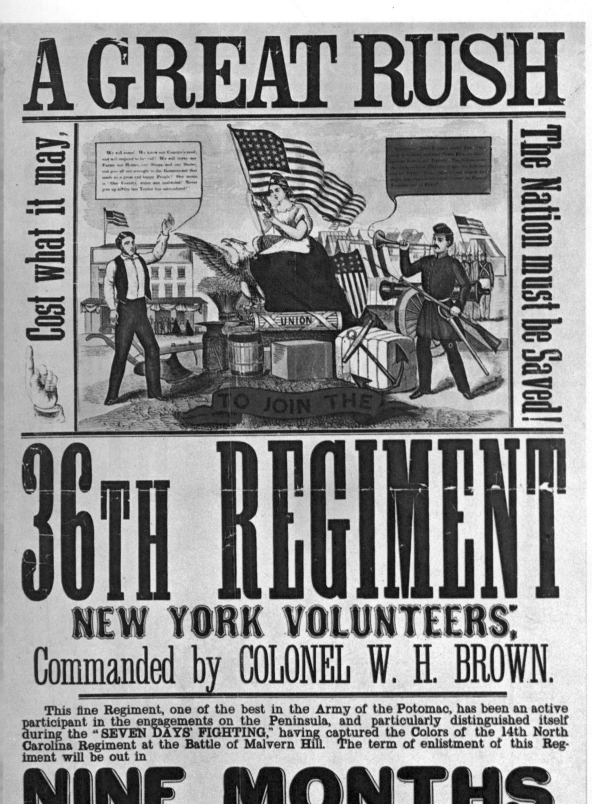

A GREAT RUSH

Cost what it may, **The Nation must be Saved!**

TO JOIN THE

36TH REGIMENT
NEW YORK VOLUNTEERS,
Commanded by COLONEL W. H. BROWN.

This fine Regiment, one of the best in the Army of the Potomac, has been an active participant in the engagements on the Peninsula, and particularly distinguished itself during the "SEVEN DAYS' FIGHTING," having captured the Colors of the 14th North Carolina Regiment at the Battle of Malvern Hill. The term of enlistment of this Regiment will be out in

NINE MONTHS.
DON'T WAIT TO BE DRAFTED!
THE USUAL BOUNTY GIVEN.

Recruiting Office, No. 17 CENTRE STREET,
BETWEEN CHAMBERS AND READE STREETS.

Lieut. G. H. MOORE, Recruiting Officer.

BAKER & GODWIN, Printers, Printing-House Square, Opposite City Hall, New York.

Northern campaign posters used a variety of appeals, but none was more effective than the promise of bounty payments to those who enlisted. The cost of the war in human sacrifice was staggering. The Union dead were estimated at 360,222 and included 110,000 who had died from wounds, while still another 275,175 lived with one leg or no legs, with one arm or no arms, among other afflictions of the battlefield. The Confederate dead were estimated at 258,000, of whom 94,000 had died in battle. The number of wounded remained unknown. During the course of the war, in all classifications, it is believed that more than 2,000,000 men supported the Union. The total number who fought for the South is a mere guess, but a popular figure is between 600,000 and 700,000.

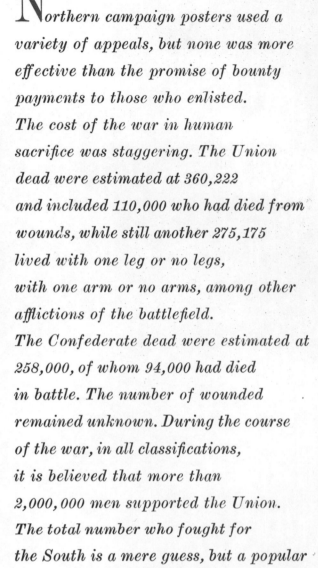

GARIBALDI GUARD!

PATRIOTI ITALIANI!
HONVEDEK!
AMIS DE LA LIBERTE!
DEUTSCHE FREIHEITS KÆMPFER!

APPEAL!

The aid of every man is required for the service of his ADOPTED COUNTRY! A Regiment of Riflemen, Bersaglieri, Honvedek, Chasseurs or Scharfschutzen, is now formed under the name of the GARIBALDI GUARD, and encamped near Washington This Regiment will be increased by order of Government to 1150.

Wanted at once,

250 ABLE-BODIED MEN!
Italians, Hungarians, Germans, and French, Patriots of all Nations,
AROUSE! AROUSE! AROUSE!
The Families of our Soldiers shall be cared for.

PER ORDER.
Col. F. G. D'UTASSY,
Lieut. Col. A. REPETTI,
Quartermaster, CHAS. B. NORTON.
Maj. GEO. H. WARING, Jr.

Headquarters, Irving Building, 594 & 596 Broadway.

BAKER & GODWIN, PRINTERS, PRINTING-HOUSE SQUARE, OPPOSITE CITY HALL, NEW YORK.

ATTENTION, TO SAVE YOUR BOUNTY!
SECOND REGIMENT
EMPIRE BRIGADE!
Col. P. J. CLAASSEN, Commanding.

☞ FIRST REGIMENT IN THE FIELD UNDER THE NEW CALL.

WANTED, 25 MEN

Between the ages of 18 and 45 years, to fill up one of the best Companies now forming,
under officers who have seen active service.

Clothing, Subsistence and Comfortable Quarters provided on enlistment.
PAY FROM $13 TO $23 PER MONTH,
TO DATE FROM DAY OF ENLISTMENT.
$50 BOUNTY GIVEN BY THE STATE.
$25 BOUNTY GIVEN BY THE U. S. GOVERNMENT.
TO BE PAID AS SOON AS MUSTERED INTO SERVICE.

☞ **$100 BOUNTY WHEN THE WAR IS OVER!**

☞ It is intended to make this one of the best Companies in the Brigade or service,
and no labor will be spared to do so. The Officers are experienced men, having been
over one year in one of the First Regiments in the service.

CAPTAIN J. H. STINER, LATE OF HAWKINS ZOUAVES.

BAKER & GODWIN, Printers, Printing-House Square, opposite City Hall, N. Y.

69TH REGT N. Y. S. M.
Col. MATHEW MURPHY.

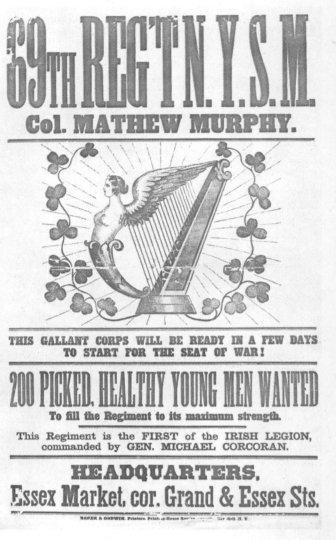

THIS GALLANT CORPS WILL BE READY IN A FEW DAYS
TO START FOR THE SEAT OF WAR!

200 PICKED, HEALTHY YOUNG MEN WANTED
To fill the Regiment to its maximum strength.

This Regiment is the FIRST of the IRISH LEGION,
commanded by GEN. MICHAEL CORCORAN.

HEADQUARTERS,
Essex Market, cor. Grand & Essex Sts.

BAKER & GODWIN, Printers, Print. House Square, N. Y.

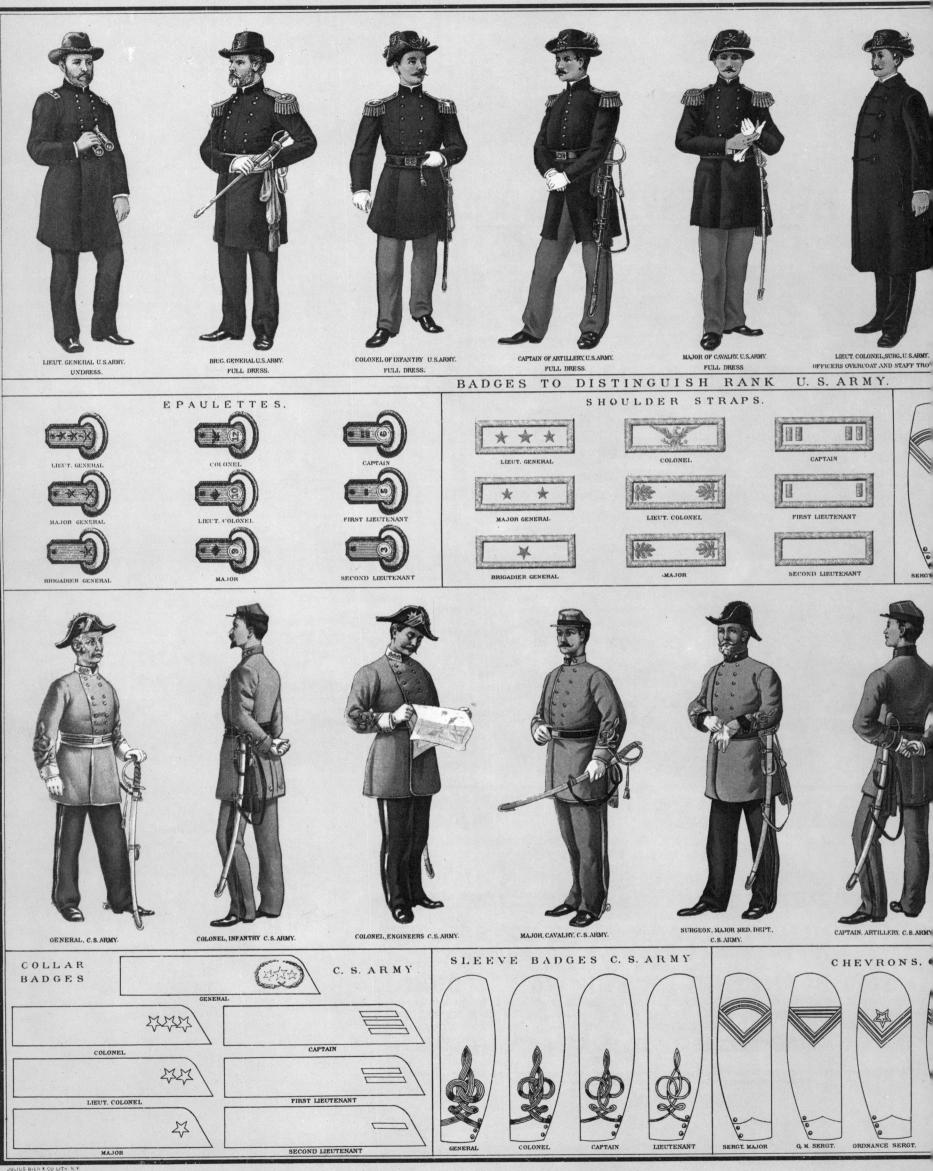

LIEUT. GENERAL, U.S.ARMY.
UNDRESS.

BRIG. GENERAL, U.S.ARMY.
FULL DRESS.

COLONEL OF INFANTRY, U.S.ARMY.
FULL DRESS.

CAPTAIN OF ARTILLERY, U.S.ARMY.
FULL DRESS.

MAJOR OF CAVALRY, U.S.ARMY.
FULL DRESS.

LIEUT. COLONEL, SURG. U.S.ARMY.
OFFICERS OVERCOAT AND STAFF TROOP

BADGES TO DISTINGUISH RANK. U.S. ARMY.

EPAULETTES.

LIEUT. GENERAL

MAJOR GENERAL.

BRIGADIER GENERAL.

COLONEL

LIEUT. COLONEL.

MAJOR

CAPTAIN

FIRST LIEUTENANT

SECOND LIEUTENANT

SHOULDER STRAPS.

LIEUT. GENERAL

MAJOR GENERAL.

BRIGADIER GENERAL.

COLONEL.

LIEUT. COLONEL

MAJOR

CAPTAIN

FIRST LIEUTENANT

SECOND LIEUTENANT

SERGT

GENERAL, C.S. ARMY.

COLONEL, INFANTRY C.S. ARMY.

COLONEL, ENGINEERS C.S. ARMY.

MAJOR, CAVALRY, C.S. ARMY.

SURGEON, MAJOR MED. DEPT.,
C.S. ARMY.

CAPTAIN, ARTILLERY, C.S. ARMY

COLLAR BADGES

GENERAL

COLONEL

LIEUT. COLONEL

MAJOR

C. S. ARMY

CAPTAIN

FIRST LIEUTENANT

SECOND LIEUTENANT

SLEEVE BADGES C.S. ARMY

GENERAL

COLONEL

CAPTAIN

LIEUTENANT

CHEVRONS,

SERGT. MAJOR

Q. M. SERGT.

ORDNANCE SERGT.

JULIUS BIEN & CO LITH. N.Y.

PLATE CLXXI

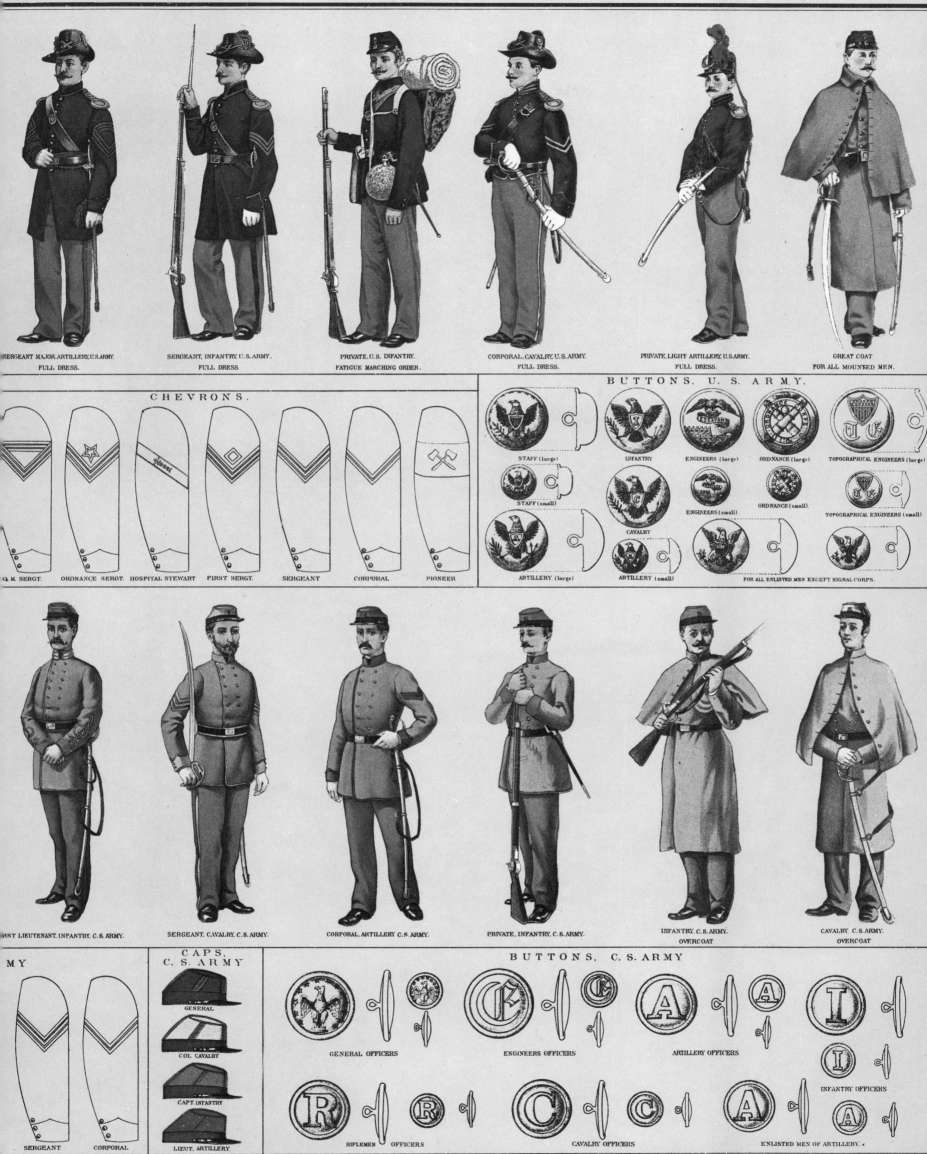

SERGEANT MAJOR ARTILLERY, U.S. ARMY.
FULL DRESS.

SERGEANT, INFANTRY, U.S. ARMY.
FULL DRESS

PRIVATE, U.S. INFANTRY.
FATIGUE MARCHING ORDER.

CORPORAL, CAVALRY, U.S. ARMY.
FULL DRESS.

PRIVATE, LIGHT ARTILLERY, U.S. ARMY.
FULL DRESS.

GREAT COAT
FOR ALL MOUNTED MEN.

CHEVRONS.

Q. M. SERGT.   ORDNANCE SERGT.   HOSPITAL STEWART   FIRST SERGT.   SERGEANT   CORPORAL   PIONEER

BUTTONS, U.S. ARMY.

STAFF (large)   INFANTRY   ENGINEERS (large)   ORDNANCE (large)   TOPOGRAPHICAL ENGINEERS (large)

STAFF (small)   ENGINEERS (small)   ORDNANCE (small)   TOPOGRAPHICAL ENGINEERS (small)

CAVALRY

ARTILLERY (large)   ARTILLERY (small)   FOR ALL ENLISTED MEN EXCEPT SIGNAL CORPS.

FIRST LIEUTENANT. INFANTRY. C.S. ARMY.

SERGEANT, C.AVALRY, C.S. ARMY.

CORPORAL, ARTILLERY C.S. ARMY.

PRIVATE, INFANTRY, C.S. ARMY.

INFANTRY. C.S. ARMY.
OVERCOAT

CAVALRY C.S. ARMY.
OVERCOAT

MY

CAPS,
C. S. ARMY

GENERAL

COL. CAVALRY

CAPT. INFANTRY

LIEUT. ARTILLERY

SERGEANT   CORPORAL

BUTTONS, C.S. ARMY

GENERAL OFFICERS   ENGINEERS OFFICERS   ARTILLERY OFFICERS

INFANTRY OFFICERS

RIFLEMEN   OFFICERS   CAVALRY OFFICERS   ENLISTED MEN OF ARTILLERY.

* For all other enlisted men the same as for Artillery, except that the number
of the regiment in large figures will be substituted for the letter A.

CAMP "N. P. BANKS,"
COL. COLLIS' REGIMENT OF ZOUAVES D'AFRIQUE,

L. N. Rosenthal, Lith., 327 Walnut St., Philad'a.

Boys wearing the blue and the gray waited in camp, drilled, marched, waited
again while generals argued over strategy and tactics. A leisurely scene
in an unidentified Confederate camp (upper left), awaiting the evening mess.
A new sight invades the German-populated farm country of Pennsylvania
(lower left). The officers of the 10th Maine make merry at Camp Kelsey (top),
while at a Confederate military post (below) at Anderson,
Tennessee, war appears to have no more reality than mere newspaper headlines.

The Army

The Army of the Potomac crossing the Rapidan. At full strength, whenever this great fighting organization moved, the effect was the same as though a city like Albany or Columbus or Indianapolis arose one morning and walked away complete in every detail—clothing, food, medicine, horses, wagons, people. Seldom did this great army of the North move with less than 100,000 men, and at times its strength swelled to a majestic total of 125,000.

the Potomac

LITH. OF J.H. BUFFORD, BOST.

The beautiful Shenandoah Valley (upper left) where Stonewall Jackson
(above) rode to fame as the avenging Joshua in gray. But the war changed and into
these peaceful mountains came Little Phil Sheridan, bringing a scorched-earth
policy that became one of the bitterest memories for the South of the tragic years from
1861 through 1865. Hard though the scene after a battle could be (upper right), with the
maimed to care for and the dead to bury (lower right), these were still clean
wounds that healed. But Sheridan in the Valley—or Columbia, South Carolina, put
to the torch by Sherman's troops—were livid scars on the spirit of the South.

Robert E. Lee (inset) and the crucial area of northern Virginia
in which the war reached its climax. Federal gunboats sailing the tidal
rivers constantly harried the Confederate rear. Rebel cavalry,
coursing the western valleys, threatened fearful Washington.
In this perspective, the capital is due north of Fortress Monroe.

Seal of War.

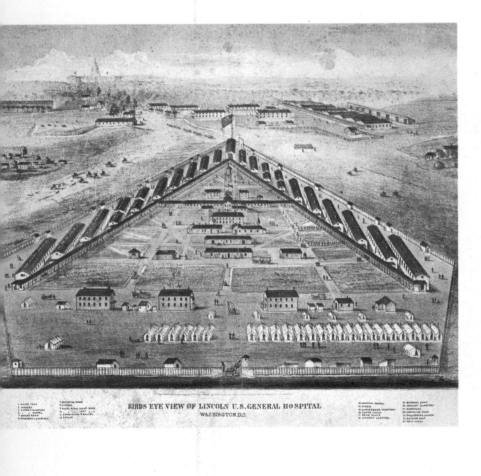

BIRDS EYE VIEW OF LINCOLN U.S. GENERAL HOSPITAL
WASHINGTON D.C.

The moods of war were many and changing. Thus, the print, "Yankee volunteers marching into Dixie" (left), captured the early spirit of a conflict that was to be all over in three months. Then the print of a Federal hospital outside Washington and the cover of a song celebrating the fighting at Bull Run (lower left) each in its way was part of the grim awakening. The picket reserves who occupied a ravine (right) tried to forget how long and weary the war could be, but at night the loneliness and homesickness that swept over both Yankee and Rebel were moods powerfully depicted in the superb lithograph by Currier & Ives (shown below).

PUBLISHED BY CURRIER & IVES.

152 NASSAU ST. NEW YORK.

THE SOLDIER'S DREAM OF HOME.

Stretched on the ground the war worn soldier sleeps.
  Beside the lurid watch fire's fitful glare;
And dreams that on the field of fame he reaps,
  Renown and honors, which he hastes to share.

With those beloved ones who gathering come,
  To bid their hero husband father "welcome home";
Fond dreamer may thy blissful vision be,
  A true fore shadowing of the fates to thee.

UNION PRISONERS

Lith of SARONY MAJOR & KNAPP, 449 Broadway N York.

DRAWN FROM NATURE BY

Federal prisoners at Salisbury, North Carolina, while away the hours playing baseball, a popular sport in both the North and South. Football was beginning to gain popularity, and the first intercollegiate game between Princeton and Rutgers, launching the sport as a second national pastime, would be played in 1869. Other forms of athletics, commonly seen in camp and prison included foot racing, wrestling, boxing, leapfrog, and ten pins played with cannonballs. The "Ring Tournament," derived from the days when knighthood was in flower, had many devotees among Confederate cavalrymen.

T SALISBURY, N. C.

R OTTO BOETTICHER

In the bloodiest months of the war, with Grant stuck in the mud before Vicksburg and Lee conceiving of the campaign into Pennsylvania that led to Gettysburg, two great romances captured the hearts of America. By all odds, the wedding of Tom Thumb to Lavinia Warren was the sensation of the war years. Observing the circus people at the ceremonies, the New York Herald said: "Never before was the scarlet lady seen to such advantage. Babylon was a rag fair of it." Americans were almost equally entranced by the marriage of the Prince of Wales to the Princess Alexandria (right) in St. George's Chapel, Windsor, on March 10, 1863. Harper's Weekly reported seven women "crushed to death" cheering the couple.

THE PRINCE AND PRINCESS OF WALES.

Wiedereroberung von York-Town.

Beim Ausbruch des nordamerikanischen Bürgerkrieges im Jahre 1861 waren die südlichen Staaten besser und vollständiger zum Kriege gerüstet als die nördlichen. Denn sie hatten schon lange auf Abfall in Folge davon das Kriegsglück sich ihnen wieder zuzuwenden begann, richteten sie ihr Augenmerk vor Allem auf die Wiedereroberung von York-Town, und sandten ein Heer ab, um dieselbe zu versuchen.

A typical scroll (opposite page, top) that was "suitable for framing" and hung over many a fireplace long after the war had ended. Lithographers did not ignore the large German populations in cities like St. Louis, Missouri, who loyally supported the Union (below). A popular print of the war was the Soldier's Home in Washington, D.C., (above, left), where Abraham Lincoln often went to escape the heat of the White House during humid summer months. Another favorite, especially after the surrender of Vicksburg, was the print of General Ulysses S. Grant on his horse (at left). Every occasion of the war, from draft to battle, encouraged songwriters to new efforts. The song cover above is one of thousands that appeared during "the singing Sixties."

During the summer of 1864, the number of prisoners confined in the stockade at Andersonville, Georgia (above), was 32,899; buried in the National Cemetery there are 12,912 who did not survive. Another name that struck terror in northern hearts was Libby Prison in Richmond (upper right), yet Federal prisons also were notoriously mismanaged and feared. Camp Douglas in Chicago (lower right) is shown as it appeared in 1864 when it accommodated as many as 6,000 prisoners. The stockade was situated four miles south of the Court House and covered sixty acres.

LIBBY PRISON, RICHMOND, Va

Campaign posters of 1864 when Lincoln decided to stand for re-election despite
the advice of many friends that he should use the war emergency to avoid
the risk of a defeat. The President contended that unless the people could decide who
should occupy the White House, the purpose for which the war was being waged
had already been forfeited. Apparently the McClellan poster (center) was effective, for
Democratic rallies in New Jersey such as this one carried the state for
the General. The only other states Lincoln lost were Delaware and Kentucky.

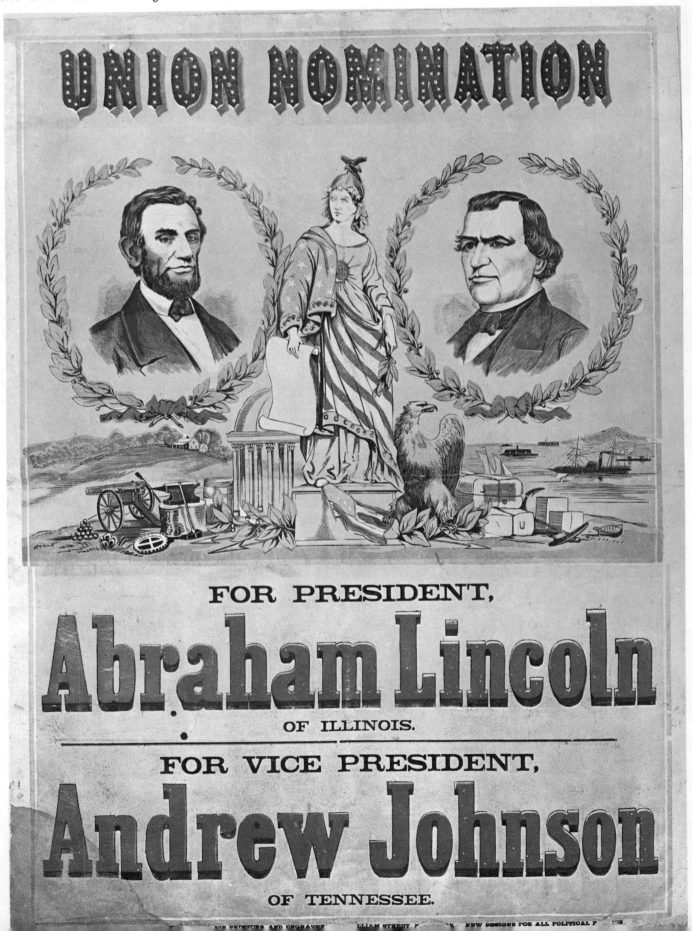

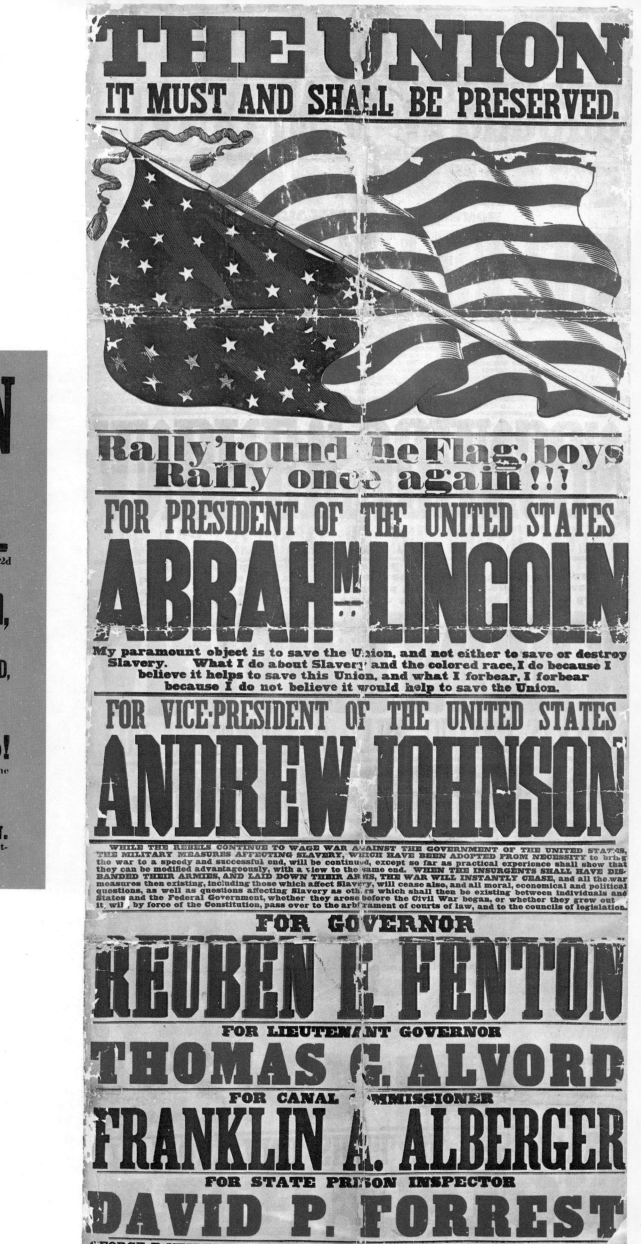

McCLELLAN MEN, ATTENTION!

There will be a Meeting of the Democracy, of the 2d Assembly District, of Bergen County, on

Tuesday Ev'g, Sept. 20th,

At 7 1-2 O'CLOCK, at the

DRILL-ROOM OF THE NATIONAL GUARD,

FOR THE PURPOSE OF ORGANIZING A

Democratic Campaign

McClellan Club!

For the 2d Assembly District, of Bergen County. The following Speakers will address the meeting.

Hon. A. J. ROGERS,
Hon. RODMAM M. PRICE,
Hon. DAN. HOLSMAN.

All Conservative, Constitutional Men are invited to attend. **By order of COMMITTEE.**

Paterson Guardian Print, S. E. Cor. Broadway & Main Street.

THE UNION

IT MUST AND SHALL BE PRESERVED.

Rally 'round the Flag, boys Rally once again!!!

FOR PRESIDENT OF THE UNITED STATES

ABRAHᴹ LINCOLN

My paramount object is to save the Union, and not either to save or destroy Slavery. What I do about Slavery and the colored race, I do because I believe it helps to save this Union, and what I forbear, I forbear because I do not believe it would help to save the Union.

FOR VICE-PRESIDENT OF THE UNITED STATES

ANDREW JOHNSON

WHILE THE REBELS CONTINUE TO WAGE WAR AGAINST THE GOVERNMENT OF THE UNITED STATES, THE MILITARY MEASURES AFFECTING SLAVERY, WHICH HAVE BEEN ADOPTED FROM NECESSITY to bring the war to a speedy and successful end, will be continued, except so far as practical experience shall show that they can be modified advantageously, with a view to the same end. WHEN THE INSURGENTS SHALL HAVE DISBANDED THEIR ARMIES, AND LAID DOWN THEIR ARMS, THE WAR WILL INSTANTLY CEASE, and all the war measures then existing, including those which affect Slavery, will cease also, and all moral, economical and political questions, as well as questions affecting Slavery as others which shall then be existing between individuals and States and the Federal Government, whether they arose before the Civil War began, or whether they grew out it, will, by force of the Constitution, pass over to the arbitrament of courts of law, and to the councils of legislation.

FOR GOVERNOR

REUBEN E. FENTON

FOR LIEUTENANT GOVERNOR

THOMAS G. ALVORD

FOR CANAL COMMISSIONER

FRANKLIN A. ALBERGER

FOR STATE PRISON INSPECTOR

DAVID P. FORREST

GEORGE F. NESBITT & CO., PRINTERS, CORNER PEARL AND PINE STREETS, N

THE OLD FLAG AGAIN, WAVES OVER SUMTER.

Lith. by Kimmel & Forster 254 & 256 Canal St. N.Y

PUB'D BY CURRIER & IVES.   Entered according to Act of Congress AD. 1865. by Currier & Ives, in the Clerks Office of the District Court of the United States, for the Southern District of N.Y.   152 NASSAU ST. N.Y.

THE FALL OF RICHMOND, V.ª ON THE NIGHT OF APRIL 2.ᴺᴰ 1865.

This strong hold and Capital City of the Davis Confederacy, was evacuated by the Rebels in consequence of the defeat at "Five Forks" of the Army of Northern Virginia under Lee; and capture of the South side Rail Road, by the brave heroes of the North, commanded by Generals Grant, Sheridan and others.— Before abandoning the City the Rebels set fire to it, destroying a vast amount of property; and the conflagration continued until it was subdued by the Union troops in the following morning.

Capt. H. M. Bragg carried the United States flag as the Union Army retook the ruined Fort Sumter (left). The official honor fell to Brevet Maj. Gen. Anderson (see p. 24), who, on April 14, 1865, raised the same flag that had flown during his defense of the fort exactly four years before. With Richmond doomed by Grant's breakthrough before Petersburg, citizens of the capital burned and looted the city before Federal forces of occupation arrived. By every available type of conveyance (above) they fled from the inferno they had touched off.

The McLean farm at Appomattox Court House (left), where on a quiet Palm Sunday in 1865 Generals Grant and Lee met to arrange the terms of surrender of the Army of Northern Virginia. The story that Lee offered Grant his sword, shown lying on the table (lower left), was not true. General Sherman meets with General Joseph E. Johnston (below) to arrange terms of surrender for Confederate forces in North Carolina. When in late May forces in the Trans-Mississippi Department laid down arms, northern newspapers announced: "The old flag waves from Maine to the Rio Grande!"

HOME FROM THE WAR.

THE WAR ON THE MISSISSIPPI

*Grant, rewriting the
rules of war, breaks a stalemate
before Vicksburg's bluffs*

December, 1862–May, 1863

In one of the strangest double plays of the war, while Grant's army was launching a campaign into Mississippi with Vicksburg as its principal objective, Lincoln authorized an old friend from Springfield, General John A. McClernand, to recruit troops in Indiana, Illinois, and Iowa for the same purpose. Learning from the newspapers that McClernand was to conduct his own campaign, Grant said huffily: "Two commanders on the same field are always one too many." On December 30, 1862, McClernand moved down river to claim command of the troops he had raised. Since his new bride came with him, he planned his arrival as the high point of his honeymoon. But no army waited at Memphis. Sherman, on Grant's orders, had run off with it!

Grimly, McClernand and his bride set off to find his "stolen" army. Something less than cheerful news awaited the couple, for in assaults on the strong fortifications of Vicksburg from Chickasaw Bayou and Haynes Bluff, Sherman's 30,720 effectives had suffered 208 killed, 1,005 wounded, and 563 missing and were not an inch nearer the objective. McClernand took over command, and planned to gain quick honor in a thrust up the Arkansas River to capture Fort Hindman. The co-operation of the river fleet under David Porter was essential to the expedition, and the admiral, who bluntly said that he disliked McClernand, was something less than cordial. He was short of coal and could not use wood in his ironclads, Porter grumbled. Sher-

PORTER'S GUNBOATS ATTACK FORT HINDMAN ON THE ARKANSAS RIVER, USING SHRAPNEL FROM SMALL SHELL GUNS.

man took credit for persuading the recalcitrant admiral to put aside his "strong prejudice" for the sake of a combined naval and military exploit that promised real success to the cause of the Union.

McClernand's army, convoyed by Porter's gunboats, reached the mouth of the White River on January 8, steamed next day through the cut-off to the Arkansas and dropped anchor just below Fort Hindman. After two days of rugged fighting, in which Porter's gunboats did a full share by running up close to the fort in slack water, the Confederates surrendered. But there was no lessening of the clash of personalities within the Union command. By Sherman's account: ". . . I found General McClernand on the

Tigress, in high spirits. He said repeatedly: 'Glorious! glorious! my star is ever in the ascendant!' . . . I was very hungry and tired, and fear I did not appreciate the honors in reserve for us. . . ." Porter claimed that since the fort belonged to the Confederate navy, it would surrender only to the Union navy, which somewhat shortened the ascent of McClernand's star. Grant, arriving before Vicksburg, made the ascent shorter still and placed McClernand's troops within his own command. The bridegroom-general wrote a bristling letter of complaint to Lincoln, but the President, as usual, stood by Grant. Before the arrival of spring, tempers at Vicksburg would be boiling even higher.

THE REBELS, SETTING THEIR RANGE BUOYS FOR GUNNERY PRACTICE AT 1,200 FEET, LET PORTER COME IN CLOSE.

In an effort to give Union gunboats a chance to operate beyond the range of Rebel batteries on the bluffs of Vicksburg, Union soldiers undertake to dig a canal across a strip of land about a mile wide. Sherman, in charge of the venture, was glad the men didn't all drown. The project failed, but men kept busy.

On a train crowded with officers, a reporter for the Chicago *Times* heard a derisive analysis of Grant as a general: "He has been kicked out of the United States Army once, and will be again. He is nothing but a drunken, wooden-headed tanner that will not trouble the country very long."

There were many critics after January, 1863, who cried both in and out of Congress that Grant was hopelessly stuck in the mud of Mississippi, and the less informed these detractors were, the louder they shouted. But with good reason Jefferson Davis had called Vicksburg "the Gibraltar of America." This city, standing on a hairpin bend of the Mississippi River, occupied cliffs that rose sharply for 200 feet above the water. Formidable batteries frowned down on the river, for unless Vicksburg was held, the Mississippi could become a knife cutting the eastern sector of the Confederacy from the western. The Cincinnati *Commercial* could claim that either "negligence" or "imbecility" must account for the stand-off developing before Vicksburg, but the truth was that Grant fought both terrain and the weather. High water in the Mississippi and its tributaries forced Grant's armies to spread their camps over a distance of sixty miles in the search for dry ground; the water even popped coffins back to the surface of their burial spots.

Grant kept probing for a way into Vicksburg. Were the Rebel batteries as formidable to the river fleet as they seemed? To answer this question on which much could depend, the Union ram, *Queen of the West,* was sent down river on a test run early in February. A day later the *Queen* had reached Natchez. Other schemes to reach Vicksburg were tried—the digging of the canal to bypass its batteries, the clearing of passageways through old bayous—but all were failures except that Grant "let the work go on, believing employment was better than idleness for the men."

The imaginative Porter, intrigued with the fact that dry land was now covered with water deep enough to float gunboats, proposed a novel naval and military expedition over a watercourse that normally would have presented difficulties to floating a canoe. Let him find an approach to the city, Porter pleaded, reminding Grant that he had nothing to gain "in sitting down before Vicksburg and simply looking at it." Grant could not disagree on this score and Porter was permitted to sail with his steamers into a dense forest where they "could ply among the trees with perfect impunity ... as much at home as the wild denizens of the forest would be in dry times."

Porter was having the time of his life among the trees in a world that "had suddenly got topsy-turvy." The admiral wrote with an almost boyish wonderment: "It was a curious sight to see a line of ironclads and mortar boats, tugs and transports, pushing their way through the long, wide lanes in the woods without touching on either side, though sometimes a rude tree would throw Briarean arms around the smokestack of the tinclad *Forest Rose,* or the transport *Molly Miller,* and knock their bonnets sideways."

Porter enjoyed knocking down bridges with 800 tons of ironclad. The admiral chuckled at the Negroes who watched with amazement "the doings of 'Mas' Linkum's gunboats,'" and he scoffed at Sherman's warning that before this expedition was finished they'd all encounter "a devil of a time." But Porter was a great admirer of Sherman, whose corps "could catch, scrape, and skin a hog without a soldier leaving the ranks."

Later Porter would have good reason to remember Sherman's warning. Rafts sunk in the mud, old logs floating treacherously beneath the water, then willow withes began to hold back the vessels "as if in a vise." To add to Porter's concern, his fleet was moving far in advance of Sherman's troops.

Flood water in the Mississippi that winter added to Grant's troubles and gave the Confederates a sense of security in their terraced city. On the night of February 3, 1863, came the first warning that Grant would try to break the stalemate in any way possible. The Federal ram, Queen of the West, attempted to demonstrate that the batteries of Vicksburg could be passed, and not only succeeded but also managed to damage a Rebel steamer tied up at the wharf (above). One of Grant's best friends was David D. Porter, the energetic admiral of the river fleet (right).

Stuck among the trees, with Rebel gunners beginning to pepper his decks, Porter badly needed Sherman, whom he once described admiringly as "half sailor, half soldier, with a touch of the snapping turtle." The admiral dispatched an urgent note:

"Dear Sherman: Hurry up, for Heaven's sake. I never knew how helpless an ironclad could be steaming around through the woods without an army to back her."

In the nick of time, Sherman arrived to save Porter from disaster. He led the fleet back to Grant while his boys kept up a constant stream of catcalls at Porter's crews:

"Halloo, Jack, how do you like playing mud turtle?"

"Where's all your sails and masts, Jack?"

The failure of Porter's scheme, in Sherman's estimation, was a sad disappointment to Grant, who, if he wanted further proof that he was a general on trial in Washington, in early April received a "special observer" from the War Department. But though Charles A. Dana might grumble that Grant "violates English grammar at every phrase," he was soon captivated by the bold, new plan of campaign that the general proposed. He would transport his entire army down river past the Vicksburg batteries, Grant said. If he couldn't get at the Confederate army under General John C. Pemberton inside Vicksburg, then he would cross the river and land "at or about" Grand Gulf. Here he could threaten both Vicksburg and the state capital of Jackson, and would force Pemberton to come out of his fortified city and fight him.

Sherman was sure that Grant's plan must fail and said so in a stormy outburst which, when Sherman was finished, found Grant as "dead set" to carry through the scheme as he had been before. On the night picked for taking the army below Vicksburg, the stubborn Sherman ordered four yawls rowed out on the river where he waited "to pick up any of the disabled wrecks as they floated by." A mass of "black things,"

the armada started down river about ten o'clock at night. Seven ironclad turtles and a heavy armed ram led the squadron. Two side-wheel steamers and one stern-wheeler, with twelve barges in tow, came next. Far astern followed the ammunition boat.

Quickly, with the flash of the upper batteries, Confederate guns sprang into action along a four-mile front. Burning tar barrels along the shore, and the railway station soon ablaze, lighted the river as though it were mid-morning. Sherman's vantage point on the river was an excellent position from which to describe the breathless scene:

". . . As soon as the rebel gunners detected the *Benton,* which was in the lead, they opened on her, and on the others in succession, with shot and shell; houses on the Vicksburg side and on the opposite shore were set on fire, which lighted up the whole river; and the roar of cannon, the bursting of shell, and finally the burning of the *Henry Clay* [struck in her cotton barricades by an exploding shell and] drifting with the current, made up a picture of the terrible not often seen. Each gunboat returned the fire as she passed the town, while the transports hugged the opposite shore. . . . One of my yawls picked up [the *Henry Clay's*] pilot floating on a piece of the wreck. . . . The bulk of her crew escaped in their own yawl-boat to the shore above."

Porter had ordered the weak points on his vessels protected by heavy logs, one reason why his armada came through so well. The admiral also cited another reason: "The enemy's shot was not well aimed; owing to the rapid fire of shells, shrapnel, grape and canister from the gunboats, the sharpshooters were glad to lay low, and the men at the great guns gave up in disgust when they saw the fleet drift on apparently unscathed."

Next morning Dana went with Grant to visit the squadron at New Carthage, on the Louisiana shore. The vessels were "all in fighting condition . . . . Not a man had been lost."

Porter's gunboats, sailing through flooded forests where ordinarily not even a canoe could navigate, found smokestacks knocked down and even pilothouses carried away (above). The imaginative Porter tests the accuracy of Rebel gunners by floating a "dummy monitor," made of planks and tar barrels, down river (below).

Running the Vicksburg batteries the night of April 16, 1863: "They floated down the Mississippi darkly and silently [wrote Dana], showing neither steam nor light, save occasionally a signal astern, where the enemy could not see it." Grant's gamble paid. Not a man was lost.

Grant's next objective was to find a crossing point from Louisiana to Mississippi. Bald Head, a Confederate bastion at Grand Gulf, set on a promontory at the head of the river, led Porter to argue that the place was far too formidable for a direct assault, but Grant wanted to strike the Rebels while they were off balance, and he waved aside the admiral's objections.

The battle, lasting five-and-a-half hours, proved as grim as Porter had feared: the *Tuscumbia* suffered eighty-one hits, the *Lafayette* forty-five, the flagship *Benton* forty-seven. Convinced at last that a crossing at Grand Gulf would only expose his troops to a murderous assault from the gunners on Bald Head, Grant called off the attack while Porter faced the "melancholy duty of burying the dead."

Grant, remaining cheerful, quickly revised his plan. He would debark his troops and march across the peninsula south of Grand Gulf until out of reach of the Confederate batteries. An old Negro told Grant that he could save time crossing at Bruinsburg, and the general rode over to inspect the suggested embarkation point at De Shroon's plantation. Dana, sharing that night-time ride, remembered that once Grant's horse stumbled, threatening to pitch the general over its head. "For an instant," Dana recalled, "his moral status was on trial; but Grant was a tenacious horseman, and instead of going over the animal's head, as I imagined he would, he kept his seat. Pulling up his horse, he rode on, and, to my utter amazement without a word or sign of impatience."

Like so many others, Dana was learning that to know Grant was to realize how little the croakers in Washington understood the innate qualities of the man. To Grant's delight, the old Negro was quite correct. Bruinsburg, some sixty miles south of Vicksburg, offered a fine crossing point. Grant took three divisions across the river on April 30, and standing at last "on dry land on the same side of the river with the enemy," admitted that he "felt a degree of relief scarcely ever equaled since." True, Vicksburg was not yet taken, nor its defenders "demoralized." But Grant now believed that "all the campaigns, labors, hardships and exposures from the month of December previous to this time that had been made and endured, were for . . . this one object."

Union gunboats locked in a vicious duel with Confederate batteries at Grand Gulf (above, left). In the current, Porter said, the ironclads—"clumsy vessels at best"— often would be turned completely around, thus "presenting their weak points to the enemy." The Battle of Raymond, fought May 12, 1863 (left), carried Grant to within quick reach of Jackson, capital of Jefferson Davis's home state. For the Confederacy, the fall of Raymond and Jackson was more than a sentimental loss. Grant now was between two Confederate armies.

SHERMAN'S TROOPS, OCCUPYING JACKSON, PUT TO THE TORCH ANY MILITARY BUILDING—AND SOME THAT WERE NOT.

Grant pushed rapidly inland, and about five miles west of Port Gibson collided with a determined but small Confederate force in the Battle of Thompson Hill. The contest was bitter while it lasted, but Grant swept back the Missourians and Mississippians under General John S. Bowen, who opposed him, and on May 3 rode into Grand Gulf. Here for the first time in a week he could bathe and change his underclothing. A day writing dispatches did not dull his eagerness to push on. At midnight he started for Hankinson's Ferry.

When Grant had arrived at Grand Gulf, his intention had been to detach McClernand's corps to co-operate with a force under Banks (then operating on the Red River) in the reduction of Port Hudson. But news had reached Grant that Banks could not be in Port Hudson before May 10 — an extremely valuable week wasted, in Grant's view. By the time the Port Hudson assault was completed he could reckon, really, on losing a month. Meanwhile, Joseph E. Johnston was recruiting an army to reinforce Pemberton in Vicksburg, so that Grant ran the risk of having any reserves he secured from Banks outnumbered by the troops which, with time, Johnston could bring to Pemberton.

Grant made the decision upon which his fame rested: "I therefore determined to move independently of Banks, cut loose from my base, destroy the rebel force in rear of Vicksburg and invest or capture the city." By May 7, Grant had moved his headquarters to Rocky Springs, whence he expected to jump off on the campaign that would carry him to the state capital at Jackson. Sherman was filled with violent objections to the entire plan. How reasonably did Grant expect to operate in enemy country without waiting for his army to be partially supplied from an established base? Sherman could quote from Jomini, Napoleon, or any other authority that Grant might respect to prove that no general in his right mind fought this way. Then, Grant replied quietly, he would fight differently, making the country support him as he traveled.

Grant knew that Washington would "disapprove" of his course and commented slyly: "The time it would take to communicate with Washington and get a reply would be so great that I could not be interfered with until it was demonstrated whether my plan was practicable." He cut loose from Rocky Springs and by May 12 one of his columns approached Raymond, eighteen miles west of Jackson. At first the 5,000 Rebels under General John Gregg mistook the appearance of the Federals in Raymond as "a brigade on a marauding excursion." But as the Union strength continued to mount (illustration, pages 188-189), Gregg had to admit that unless he pulled out quickly for Jackson he would be cut to pieces, and suddenly the Confederate line "broke and fled in confusion."

Grant was at Sherman's headquarters when he received the news that Raymond had been captured. Sherman had to confess the old man

GRANT FINALLY MEETS PEMBERTON HEAD-ON AT CHAMPION'S HILL.

had played a smart game. Gregg, like Pemberton and Johnston, had no precedent by which to fight an army that operated without a base of supplies. Grant had the Confederates virtually marching in circles to cut off supply lines that didn't exist. Meanwhile, each nightfall, the wagons of Grant's army, returning from their foraging expeditions, groaned under the weight of their impressments.

Joe Johnston was in Jackson when Gregg's boys fled in retreat from Raymond. All the reports that reached him in the next two days simply added to the confusion. Then, as rain came down in torrents on the night of the fourteenth, Johnston could hear the guns of Grant's columns advancing on the capital. Johnston left while he could. Grant, arriving in Jackson, recalled cheerily: "I slept that night in the room that Johnston was said to have occupied the night before."

To Sherman fell the provost duty of the capital of Jefferson Davis's home state. The ruins of the arsenal buildings, foundry, and gun-carriage shop gave Sherman no little satisfaction, but many other buildings were burned, among them the penitentiary and a cotton factory, because, Sherman insisted, "some convicts . . . had been set free by the Confederate authorities." A reporter for the Chicago *Times* drew a picture of the occupation of Jackson:

"The Negroes, poor whites—and it must be admitted — some stragglers and bummers from the ranks of the Union army—carried off thousands of dollars worth of property from houses, homes, shops and stores. . . . The streets were filled with people, white and black, who were carrying away all the stolen goods they could stagger under, without the slightest attempt at concealment, and without let or hindrance from citizens or soldiers. . . . The convicts . . . set all the buildings connected with the prison on fire, and their lurid flames added to the holocaust elsewhere prevailing. . . ."

An intercepted message gave Grant the plan Johnston had suggested to Pemberton for deploying his forces to attack the rear of the Federals. In sending McClernand's corps to check the Confederates, Grant wrote: "It is evidently the design of the enemy to get north of us and cross the Big Black and beat us into Vicksburg. We must not allow them to do this." Then Grant settled down to a comfortable night's rest at the Bowman House, and the correspondent for the Chicago *Times* was highly amused next morning when the proprietor rendered a bill of $60 for lodging the general's staff. Offered $100 in Confederate money, the hotelkeeper was "thunderstruck," saying he had expected payment in U.S. coin or greenbacks "or the charges would have been much higher." He could charge what he pleased, the general's orderly replied, but as a Confederate he would be paid in Confederate money and so "it was finally settled on the latter basis at ninety dollars." The *Times* reporter chuckled wryly, for his own Confederate wad had "cost me nothing."

On the morning of May 16, 1863, Grant found Pemberton entrenched across the green slopes of the Champion plantation. The Rebels, dug in along a ridge with a ravine and a creek protecting one flank and a belt of timber screening the other, offered a position that promised a nasty battle. Grant expected a bitter, hard-contested morning, and was not disappointed. By noon the fighting centered around a meadow sloping down to the belt of timber, and, unexpectedly, a Union soldier beheld Grant: "He now stood, leaning complacently against his favorite steed, smoking —as seemed habitual with him—the stump of a cigar. . . . In front of us was an enemy; behind us, and about us, and liable to overcome and crush us, were his reinforcements. . . . I am sure everyone who recognized [Grant] wished him away; but there he stood—clear, calm and immovable."

An orderly approached Grant, handing him a communication. "Then followed an order to move rapidly to the left, and into the road. The fire grew heavier, and the air seemed too hot to be borne." Suddenly the battle erupted into a vicious seesaw of charge and countercharge, of men running and weeping and slashing with fixed bayonets, until, in headlong flight, the Union boys swept back over the very spot where, a half hour before, Grant had been smoking his cigar:

The road leading down to Baker's Creek offered the chance to cut the only route by which the Confederates could retreat from Champion's Hill, and terrific fighting occurred here (below). Sherman's troops (right) freed slaves from plantations belonging to the Davis family and found a copy of the Constitution once owned by Jefferson Davis.

"Thank God! he was gone. The dead were still there, and the wounded called pitiably to us to halt and help them as we ran headlong to the rear. Like ten thousand starving and howling wolves the enemy pursued, closer and closer, and we scarcely dared to look back to face the fate that seemed certain. Grant had seen it all, and in less time than I can tell it a line of cannon had been thrown across our path, which as soon as we had passed, belched grapeshot and canister into the faces of our pursuers. They stopped, they turned, and they, too, ran, and left their dead side by side with our own. Our lines, protected by the batteries, rallied and followed, and Champion hills was won. . . ."

Increasingly, soldiers who fought under Grant learned to trust his use of reserves—"feeding a fight," he called it. The Champion's Hill victory animated Grant, for good reason: "We were now assured of our position between Johnston and Pemberton, without a possibility of a junction of their forces." Yet Pemberton had escaped with his army intact—as, indeed, he would escape again next day in a second brisk battle at the bridge over the Big Black—and Grant would find that the entrenchments of Vicksburg offered little hope of the quick victory that he wanted. So Grant, breaking one stalemate, found in the entrenchments before Vicksburg what he least wanted—another stalemate.

FROM NORTH WOODS TO GULF

New patterns of war:
Indian massacre, vessels blown up,
Mud March, Old Jack dies

December, 1862–May, 1863

While Grant was slugging his way up the Mississippi and across country to Jackson and Vicksburg, a great deal of war was being fought in other parts of America. In the east, Lincoln had grown weary of McClellan and his "slows," and so in chill December of 1862 the Army of the Potomac moved to its next battle under a new commander, General Ambrose E. Burnside, already famous for giving his name to a style of side whiskers. From the Federal encampments in the rolling hills of Stafford Heights, across the Rappahannock from Fredericksburg, Virginia, Burnside looked at the outposts of Lee's army and wondered if he were equal to the task before him. With all earnestness, Burnside had confessed to Lincoln doubt in his own fitness to command this Army of the Potomac.

But Lee also was depressed. His soldiers were in need of almost everything, and around him the Virginia countryside showed the ravages of war in fences burned, meadows trampled, crops unharvested, homesteads in ruins, and grim old people huddled around sparse fires. As soon as the Federals had assembled a sufficient number of pontoons, Lee knew, Burnside's troops would force a crossing of the Rappahannock. In a letter to Mary Lee in Richmond, the general revealed his misgivings: "I tremble for my country when I hear of confidence expressed in me. I know too well my weakness, and that our only hope is in God."

When the haze lifted on the morning of December 11, the Federal cannon on Stafford Heights opened, belching death within Fredericksburg, rocking buildings until walls crumbled. "These people delight to destroy the weak and those who can make no defense," Lee said bitterly. "It just suits them!" The Federal pontoniers swarmed down to the river, where a Mississippi brigade sniped at them from behind the heaps of rubble. Finally, Yankee infantrymen in bateaux forced a passage and screened the operations of the bridge builders. That night the Federals held the ruined city.

Federal troops scaling the river bank at Fredericksburg after the Yankee artillery on Stafford Heights unlimbered—a hundred guns, firing fifty rounds each—and nearly every house along the river had been knocked down or burned (left). That night Burnside held Fredericksburg (above). Next morning Lee, standing beside Jackson, looked down on columns of Yankees crossing on their pontoon bridges with their sheeted wagons and rumbling caissons. "We hold the hills," Lee told Jackson. Later, Longstreet came up alongside to ask: "Jackson, what are you going to do with all those people over there?" Quietly, Jackson answered: "Give them the bayonet!" The ground was clean and sparkling white with fresh-fallen snow.

The Battle of Fredericksburg rose to a blazing climax on the slopes of Marye's Heights on the afternoon of December 13, 1862. Behind a stone wall on top of that crest Longstreet had placed heavy guns and about 2,500 seasoned troops. Burnside did not seem to realize the hopelessness of his orders that sent blue-clad columns in a charge up Marye's Heights. "With our artillery from the front, right and left tearing through their ranks," Longstreet recalled in admiration, "the Federals pressed forward with an almost invincible determination, maintaining their steady step and closing up their broken ranks."

Longstreet saw them, coming within reach of the guns behind the stone wall: ". . . a storm of lead was poured into their advancing ranks and they were swept from the field like chaff before the wind. A cloud of smoke shut out the scene for a moment, and, rising, revealed the shattered fragments recoiling from their gallant but hopeless charge. The artillery still plowed through their retreating ranks and searched the places of concealment into which the troops had plunged. A vast number went pell-mell into an old railroad cut . . . and the shells began to pour down upon the Federals with the most frightful destruction."

Six times Burnside sent his columns in a suicidal assault on Marye's Heights. To Longstreet,

watching the Union boys falling "like the steady dripping of rain from the eaves of a house," this wasn't an assault at all, but a death march. Even Burnside seemed to understand at last his dreadful blunder, but not until months had passed would the staggering cost of Fredericksburg to the Union be calculated: 12,653 casualties against 5,309 for the Confederacy. On Marye's Heights the Federal loss was 9,000.

Observing the fearful carnage at Fredericksburg, a correspondent for the London *Times,* permitting wish to become mother of the thought, believed that he had witnessed "a memorable day to the historian of the Decline and Fall of the American Republic."

In successive waves, game, but doomed to merciless destruction from Longstreet's guns, the Federals charged at Fredericksburg and, observing the slaughter, Lee said: "It is well that war is so terrible — we should grow too fond of it." In his report to Washington, Burnside knew where to place the blame: "I am responsible." Lincoln answered him consolingly: "...the attempt was not an error, nor the failure other than accident." But those who had fought there knew better.

When the first reports reached St. Paul of massacre along the Yellow Medicine River, nobody would believe them. Then the first bedraggled, stunned, terrorized victims made their way back to civilization. In hollow voices they told of the Sioux outrages under the instigation of power-crazed Little Crow.

Some were mere children, frightfully mutilated, who in a daze had been wandering over the prairies.

Some were women, who spoke in broken voices of seeing the heads of babies bashed against a wagon wheel, of the aged and sick burned to death in their beds, of daughters thrown to the ground and assaulted by a dozen drunken, screaming warriors.

Some had lost all contempt for the savage Sioux because of the deeper hatred burning within them for husbands who, in a wild flight to save their own necks, had deserted their womenfolk and children to the depravities of the Indians.

Somewhat abortively, Secretary of the Interior Caleb Smith gave semi-official support to the charge that the Sioux uprising had been in-stigated by the Confederacy (but no evidence ever has sustained that vicious accusation). Nor would the ravages of the Indians have been so extensive if the military expedition under Henry H. Sibley, ex-governor of the territory, had pursued the Sioux as vigorously as the German settlers of New Ulm, who whipped them to a standstill. The final act of the bloody tragedy came in December when thirty-eight "Indians and half-breeds" were hung at Mankato, at the order of President Lincoln. The St. Paul *Press* described the end:

"As they commenced the ascent of the scaffold, the death-song was again started, and when they had all gone up, the noise they made was truly hideous. It seemed as if pandemonium had broken loose. It had a wonderful effect in keeping up their courage. One young fellow who had been given a cigar by one of the reporters, just before marching from their quarters, was smoking it on the stand, puffing away very coolly during the intervals of the hideous 'Hi-yi-yi,' 'Hi-yi-yi,' and even after the cap was drawn over his face, he managed to get it over his mouth and smoke. Another was smoking a pipe...."

A boy who witnessed the murder and outrage of mother and sisters during the Sioux uprising in Minnesota points an accusing finger (above) at the attacker. On December 28, 1862, by Lincoln's orders, thirty-eight redskin marauders died on the gallows at Mankato, Minnesota (below). To the end the Indians sang a death dirge.

Late December and early January brought terrific fighting in Tennessee when General William S. Rosecrans and his Army of the Cumberland left Nashville to find Rebel forces under Braxton Bragg. Rosecrans discovered his quarry astride Stone's River, protecting Murfreesboro. Bragg rolled the Union's right back against the river and a turnpike, but Rosecrans rallied and the battle became a futile stalemate. Both armies needed a rest.

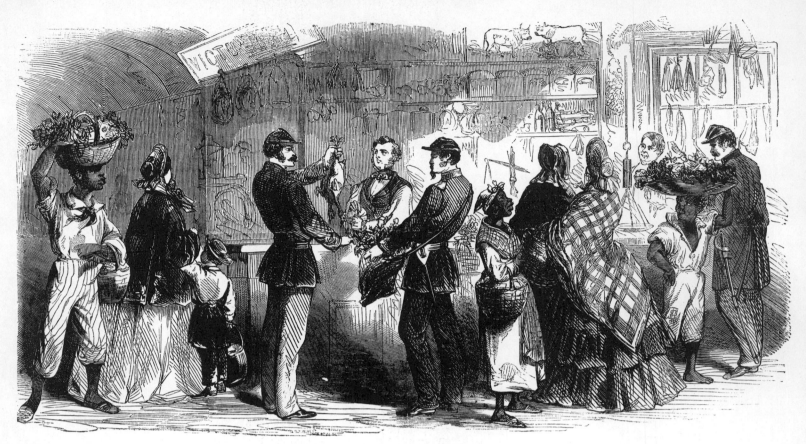

With New Orleans occupied, the Union late in 1862 was encouraged to take another successful nibble from the Confederate Gulf Coast by striking at Galveston, Texas. Not only had Rebel defenders been driven from this important port of the Confederacy, but even the railroad bridge connecting the city-island from the mainland had been isolated. Off shore stood only the *Harriet Lane*, mounting eight guns, which could, if the occasion necessitated, lob its shells into a Confederate force attempting to retake the port.

Obviously, one ship couldn't guard the port. Washington ordered up troops stationed on Ship Island in the Gulf—the Massachusetts 42nd, the Connecticut 23rd, a Vermont battery—to strengthen the defenses of Galveston. On a starlit January 1, 1863, only three companies of the Massachusetts 42nd had reached Galveston, although the transports carrying the other troops and several ships of the blockading squadron now had joined the *Harriet Lane*. What Washington did not know was that the Confederacy recently had sent General John ("Prince John," so named because he was an amateur Shakespearean actor) Magruder from Virginia to Texas to retake Galveston. A hastily collected land force, aided by a hodge-podge of tenders and packets padded with cotton, gave "Prince John" his striking power, and at about five o'clock in the morning, in the words of the Houston *Telegraph*, "the ball opened." An artillery duel between ships and shore batteries became "one of the most terrific on record." Then:

"The scene was at once sublime and appalling. Our men [the Confederates] were once driven from their guns, but rallied and fought nobly on. As dawn approached the fire of the enemy appeared to increase in severity, and fearing that our men would be unable to withstand it after daylight gave the enemy a better view of our position, orders were prepared to withdraw. Just as they were about to be issued, however, at about six o'clock, the welcome announcement was made at headquarters that the *Bayou City* and *Neptune* had arrived, and opened on the *Harriet Lane*. Immediately new vigor was infused in our men; they played their pieces with redoubled energy, and seemed determined that the victory should be ours."

The Union flagship, *Westfield*, grounded and her crew hastened to burn her before capture. When the fire reached the magazine, the New York *Herald* reported, she was "scattered through the air in ten thousand fragments." Thus went most of the battle until the Federal gunboats, in the eloquent phrase of the Houston *Telegraph*, "drew off, and escaped out of the harbor, utterly routed and defeated."

This drawing (left), its artist, Theodore Davis, wrote Harper's Weekly, "represents our troops in New Orleans 'swapping' their rations of flour for tropical fruits and other farm produce.... Flour has long been scarce at New Orleans; our brave boys, who receive a fair modicum of it daily as part of their ration, manage to dispose of it in market in such a way as, to use their own words, 'to live like fighting cocks.'" Early in the fall of 1862, a Union naval squadron had pounded its way into Galveston, Texas, and forced the evacuation of one of the most important ports of the Confederacy. In late December, to strengthen the defense of Galveston, the Union ordered troops on Ship Island in the Gulf transferred to the city. In the starlight of January 1, 1863, the Rebels attacked the Union gunboat flotilla with devastating consequences.

The loss of Galveston was not the least of the bad news that January brought to the North. Attempting to find Lee's army during two days of rain, Burnside had embarked on his famous "Mud March"—struggling over roads turned into sticky bogs, with only the fatigue of his troops to show for the effort. Nothing had been gained, men grumbled. But much had—Burnside had lost the army's command.

"FIGHTING JOE" HOOKER

Always a stern Christian, who took as a favorite Bible text: "We know that all things work together for good to them that love God," General Stonewall Jackson (1, right) leads his camp in prayer before the Battle of Chancellorsville—General A. P. Hill (2), General Richard Ewell (3), Colonel A. J. "Sandy" Pendleton (4), Major Henry K. Douglas (5), Dr. Hunter McGuire (6), Colonel William Allen (7), Captain J. Smith (8) and Major William J. Hawks (9). Christianity was the only allegiance Jackson placed above the Confederacy. He never smoked, drank, or played cards, he prayed awkwardly, stiffly. Often he perspired at prayer, but never faltered.

With spring, the Army of the Potomac had a new commander—Joseph E. Hooker (above), Class of 1837 at West Point, a veteran of the Florida wars against the Seminoles, a frontier fighter, an officer who had earned three brevets in the Mexican War. Tall, robust, bronze-haired, affable, likable, "Fighting Joe" had been an especially sharp-tongued critic of Burnside. Stories had reached Lincoln that Hooker was a heavy drinker and, in appointing him to command, the President had confessed reservations as to whether Hooker could " 'keep tavern' for a large army." The phrase, apparently, was well chosen, for Charles Francis Adams, Jr., called the army's headquarters under Hooker, "a place to which no self-respecting man liked to go, and no decent woman could go. It was a combination of barroom and brothel."

Lee had to fight the general and not the convivial spirit, and soon he was complaining in his letters home that Hooker was "playing the Chinese game, trying what frightening will do. He runs out his guns, starts his troops up and down the river, and creates an excitement generally." But nothing happened and, in exasperation, Lee wrote Mary: "I owe Mr. J. E. Hooker no thanks for keeping me here [before Fredericksburg]. He ought to have made up his mind long ago what to do." By late April, however, a raid on Port Royal indicated that Hooker had made up his mind. His cavalry was concentrating on the upper Rappahannock and troops were coming up from the rear. By the twenty-ninth, Hooker was throwing his pontoons across the river.

For two days, Lee tried to guess Hooker's game, but once the Federal columns began to deploy, it became clear that Hooker was moving above Fredericksburg toward Chancellorsville and that sunless part of Virginia known as the Wilderness. Hooker was telling his own soldiers, as they moved, that Lee's troops had been outmaneuvered and "may as well pack up their haversacks and make for Richmond." But Hooker knew little of the desolate region of owls, whip-

poorwills, and water moccasins toward which he moved. The Wilderness was described as "this jungle," as "a wolf's den" and, said a contemporary, "Artillery could not move; cavalry could not operate; the very infantry had to flatten their bodies to glide between the stunted trees."

Lee, following doggedly after Hooker, met Jackson on the night of May 1. They debated whether Hooker really meant to fight in this thicket, which Lee believed and Old Jack rather doubted. Then Jeb Stuart brought news that the Federal right, extending west beyond Chancellorsville, was "in the air." All that was needed to turn that flank was to reach it, and Jackson proposed to do exactly that by marching over a little-known road deep into the Wilderness. What troops would he need, Lee asked.

"My whole corps," Jackson answered.

"What will that leave me?" Lee persisted.

"The divisions of Anderson and McLaws," Old Jack said.

In round figures, Lee thought, about 20,000

troops with which to hold off perhaps 50,000 on Hooker's front. Then, calmly, Lee decided.

"Well, go on," he said.

At seven o'clock Jackson plunged into the sunless jungle. Not until "near 3 p.m." did Jackson scrawl a message to Lee. He was around on the Federal flank, hoping to attack soon and trusting "that an ever kind Providence will bless us with great success." While Lee, hoping every bit as earnestly, waited, the sun started to arch downward. Then across the Wilderness came the rumble of Jackson's guns. The moon came up and the sky was flecked with the flashes of Old Jack's exploding shells. Wolburn, the signal officer, rode into Lee's headquarters with the almost unbelievable account of how Jackson had caught the Yankees, about a mile above Wilderness Church, with arms stacked while they cooked supper. Out of the woods the Rebels had charged, yelling to beat hell. And down the road —again to beat hell—the Yankees had taken off, in a flight that amounted to panic.

Lee, waiting for the sound of Jackson's guns, knew the gamble he took. In places his lines were so thin that his men stood only six feet apart. After a time, across the Wilderness came the sound of Old Jack's attack, and Lee threw his sparse ranks across the road in a superb game of bluff. Soon the 6th Virginia was back, bringing him the colors of the 107th Ohio as proof of their penetration of Hooker's lines. Rebel yells had the ring of triumph.

Wolburn also brought staggering news for Lee: Jackson, riding ahead of his column, had been fired upon through a mistake by his own men and wounded three times in the arm. Under heavy fire, Jackson had been carried back to a surgeon. His pain was severe. Lee made no effort to brush away the tears that stung his eyes.

"Don't talk about it," he said. "Thank God it is no worse!"

Jeb Stuart took command of Jackson's troops and next day hammered his way to a juncture with Lee's thin columns, an incredible feat in the circumstances. The Yankees huddled in confusion when Confederates stormed into Chancellorsville with exultant yells, overrunning earthworks, sweeping the Wilderness clear of Federals—a scene, one Rebel said, "of singular horror." He drew a picture of his commanding general in that moment of triumph:

"Lee had ridden to the front of his line, following up the enemy, and as he passed before the troops they greeted him with one prolonged,

unbroken cheer in which those wounded and dying upon the ground united. In that cheer spoke the fierce joy of men whom the hard combat had turned into bloodhounds, arousing all the ferocious instincts of the human soul. Lee sat on his horse, motionless, near the Chancellorsville House, his face and figure lit up by the glare of the burning woods, and gave his first attention, even at this exciting moment, to the unfortunates of both sides, wounded and in danger of being burned to death...."

Though hard fighting remained at Chancellorsville, Hooker, knocked unconscious and carried from the field, was clearly "a doomed fly." Lee was waging a much more exhausting battle within his heart, for Jackson's arm had been amputated. The old warrior seemed to rally, then on May 7, symptoms of pneumonia developed. Next day Old Jack's lungs were filling up, and he lapsed into moments of delirium, muttering: "Tell Major Hawks to send forward provisions for the men."

In anguish, Lee spent the day virtually alone, sending Jackson a special message: "When a suitable occasion offers, give him my love, and tell him that I wrestled in prayer for him last night, as I never prayed, I believe, for myself." Through Sunday, deep in delirium now, Jackson spoke softly through feverish lips: "A. P. Hill, prepare for action. I must find out ... whether there is high ground ... between Chancellorsville and the river." Many turned away, knowing the end was close for Old Jack—but, stubbornly, Lee refused to believe: "God will not take him from us, now that we need him so much." Jackson slept, awoke, and stared distantly at a scene that he alone seemed to perceive. Falteringly, the mighty Stonewall said his last words:

"Let us pass over the river, and rest under the shade of the trees."

The lips then were quiet, the bearded face composed. Jackson had won his victory. He had conquered the Dark Valley.

All battles end raggedly, too often in pain and death far behind the lines. And so it was at Chancellorsville, in balmy May of 1863, where in killed, wounded, and missing the Union lost 16,845 and the Confederates 13,156. Grief-stricken, the South received the startling news that among its dead was Stonewall Jackson.

COUNTERBALANCE

A military seesaw:
Grant besieges Vicksburg and
Lee strikes Gettysburg

May–July, 1863

Lincoln recoiled from the reports that came to him from Chancellorsville. In carpet slippers, looking gaunt and haggard, the President paced the floor of the White House, moaning: "My God! My God! What will the country say? What *will* the country say?" Why was there no general who could win with the tremendous fighting organization that had been created in the Army of the Potomac? Again, as friends said Lincoln had acted after Second Manassas, the President was "wrung by the bitterest anguish." The war was a mystery that he could not probe, though he pondered long upon it, even writing down his meditations:

"The will of God prevails. In great contests each party claims to act in accordance with the will of God. Both *may* be, and one *must* be wrong. God cannot be *for*, and *against* the same thing at the same time. In the present civil war it is quite possible that God's purpose is something different from the purpose of either party—and yet the human instrumentalities, working just as they do, are of the best adaptation to effect His purpose. I am almost ready to say this is probably true—that God wills this contest, and wills that it shall not end yet. By His mere quiet power, on the minds of the now contestants, He could have either *saved* or *destroyed* the Union without a human contest. Yet the contest began. And having begun He could give the final victory to either side any day. Yet the contest proceeds."

Nowhere did the war proceed more furiously that May of 1863 than before Vicksburg, where on the nineteenth, in an optimistic mood, Grant ordered an assault on Pemberton's entrenchments. Rudely, the Federals were thrown back, and for two days Grant had to take stock. Considering the gullies and ravines that offered natural protection to Vicksburg, could he ever hope to take the city by direct assault? Grant must have thought he could—or, at any rate, good reasons existed in Grant's mind for trying again to storm the place:

"...Johnston was in my rear, only fifty miles away, with an army not much inferior in numbers to the one I had with me, and I knew he was being reinforced. There was danger of his coming to the assistance of Pemberton, and after all he might defeat my anticipations of capturing the garrison if, indeed, he did not prevent the capture of the city. The immediate capture of Vicksburg would save me sending the reinforcements which were so much needed elsewhere, and would set free the army under me to drive Johnston from the State. But the first consideration of all was—the troops believed they could carry the works in their front, and would not have worked so patiently in the trenches if they had not been allowed to try."

A second attack on the Confederate lines was ordered for ten o'clock on the morning of May 22. Corps commanders set their watches in time with Grant's and waited for the agreed-upon opening of the ball—"a furious cannonade from every battery in position." The big guns began to roar on the dot of ten, and the troops sprang to the assault. Small parties went ahead with planks to throw across the ditches. Behind came the lines of infantry, advancing rapidly. Concealed by a parapet, the Rebel line waited until the Federals came into view, when the Confederates rose up and poured a devastating fire into the charging bluecoats. "For about two hours," Sherman reported, "we had a severe and bloody battle, but at every point we were repulsed. In the very midst of this, when shot and shell fell fast and furious, occurred that little episode which has been celebrated in song and story, of the boy Orion P. Howe, badly wounded, bearing me a message for cartridges, caliber 54."

Grant joined Sherman on the off slope of a spur, seeing for himself that everywhere the troops under Sherman had been "badly beaten back." Then came a message from McClernand: "I am hotly engaged with the enemy.... A vigorous blow by [General James B.] McPherson would make a diversion in my favor."

Other messages came from McClernand, who alone claimed to be carrying the assault against Vicksburg to a promised victory. "We are hotly engaged with the enemy," McClernand wrote Grant at noon. "We have part possession of two forts, and the Stars and Stripes are floating over them. A vigorous push ought to be made all along the line." For Grant a quandary arose. Could he believe these claims?

Looking over the field, Grant said of McClernand's dispatches: "I did not see the success he reported." Still, Grant sent the reinforcements demanded. McClernand won no victory. Grant listened with his "usually placid countenance" filled with a "grim, glowering look of disappointment and disgust" as a reporter for the Chicago *Times*, who insisted he had seen McClernand's advance on the Confederate works, said that "a straggling line, continually growing thinner and weaker, finally reached the summit, when all who were not instantly shot down were literally pulled over the rebel breastworks as prisoners. One stand of our colors was planted half way up the embankment and remained there till they could crawl away covered by darkness."

Grant and McClernand obviously approached a parting of the way, though bitter charges and countercharges between the two generals—and between Vicksburg and Washington—remained to be exchanged. Meanwhile, Grant had to be content to achieve with bellies what he could not win with bullets: he must take Vicksburg by siege and hunger.

In the weeks that followed, Vicksburg became a "city of caves," and Yankees referred to it derisively as "the prairie dog's village." Grant's guns ringing the city, Grant's boats prowling the river, poured in shells by night and day. Houses, schools, stores, factories, and hospitals were pounded into rubble. The hope that Johnston was coming to relieve Pemberton sustained civilians as they ran for the holes they had dug in the hillsides at every explosion of the siege guns. Toward late June, it was said, as many as 150,000 shells fell upon Vicksburg in a single day. An astonishing discovery after a time was the fact that neither a dog nor a cat could be found in the streets of Vicksburg. Then, equally astonishing, was the realization why—they all had been killed. After the tenth day of siege, even the Confederate soldiers were living on half rations, and with food shortages appeared extortioners, charging $5 a pound for flour, $10 a gallon for molasses, $10 a bushel for corn—vandals, in the opinion of the editors of the Vicksburg *Daily Citizen* (which was published occasionally on the reverse side of thin strips of wallpaper), who should be punished with a brand placed upon their brows so that "humanity may scorn and shun them as they would the portals of hell."

"A week of their wonderful life there would have made their tongues eloquent forever perhaps," a victim of the siege told Mark Twain in after years, "but they had six weeks of it, and that wore the novelty all out." So every day became Sunday—seven Sundays in the week. At first it was amusing to pile up the iron fragments from the shells in the front yard as a kind of souvenir, but after a while that pastime dulled and the debris lay where it fell.

And the informant recalled a morning, leaving church, when he said to an old friend, "Drop into the cave tonight, after bombardment; we've got hold of a pint of prime wh—" Whiskey, he meant to say, but, "A shell interrupted. A chunk of it cut the man's arm off, and left it dangling in my hand. And do you know the thing that is going to stick longest in my memory . . . is the mean thought I had. It was, 'the whiskey is *saved.*'" Yet, hang it, there wasn't another drop in all Vicksburg!

With the failure of the assault on May 22, 1863, Grant had what he least wanted —no choice but "to outcamp the enemy." Soon the hills around Vicksburg were dotted with huts that Yankees built against a broiling Mississippi sun (right, above). Negroes took over the deserted plantations, dressed in the "fine clothes" once worn by their masters, and, gay of heart, held their own plantation parties (below).

TO ARMS! TO ARMS!

Lee's invasion of Pennsylvania found Philadelphians rallying to the all-important need
to defend their city (above). Baltimoreans
also believed (right) that Lee's army would
appear along their cobbled thoroughfares.

Pennsylvanians, expecting to feel the hard heel of war, closed their businesses in mid-afternoon and dug trenches to protect cities as widely separated as Philadelphia and Harrisburg, the state capital (above). As Lee's hungry soldiers advanced into Pennsylvania, a land of rich farms, a Confederate general wrote home: "It's like a hole full of blubber to a Greenlander!" Meanwhile, pursuing Union troops reached Wrightsville (below) under still another commander, Pennsylvania-born George Meade.

The peril that faced the Confederacy at Vicksburg led Davis to summon Lee to a meeting of the Cabinet in Richmond. Should troops be detached from Lee to help the embattled Pemberton? The general shook his head, knowing how desperately his army needed food, shoes, fodder, and horses that war-torn Virginia no longer could supply. Lee's answer to taking the pressure off Vicksburg was to confront the North with another invasion—this time into Pennsylvania, where soon the young green stalks of corn would be standing straight and firm. Alone of the Cabinet members, Postmaster-General Reagen hedged. But Lee, the man who won, had his way.

Lee planned carefully for his invasion, but what he could not calculate was the fact that in the cool dawn haze of June 9 a detachment of Federal cavalry would slip across the Rappahannock and, catching Stuart and his boys at a dance, would give Stuart one of the nastiest fights—and frights—of his military career. After several hours, the bluecoats were driven off, but Stuart felt the sting of such comments as that which appeared in the Richmond *Examiner*: "If the war was a tournament, invented and supported for the pleasure of a few vain and weakheaded officers, these disasters might be dismissed with compassion." Stuart, having lost face, meant to regain it at the first chance, and that was why on June 27, seeing an opportunity to capture a Federal wagon train, he raced off through Maryland until within sight of Washington when his job was to screen the movement of Lee's troops into Pennsylvania and report the whereabouts of pursuing Federals.

Thus Lee entered Pennsylvania, deprived of the "eyes" of his army. And meanwhile Lincoln played his old trick of switching commanders of the Army of the Potomac, replacing Hooker with Pennsylvania-born George Gordon Meade, who as a boy in Philadelphia had numbered among his playmates McClellan and the turncoat Pemberton, who was now holed up inside besieged Vicksburg.

THE OPENING OF THE BATTLE OF GETTYSBURG ON JULY 1, 1863. IN THE DISTANCE, RIGHT, IS THE SLEEPY

Meade followed Lee stoically, setting up his headquarters at Taneytown while Lee pitched his tents at Cashtown. Between them was Gettysburg, a drowsy college town. The place had absolutely no military significance to Lee, except possibly that its stores could supply shoes for his almost barefoot troops. On the morning of July 1, a division under General Henry Heth swung down the road toward Gettysburg with only shoes on their minds. About a mile and a half from town, where Willoughby Run crosses the Chambersburg Pike, they found something more — one of the greatest battles that the war produced.

At Cashtown, Lee listened to the sounds of distant gunfire, wondering. But a spy soon ended his doubts with the information that Gettysburg contained "a pretty tidy bunch of blue-bellies." Lee spurred his horse along the pike, and the reports that came to him were all bad. The Yankees, surprising Heth, had handled him roughly, and by the time Heth was able to regroup his stunned troops at Willoughby Run any hope for

Confederate success depended on how quickly General Ewell, then marching his corps from Fayetteville to Cashtown, could swing his columns and come to Heth's rescue.

Hold on, Lee urged, and hold on Heth did in a brilliant countercharge at Willoughby Run, while troops under Robert Rodes held off two Yankee brigades on Seminary Ridge. When Ewell threw his full strength into the contest, the Union boys were down in an old railroad cut with smoke-blackened cannoneers screaming, "Feed it to 'em, God damn 'em." But the Yankees did not feed the Rebels enough, and all at once the Union lines began to yield.

Then the rout was on, with the Yankees hopping like scared rabbits through the town ahead of their Rebel pursuers. A schoolteacher remembered a horseman galloping up to her gate and calling, "For God's sake, go into the house! The Rebels are in the other end of town, and all will be killed!" The teacher fled to the cellar, and, in a few minutes, "the town was full of filthy Rebels." Ewell pressed the drive into

OLLEGE TOWN WHERE NEITHER LEE NOR MEADE EXPECTED TO FIGHT. THE CEMETERY IS AT LEFT.

Gettysburg, but here, mingling with exuberant soldiers waving pilfered wine bottles, the general lost his zest for the chase. Young officers, pleading with him not to permit the Yankees to entrench in the heights beyond the town, were waved aside. Ewell was more than pleased with the day's accomplishments as he looked upon streets strewn with clothes, blankets, knapsacks, cartridge boxes, and dead men and horses.

Up on Cemetery Ridge that night, exhausted Yankees slept among the tombstones, and when next morning Longstreet looked over the Union position, he advised Lee to quit Gettysburg. Longstreet, pointing to the heights occupied by the Federals, wondered why Lee couldn't see that Gettysburg had become Fredericksburg and Marye's Heights in reverse. Years afterward, Longstreet was still trying to explain Lee's stubbornness: "He seemed under a subdued excitement, which occasionally took possession of him when the 'hunt was up,' and threatened his superb equipoise."

Overcast skies on July 2 brought a murky dawn, promising a sultry day and perhaps rain. Lee, up early, told General Hood: "The enemy is here, and if we do not whip him, he will whip us." Hood went back to Longstreet, muttering that Lee seemed "a little nervous this morning," a point on which Longstreet was not in any mood to disagree. Lee wanted to start an assault at daybreak, but the morning passed without a sound beyond the usual skirmishing on the outposts. The Yankees were dug in now, and by the testimony of Frank Haskell quite recovered from yesterday's rout:

"Our arms were still stacked, and the men were at ease. . . . The storm was near, and we all knew it well enough by this time, which was to rain death upon those crests and down their slopes, and yet the men who could not, and would not escape it, were as calm and cheerful, generally, as if nothing unusual were about to happen. . . ."

Then the cannon opened fire, and all along a six-mile front the air suddenly seemed to be full of shells.

THE LOUISIANA TIGERS AT GETTYSBURG IN FIGHTING THAT RIPPED APART A UNION CORPS.

In the midst of the cannonade, a British observer recalled, a Confederate band began to play polkas and waltzes "which sounded very curious accompanied by the hissing and bursting of shells." Then the guns fell silent and Longstreet led his troops in what, he afterward insisted, was "the best three hours of fighting by any troops on any battle field."

Nor was Longstreet far from the truth. On this day men fought and died on the ragged slopes of Little Round Top, Big Round Top. They charged and died in that rock-strewn declivity called Devil's Den. With bayonets fixed, with defiant yells filling the air, they rolled in successive waves of death and glory through the Peach Orchard, across the Wheatfield. These names still live in American history, and the story they tell is of how at the last possible moment the Federals awoke to the Round Tops as the key to the position they held, and in a desperate struggle wrested them from charging Confederates; of how on this day—very likely Longstreet's greatest day—howling Rebels in the Wheatfield and Peach Orchard ripped to shreds the Union's Third Corps and kept alive the hope for a Confederate victory on the morrow; and how, as night closed down upon the moans of the wounded and the twinkling lanterns of the litter-bearers, Meade called his generals together to ask if he should risk another day's fighting.

The Union generals advised Meade to stand where he was. Lee also decided to stay, for if he could throw the Federals off their ridges, he would open the roads to Baltimore and Philadelphia. Pickett's division, fresh, full of fight, was coming up now. They would turn the balance on the morrow.

Lee next morning pointed to the 1,400 yards of ground separating the two armies. There was the field that Pickett must take. Longstreet, who had never awakened "so depressed" as on this third of July, answered curtly: "It is my opinion that no 15,000 men ever arrayed for battle

THE BATTLE IN THE PEACH ORCHARD WHEN LONGSTREET ROSE TO HIS GREATEST DAY OF WAR.

can take that position!'' Lee said a bombardment would clear the way. He would use Ewell and Stuart (who had at last reached the field) to occupy the Federals and draw off forces from the point of Pickett's charge.

In theory it was fine—except that Ewell was late in launching his assault and became involved in a series of murderous charges and countercharges that achieved nothing, while Stuart's cavalry was beaten back. So Pickett's boys waited, in no real sense supported, as Lee unleashed the greatest cannonade of the war. On Cemetery Ridge the havoc was unbelievable. "...we see [wrote Haskell] the poor fellows hobbling back from the crest, or unable to do so, pale and weak and lying on the ground with the stump of an arm or leg, dripping their life-blood away; or with a cheek torn open ...''

Then the guns stopped. Pickett's soldiers— moments before they had pelted one another with green apples—started across the 1,400 yards of open ground toward the Federals in the en-

trenchments on the ridge. Under a blistering sun, Pickett's boys went forward, here dressing to the right, there giving way to the left, and remembering: "Steady, not too fast—don't press upon the center.'' The slope seemed surprisingly gentle until, with an ominously growlish rumble, the guns of the Federals breathed a line of flame. The ranks of the Confederates appeared in that moment to melt away, the line to grow unsteady. The men moved closer, but from the ridge now volley after volley of musket balls crashed down.

The marvel was that so many still lived. And then there was a greater marvel—just thirty yards to go. Pickett's boys had not yet fired, and with a rousing southern yell they broke into a run. Upon the ridge Haskell saw them coming: "The jostling, swaying lines on either side boil and roar and dash their flaming spray, two hostile billows of a fiery ocean. Thick flashes stream from the wall, thick volleys answer from the crest. No threats or expostulations now, only example and encouragement....''

Longstreet assaults the Union left-center on July 2. The spirit of the Battle of Gettysburg was captured by a Union soldier who said, in the closing moments, when Pickett's hopeless charge sealed Lee's defeat: "The men do not cheer or shout; they growl, and over that uneasy sea, heard with the roar of musketry, sweeps the muttered thunder of a storm of growls."

THROUGH THE FLASHES OF FIRE COULD BE SEEN DARK OBJECTS—MEN, GUN-CARRIAGES!

Before Vicksburg, Grant's patience grew increasingly shorter. In mid-June he approved a plan to tunnel under the defenses of Vicksburg to blow the Confederates into submission. By night the Federals dug, by day they deepened their tunnel, and Porter, who always liked "new" ideas, supplied 2,200 pounds of powder for the explosion. On June 25, a hot and misty day, Grant brought up his troops in battle line and gave the order to fire the powder.

By the testimony of Wilbur Crummer of the 45th Illinois an awesome scene resulted: "Huge masses of earth were thrown in the air, and the ground was shaken as by an earthquake. As soon as the earth was rent, a bright glare of fire issued from the burning powder, but quickly died

away." To Major Andrew Hickenlooper, the fort, breaking into fragments, "looked like an immense fountain of pulverized earth, mingled with flashes of fire and clouds of smoke, through which could occasionally be caught a glimpse of some dark objects—men, gun carriages, shelters."

Confederate soldiers, hurled into the air, came down into the Union lines. A Negro boy named Abraham, who fell into the company of the 45th Illinois, replied when asked how far he had traveled, "Don't know, Massa. 'Bout free miles, I guess."

Grant's guns opened then—150 cannon and 50,000 muskets, by Hickenlooper's estimate—and when the smoke and dust cleared partly away, the command sounded: "Forward!"

By the time sunset ended the fighting in that man-made crater, Grant and his soldiers had to face a grim reality: days of half rations had not knocked the fighting spirit out of the defenders of Vicksburg. Waves of Federals were thrown into the fight and were "literally torn to pieces by the shots of the enemy." General John A. Logan, who commanded the attack, wept as he watched his wounded men carried away. "My God!" Logan cried. "They are killing my bravest men in that hole!"

Next morning Grant called off the assault and Vicksburg settled back to the routine of its siege. But within the city Pemberton knew the end was near. The hope of reinforcements from Johnston had become a chimera. Either his garrison must surrender or starve. On July 1, the day when Lee was encountering an unexpected battle at Gettysburg, Pemberton conferred with his officers and accepted the sad reality. On July 3—the day when Pickett's soldiers made their futile charge—Pemberton and Grant met "near a stunted oak tree" and arranged the terms of surrender.

For the North, with Gettysburg and Vicksburg to celebrate, it was a Glorious Fourth. Along the Mississippi alone, Grant had bagged almost 30,000 prisoners!

And yet the war went on. Apparently winning battles wasn't enough to end it.

GENERAL GRANT MEETS WITH GENERAL PEMBERTON TO ARRANGE FOR THE SURRENDER OF VICKSBURG AND ITS GARRISON.

THE MANY MOODS OF WAR

A New York riot, a Kansas massacre are symptoms of the explosive pressures of the conflict

July–December, 1863

Violence became unpredictable. In New York, now a city of 800,000, where recently a dock strike had been broken by employing abundant, cheap Negro labor, pressure was building up and hard times for the average worker increased the strain. Since Sumter, roast beef had jumped from eight cents a pound to sixteen, eggs from twelve-and-a-half cents for thirteen to twenty-five cents a dozen, while wages had remained static. New York City, therefore, was one kind of breeding ground for violence. In Kansas, where a generation of outlaws was in the making, another kind of violence erupted. Meanwhile, of course, the legitimate practices that went with the art of killing one's fellow man continued unabated. A new theater of operations from August through December, 1863, was Charleston, South Carolina, besieged by a Federal fleet that stoically bombarded the city.

Major Henry Bryan, Assistant Inspector-General in Charleston, listed with equal stoicism the cost in human life as "the Abolition army" lobbed its shells into the city: "Mrs. Hawthorne, No. 70 Church Street, wounded by shell in right side, and died six weeks after; Miss Plane, corner Meeting and Market, left foot crushed by shell and died in six days; Mr. William Knighton, corner Meeting and Market, right leg taken off and died in four days; Mr. John Dorcher, of German Fire Company, wounded at fire of December 25, and since died; Rebecca, slave of Mr. Lindsay, No. 5 Beaufair Street, killed instantly by shell...." With similar dispassion, Major Bryan kept his statistics:

Shells striking houses—145
Shells striking yards—19
Shells striking in the streets and on the
edge of burned districts—61

How civilization could justify such acts puzzled Major Bryan.

CITIZENS OF CHARLESTON, SOUTH CAROLINA, RUN FOR COVER AS SHELLS FROM FEDERAL BOATS RAKE THEIR CITY.

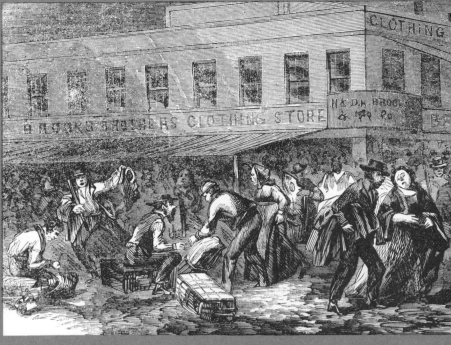

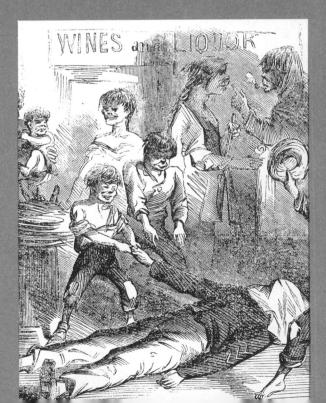

Sunday, July 12, 1863, was a sullen day in New York City. Resentment had been growing ever since the Conscription Act had made all males between the ages of eighteen and forty-five (including Indians and Negroes) subject at the spin of a lottery wheel to military service for three years. Now on a murky Sabbath men read their names on the lists of those drawn for the hardships of army life and tempers began to boil. That afternoon a detective sent a note to his police precinct headquarters:

"Sergeant Young: A man named John Andrews is stirring the people to action against the draft and the colored. He is making treasonable speeches about the 10th Ward and especially along Allen Street. I am sticking with him. Dusenberry."

What Detective Dusenberry's note failed to add was the fact that Andrews was not only a well-known Copperhead, but also that wherever he went Ross Lane, a Richmond agent, was close on his heels. By Monday the mob that followed Andrews carried long-handled axes, and waterfront workers pulled off their belts and turned the buckles outward. As this crowd started marching uptown it picked up recruits at every corner until some observers estimated its number at 10,000. It moved like a hostile army.

The draft office of the ninth district at 677 Third Avenue became a focal point for a segment of the mob, and here a stone thrown through a window unleashed a bloody reign of terror that lasted four days. Fires set to apart-

Draft rioters in New York City sack a drugstore on Second Avenue (top, left) and loot a clothing store (top, right). The police charge the rioters in a free-for-all in front of the offices of the Tribune *(center). A Negro is hanged (bottom, left) in Clarkson Street and the unruly mob jeers a dead sergeant (bottom, right).*

ment houses imperiled the lives of hundreds. Telegraph lines were cut and hook-and-ladder brigades prevented from extinguishing the fires. The city's small police force, reported *Frank Leslie's Illustrated Newspaper,* "were speedily attacked, and, after they had fired a volley of blank cartridges, disarmed and routed, many of them horribly beaten."

Harper's Weekly told how one of the first victims of "the insane fury of the rioters" was a Negro cartman residing on Carmine Street:

"...A mob of men and boys seized this unfortunate man on Monday evening, and having beaten him until he was in a state of insensibility, dragged him to Clarkson Street, and hung him from a branch of one of the trees that shade the sidewalk by St. John's Cemetery. The fiends did not stop here, however. Procuring long sticks, they tied rags and straws to the ends of them, and with these torches they danced round their victim, setting fire to his clothes, and burning him almost to a cinder...."

An orphanage for Negro children was burned and looted, street cars overturned, the business of the city in large part suspended. Federal troops garrisoning the forts in the harbor, a company from West Point, and the New York militia regiments from the Army of the Potomac were rushed to the city to restore order. Estimates placed the killed and wounded at 1,000, the property damage at $1,500,000. A Broadway merchant, reopening his charred shop, tried to rally customers with good humor:

> *Our goods are damaged by fire*
> *And also blackened by smoke.*
> *Won't you please buy 'em,*
> *So we don't go broke!*

On August 19 the draft was resumed in New York City without incident, and throughout the North generally the Conscription Act stimulated enlistments. States, counties, cities, and towns contributed vast sums in bounties, enticing a number of men to volunteer. The national government clearly was able to fight a long war.

William Clarke Quantrill, ex-schoolteacher, was known along the frontier as a gambler, a horse thief, and a murderer. From the days of border warfare between Kansas and Missouri he had used the unsettled times to his personal advantage. Variously called Charley Hart and Billy Quantrill, this guerrilla had captured Independence, Missouri, on August 11, 1862, and four days later he had received a commission as captain in the Confederate Army. Many a western bandit—the James boys among them—began to learn his trade under Quantrill, who supplied a perfect lesson in the ruthless burning of the town and the "massacre" of its inhabitants when he led his bushwhackers into Lawrence, Kansas, on August 21, 1863.

Lawrence, reported *Harper's Weekly*, was "one of the most thriving towns between the Missouri River and the Rocky Mountains"—before Quantrill struck. The bandit chieftain knew his trade to perfection: "Guards were posted around the town so as to prevent all escape, and the work of pillage and murder at once commenced.... The citizens were massacred by the light of their burning homes, and their bodies flung into wells and cisterns. In one case twelve men were driven into a building, where they were shot down, and the house burned over their bodies.... Two banks were plundered, and the third escaped because the marauders could not force the safe in time." The correspondent for the New York *Herald*, corroborating these facts, added: "It was a sudden incursion of fiendish guerrillas—a repetition of the scenes that used

In the humid dawn of August 21, 1863, the guerrilla chieftain, William Clarke Quantrill, led a band of four hundred raiders into Lawrence, Kansas. A former schoolteacher, a horse thief and murderer, Quantrill held a regular Confederate commission as captain. The North, however, considered Quantrill and his men mere outlaws and cutthroats, and their senseless killing of unarmed citizens in Lawrence (left) convinced Harper's Weekly *that history would record the name of Quantrill with "Nena Sahib in India and Cut Nose in Minnesota"—and, indeed, history has. Those who survived the "massacre" stood among the ruins (below), wondering how "men could be such fiends." The whole number killed was perhaps 150; the property damage was estimated at $2,000,000, which seemed high.*

to be enacted on our borders by the savage Indians, when villages were given to the flames by some 'Monster Brandt, with all his howling, desolating band'."

Among the survivors of the raid was a publisher, J. S. Boughton, who remembered how Quantrill's vandals had scattered in small gangs to carry on their work quickly and efficiently. Boughton told of a judge who was discovered hiding in his basement. "...he was [shot,] driven out of the cellar into the yard and shot again. He fell mortally wounded. His wife threw herself on to him and covered him with her person to shield him from further violence. The ruffian deliberately walked around her to find a place to shoot under her, and finally raised her arm and put his revolver under, and fired

so that she could see the ball enter his head. They then fired the house...."

Quantrill escaped. In 1864, however, while en route to Washington to assassinate Abraham Lincoln, he was fatally wounded by Federal troops in Kentucky on May 10. Quantrill managed to live on for twenty days and to scrape together $500 in gold for Kate Clarke, his doxy, who prudently used the sum to establish a house of prostitution in St. Louis.

To easterners, reading of Quantrill's raid, came the same sense of shock they had felt in the accounts of the Sioux uprising in Minnesota and they would experience later in stories of the campaign along the Red River. Enormous areas of the nation were still raw frontier where human life was held to be cheap.

A remarkable pen-picture of the war by Thomas Nast. In the Far West guerrillas creep up on two pickets, not realizing that they have been seen. One senses the tense stealthiness with which the guerrillas inch forward, expecting to wipe out the unsuspecting pair, who wait in the tree above with rifles ready. Thus the hunters become the hunted, an incident of war rarely documented.

Since early January, when Rosecrans and Bragg had fought to a standstill at Murfreesboro, the war in Tennessee had fallen into a period of inactivity. With Bragg holed up in Chattanooga, Rosecrans started in August to move his Army of the Cumberland in an effort to maneuver the Confederates out of Tennessee.

There was real flair in William Starke Rosecrans. His large red nose explained why soldiers called him "Old Rosy" behind his back. He loved leisure and a good time and howled uproariously when he came upon a sign on a tent reading, "Dog-hole No. 1 . . . Sons of Bitches Within." He swore with vehemence, but insisted, as a convert to Roman Catholicism, that never did he blaspheme God. He could drink with the best topers, and could outdrink most, and he could plan a battle with cunning and sense.

"Old Rosy's" plan at Chattanooga—a sound one—was to make a feint at the Confederate position from the northwest while crossing the Tennessee River to the southwest with the main body of his army. The scheme worked perfectly at first. Rosecrans pressed down on Chattanooga and Bragg pulled out. The Rebels, by Rosecrans' calculations, were supposed to keep running, but a few miles south of the town Bragg halted as if to give battle, and Rosecrans, with his army widely dispersed, found himself in the worst possible situation.

Frantically, Rosecrans tried to pull together his scattered corps, and by September 18 had virtually completed his concentration with West Chickamauga Creek in front of the great part of the line. The center was held by George H.

Thomas, a name to remember. Virginia-born Thomas stood six feet and weighed two hundred pounds. As a cadet at West Point, where he graduated in 1840, he had been known as "Old Tom," and later when he returned to the Military Academy as an instructor his nickname had been "Slow Trot." Truly, he was a deliberate student of war—careful at times to the point of exasperation—and yet, as Thomas would soon demonstrate, he was as tenacious as he was fastidious.

The Battle of Chickamauga opened on September 19, and the arrival of Longstreet and his corps from Lee's Army of Northern Virginia gave the strength to Bragg that produced the climax next day. A drive on the Federal flank opened a gap through which Longstreet poured his corps. As the Union forces began to melt away, "Old Rosy," very likely with his heart in his throat, scampered toward Chattanooga. But at Snodgrass Hill, Thomas refused to be swept back, and henceforth no one would call him "Slow Trot." He had become instead "The Rock of Chickamauga." In a rousing piece of war reporting, General J. S. Fullerton described the closing scene of that memorable afternoon:

"... The cartridge-boxes of both our own and the enemy's dead within reach had been emptied by our men. . . . Along the whole line ran the order, 'Fix bayonets.' On came the enemy—our men were lying down. 'Forward,' was sounded. In one instant they were on their feet. Forward they went to meet the charge. The enemy fled. . . . One regiment, with empty muskets . . . broke through the enemy's lines."

GEORGE H. THOMAS

What glory the Federals could claim at Chickamauga belonged alone to Thomas and his troops. Charles Dana, attached as an observer now to Rosecrans, wired Washington: "Chickamauga is as fatal a name in our history as Bull Run." Yet for all that "Old Rosy" had lost his head and the day, the casualty figures on both sides would make sober reading. Rosecrans, with 58,222 effectives, counted 1,657 killed, 9,756 wounded, and 4,757 missing; Bragg, with 66,326 effectives, counted 2,312 killed, 14,674 wounded, and 1,468 missing.

Succeeding weeks saw Federal reserves rushed to Rosecrans. Hooker brought forces from the east and Sherman brought forces from the west. Then in late October, looking thin and still limping on an injured leg, arrived Grant. He found Rosecrans shut off from supplies unless they were hauled by a circuitous route over mountainous country. Soldiers for some time had been on half rations of hard bread and "beef dried on the hoof." Their clothes were worn out and many of them were without adequate shoes. Fuel was exhausted; even the supply of tree stumps was used up. The men were lethargic and dispirited.

Happily, General William F. Smith, an excellent engineer who had made his mark with the Army of the Potomac, recently had been transferred to Chattanooga and already had a plan for breaking Bragg's strangle hold on the Union's supply lines. Smith's scheme had a style that Grant liked instantly. Hooker, then twenty-five miles west of Chattanooga at Bridgeport on the Tennessee, was to cross to the south side. If necessary, he was to fight his way to Brown's Ferry, three miles across country from Chattanooga, where he would be met by forces

SERGEANT JOHN CLEM

that would cover his position from nearby heights. Hooker moved as ordered, catching the Confederates napping, and before Bragg realized quite what had happened, Grant had opened his famous "cracker line."

Within a week the troops were receiving full rations and, Grant said, "Neither officers nor men looked upon themselves any longer as doomed. The weak and languid appearance of the troops, so visible before, disappeared at once." Among Bragg's recent visitors had been Jefferson Davis, who had received warm assurance that the Federals' want of food and forage must bring a "speedy evacuation of Chattanooga." The destruction of Rosecrans' army, Bragg had told Davis confidently, "was only a question of time."

But now Grant was on the scene. Even Bragg realized a change had come.

General George H. Thomas (left) who won fame as "The Rock of Chickamauga." A Rebel charge (center) at Chickamauga, fought September 19 and 20, 1863. Sergeant John Clem (above), who served with the Michigan 22nd, was the Union's youngest soldier. Twelve years old, "and small even for his age," he had three bullets pierce his hat at Chickamauga. A Rebel colonel, seeing the lad in battle, cried, "Stop, you little Yankee devil!" Clem cocked his rifle and shot the officer dead. In recognition of this coolness, General Rosecrans made Clem a sergeant and assigned him to special duty at headquarters.

This point of Lookout Mountain, above the winding Tennessee River, reveals the tortuous terrain over which Grant smashed his way to the devastating victory of November 23-25, 1863. Braxton Bragg could hardly believe how his army crumbled around him: "A panic which I never before witnessed seemed to have seized upon officers and men, and each seemed to be struggling for his personal safety, regardless of his duty or his character.... No satisfactory excuse can possibly be given for the shameful conduct of our troops on the left in allowing their line to be penetrated." Bragg rocked back in humiliating defeat, retreating into Georgia, while the star of Grant blazed in the military heavens.

Lincoln could never quite put military sense before sentiment when it came to "protecting" loyal Unionists in east Tennessee, and so before Grant reached Chattanooga a Federal force of about 25,000 under Ambrose E. Burnside had been sent into east Tennessee, where about the best they could hope to achieve was to invite future trouble. In early November, when Bragg sent Longstreet with some 20,000 troops to clean out the Federals, the trouble moved up to Burnside's tent fly.

An urgent call went from Washington to Grant asking him to save the situation—somehow. No one could say what should be done, and Grant, taking a deep breath, probably wished that more than one solution promised to save this mess. Bragg occupied Missionary Ridge, east of Chattanooga and, about equally distant to the southwest, Lookout Mountain, where his forces controlled the Tennessee and the one railroad (the Nashville and Chattanooga) coming from the north. Obviously, Bragg was in a strong position and yet, realistically, how could Grant aid Burnside unless by so jarring Bragg in battle that he felt impelled to recall the forces under Longstreet?

Grant waited for Sherman to come up with the Army of the Tennessee, then on November 23 launched his attack. After three days the battle had run like a river of fire across Lookout Mountain and Orchard Knob to Missionary Ridge, where Bragg's soldiers occupied three rows of rifle pits. Treacherous Chickamauga Creek separated Bragg from his depot of supplies. Both flanks of his army were exposed.

The day was filled with anxieties for Grant, while his weary armies grappled for advantage. Fighting hand to hand and bayonet to bayonet, Sherman tried to hammer his way up a slope, but toward three o'clock, after the Rebels had started rolling down boulders to crack open Yankee heads, Sherman was willing to admit that he had been fought to a standstill. Grant turned to Thomas, "the Rock of Chickamauga."

He pointed to the center of a 200-foot ridge and told Thomas to take his men as far as the first row of Confederate rifle pits, capture them, and await further orders. Thomas and his 20,000 soldiers went up with a shout. They took the first row of pits in a quick, nasty skirmish, but with the Rebels above raining bullets down on them they forgot to wait for orders. Watching the Yankee advance, a Federal officer said: "The men away above us look like great ants crawling up, crouching on the outside of the rebel breastworks. One of our flags seems to be moving; look! look! look! Up! Up! Up! it goes and is planted on the rebel works." Private Sam Watkins of the Confederate Tennessee 1st saw that blue-clad column rolling toward him: "They kept climbing and scratching until I was in touching distance of the old Rebel breastworks, right on the very apex of Missionary Ridge.... The Yankees were cutting and slashing, and the cannoneers were running in every direction. I saw Day's brigade throw down their guns and break like quarter horses. Bragg was trying to rally them. I heard him say, 'Here is your commander,' and the soldiers hallooed back, 'Here is your mule.' "

Later Watkins felt sorry for Bragg, "he looked so hacked and whipped and mortified and chagrined at defeat." Of 46,165 effectives engaged, Bragg listed 361 killed, 2,160 wounded, and 4,146 missing, against losses for Grant, with 56,359 effectives engaged, of 753 killed, 4,722 wounded, and 349 missing. But figures alone could not tell the story of Bragg's humiliation, for he was started on a retreat destined with time to carry the war from Tennessee into the heart of Georgia.

The year had brought four great successes to the North: Gettysburg, Vicksburg, Missionary Ridge—and a general named U. S. Grant.

SAVAGE FIGHTING ON THE SLOPES OF MISSIONARY RIDGE WHERE THOMAS'S BOYS SPREAD A PANIC.

Almost from the moment the guns fell silent at Gettysburg, the movement began to establish a national cemetery honoring the soldiers who had fallen in the battle. No speaker other than the Honorable Edward Everett of Massachusetts, considered the greatest living American orator, would satisfy the members of the cemetery commission and when Everett's schedule would not permit him to speak on October 23, 1863, the date of the dedication ceremonies was changed to November 19. Many governmental and diplomatic officials were invited to the dedication, among them the President of the United States. But it was not until early in November, almost as an afterthought, that Lincoln was asked "after the oration [by Everett], to set apart formally these grounds to their sacred use by a few appropriate remarks."

"When the suggestion was made that he [Lincoln] be invited to speak," explained Clark E. Carr, the Illinois member of the cemetery commission, "while all expressed high appreciation of his great abilities as a political speaker, as shown in his debates with Senator Douglas, and in his Cooper Institute address, the question was raised as to his ability to speak upon such a grave and solemn occasion as that of the memorial services."

Lincoln apparently was more confident than the members of the commission. He accepted at once the invitation to speak. John Hay, who traveled on the special train from Washington to Gettysburg, recalled that on arriving at the little college town "the President went to Mr. Wills who expected him, and our party broke like a drop of quicksilver spilled." Judging by Hay's diary, he was more than willing to forget attending to the President. The young secretary visited the college, "got a chafing dish of oysters, then some supper," sang songs and drank no little amount of whiskey. So too did the Pennsylvania journalist, John W. Forney, who nourished a grievance with each drink. When the crowd cheered, Forney's umbrage spilled over. Turning on the carefree celebrants, he shouted:

"My friends, you gave no such cheers to your President down the street. Do you know what you owe to that great man? You owe your country—you owe your name as American citizens."

Nor, by the testimony of Hay's diary, was Forney finished speaking his mind:

"He went on blackguarding the crowd for their apathy and then diverged to his own record, saying he had been for Lincoln in his heart in 1860—that open advocacy was not as effectual as the course he took—dividing the most corrupt organization that ever existed—the proslavery Democratic party. He dwelt at length on this question and then went back to the eulogy of the President, that great, wonderful, mysterious, inexplicable man who holds in his single hands the reins of the Republic; who keeps his own counsels; who does his own purpose in his own way, no matter what temporizing minister in his Cabinet sets himself up in opposition to the progress of the age."

Next morning John Hay "got a beast" and rode with the President's suite to the ceremonies, and watched and listened as "the President, in a fine, free way, with more grace than is his wont, said his half dozen words of consecration, and the music wailed and we went home through crowded and cheering streets." No clue had come to Hay, listening, that Lincoln had defined the purpose of the war with such clear, poetic insight that history would never forget his words. Twice he had drafted this speech before he rose to speak, and then, coming to the beautiful ending, he said, adding "under God" upon the inspiration of the moment, "that this nation under God shall have a new birth of freedom..." In all, Lincoln had used 268 words, and, the editors of the Chicago *Times* thought, "The cheek of every American must tingle with shame as he reads the silly, flat and dishwatery utterances of the man who has to be pointed out to intelligent foreigners as the President of the United States."

At Gettysburg, Lincoln said:

Four score and seven years ago our fathers brought forth, upon this continent, a new nation, conceived in Liberty, and dedicated to the proposition that all men are created equal.

¶ Now we are engaged in a great civil war, testing whether that nation, or any nation, so conceived, and so dedicated, can long endure. We are met here on a great battle-field of that war. We have come to dedicate a portion of it as a final resting place for those who here gave their lives that that nation might live. It is altogether fitting and proper that we should do this.

¶ But in a larger sense we can not dedicate—we can not consecrate—we can not hallow this ground. The brave men, living and dead, who struggled here, have consecrated it far above our poor power to add or detract. The world will little note, nor long remember, what we say here, but can never forget what they did here. It is for us, the living, rather to be dedicated here to the unfinished work which they have, thus far, so nobly carried on. It is rather for us to be here dedicated to the great task remaining before us—that from these honored dead we take increased devotion to that cause for which they here gave the last full measure of devotion— that we here highly resolve that these dead shall not have died in vain; that this nation shall have a new birth of freedom; and that this government of the people, by the people, for the people, shall not perish from the earth.

TURNING POINT

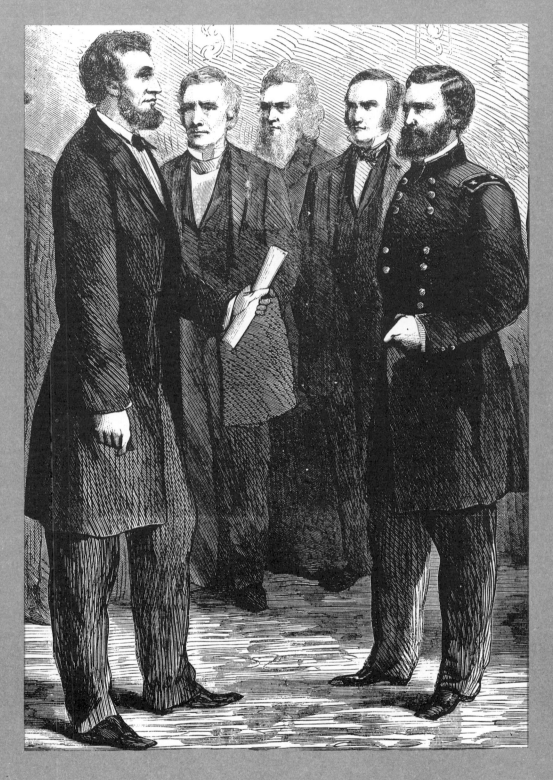

Lincoln's quest ends:
In U.S. Grant he finds a general
who has the will to win

With immortal words at Gettysburg, with a smashing victory for the North at Missionary Ridge, thus ended 1863, which, with a superb sense of history, the editors of *The Atlantic Monthly* called "The Year of the Proclamation." Sniped at by Peace Democrat and Copperhead for sustaining the new kind of Union that the Emancipation Proclamation foreshadowed, branded everything from boob to "nigger-lover" and often sorely tormented in mind over whether damaging the Rebel was worth adjusting life-long social values, the fighting Yankee had stood by his government. He had fought under Hooker at Chancellorsville, under Meade at Gettysburg, under Rosecrans at Chickamauga, and under Grant at Vicksburg and Missionary Ridge—he had never fought better. He was part now of a nation, *The Atlantic Monthly* insisted, that had been saved "by the mighty hand of God," a bounty no one could have expected "had we continued to link the nation's cause to that of oppression, and had we shed blood and expended gold in order to restore the system of slavery and the sway of slaveholders."

In a real sense, Lincoln returned from his "half dozen words of consecration" at Gettysburg with the war organized as a moral purpose. When 1864 ended he would have it organized also as a military force and a political reality. That achievement began on a March day when Grant, arriving in Washington to receive the rank of lieutenant general (formerly held only by George Washington and Winfield Scott), wrote with characteristic simplicity in the register at Willard's Hotel: "U. S. Grant and son, Galena, Ill." Then the general who would soon receive command over armies numbering more than half a million men, called during a reception at the White House, quite unprepared to find official Washington so eager to catch a glimpse of him that his mere presence nearly turned the occasion into a shambles. Asked later to a dinner by the President, the general politely declined the invitation. In all honesty, he declared, "I have become very tired of this show business."

Looking down from the advantage of an extra eight inches in height, Lincoln understood this unaffected man who, like himself, "had sprung from the common people to become one of the most uncommon of men." Between them existed a candor that was rare, and when Grant insisted on bringing Sheridan east to command his cavalry and Lincoln complained that he was "rather a little fellow," the argument ceased with Grant's quiet retort: "You will find him big enough for the purpose." Even Secretary of War Stanton could not fluster Grant—no small achievement in view of the numerous Union generals who, long years after the war ended, still shuddered every time they beheld Stanton's stern visage on a one-dollar treasury note.

On March 9, Grant, accompanied by Fred, his eldest son, returned to the White House to receive his promotion in rank. Lincoln and his Cabinet greeted their new lieutenant general (left). The President said:

"General Grant, the nation's appreciation of what you have done, and its reliance upon you for what remains to be done in the existing great struggle, are now presented, with this commission constituting you lieutenant general in the Army of the United States. With this high honor, devolves upon you, also, a corresponding responsibility. As the country herein trusts you, so, under God, it will sustain you. I scarcely need to add, that, with what I here speak for the nation, goes my own hearty personal concurrence."

Grant, plainly affected, hoped that he would not disappoint the President's expectations, then added: "I feel the full weight of the responsibilities now devolving upon me; and I know that if they are met, it will be due to those armies, and above all, to the favor of that Providence which leads both nations and men."

Next day Grant left for the headquarters of the Army of the Potomac.

Northern morale was quickened by the appointment of Grant, the man of success, to supreme command of all Union armies. Then in mid-April reports of the Fort Pillow "massacre," reaching the northern press, added anger to the resolution of the nation to prosecute the war to whatever bitter end was necessary.

These were the facts: Forty miles north of Memphis in a straight line (twice that distance if one followed the Mississippi River) stood Fort Pillow, garrisoned by a single Union cavalry brigade (from Tennessee, white) and four companies of artillery, all Negro. In round figures, less than 600 Yankee troops manned this fort against an attack on April 12 of 1,200 Confederates under command of Nathan Bedford Forrest, an ex-slave dealer from Memphis who was easily the best cavalry leader in the South (or so, at any rate, both Grant and Sherman believed). By mid-afternoon the Rebels had in-

vested the fort on its three land sides and had demanded its surrender, which was refused. In some measure what happened thereafter—by the testimony taken under oath from eyewitnesses—may have been exaggerated, but this statement by Union soldier William J. Mays is typical of the horrors reported:

"...There were also 2 negro women and 3 little children standing within 25 steps from me, when a rebel stepped up to them and said, 'Yes, God damn you, you thought you were free, did you?' and shot them all. They all fell but 1 child, when he knocked it in the head with the breech of his gun." Testified Lieutenant Mack J. Leaming, a Union adjutant: "The enemy carried our works at about 4 p.m., and from that time until dark, and at intervals throughout the night, our men were shot down without mercy and almost without regard to color. This horrid work of butchery did not cease even with

the night of murder, but was renewed again the next morning, when numbers of our wounded were basely murdered after a long night of pain and suffering on the field where they had fought so bravely...."

Wild tales? Perhaps. Yet Forrest wrote in his official report: "It is hoped that these facts will demonstrate to the northern people that negro soldiers cannot cope with Southerners."

What, really, the "facts" of the Fort Pillow affair demonstrated was that northern people had a sense of responsibility toward the Negro soldiers they had enlisted. The slave dealer as an avenging warrior supplied a symbol of propaganda that was highly salable to the North. More than ever now, there was a sense of anticipation in the telling blow that Grant would undoubtedly strike.

Grant had been to Cincinnati to see Sherman. Bragg was gone from command of the Confederate army in Georgia, and Joe Johnston had been assigned to defending Atlanta and the interior of Georgia. Grant gave Sherman the job of destroying Johnston's army, if possible, and in any event, of capturing Atlanta. Meanwhile, in the east, Grant, working with Meade, would handle Lee and the Army of Northern Virginia.

In Virginia the dogwood came into bloom. Grant selected May 4 as his jumping-off day for knocking Lee out of the war. With Federal effectives numbering 100,000—not counting the Ninth Corps under Burnside then held near the Rappahannock railroad bridge—Grant started after Lee, whose army, lying west of the Rapidan, numbered no more than 67,000 effectives. Grant moved his army across the fords at Ely's and Germanna—fords that led into the Wilderness where a year ago Hooker had floundered so miserably. Writing to his son Custis, Lee said: "If victorious, we have everything to hope for in the future. If defeated, nothing will be left for us to live for...."

Lee had two problems: Grant was no Hooker; and no Stonewall Jackson supported him now.

Above Memphis on the Mississippi River stood Fort Pillow, garrisoned in 1864 by the Union's 13th Tennessee Cavalry and four companies of Negro artillery. In all, about 557 officers and men held the fort when on April 12 some 1,200 Rebels under a onetime slave dealer in Memphis, Nathan Bedford Forrest, attacked Pillow (left). Survivors told grim stories of Negro troops brutally massacred, and Forrest reported that "the river was dyed with the blood of the slaughtered for 200 yards." The North cried for revenge. Grant and Meade (above) plan an attack to crush Lee.

On May 6, Lee and Grant clashed head-on in the Wilderness. A contemporary account explained the new kind of warfare that suddenly confronted Grant:

"...Death came unseen; regiments stumbled on each other and sent swift destruction into each other's ranks, guided by the crackling of the bushes. It was not war—military maneuvering; science has as little to do with it as sight. Two wild animals were hunting each other; when they heard each other's steps they sprung and grappled. The conqueror advanced, or went elsewhere. The dead were lost from all eyes in the thicket.... Officers advance[d] to the charge in the jungle, *compass in hand*.... Here in the blind wrestle as at midnight did two hundred thousand men in blue and grey clutch each other —bloodiest and weirdest of encounters. War had had nothing like it...."

Lee, waiting for Longstreet to come up, in-tended to drive the full force of Longstreet's right and center against the Federal left. It was late in the game that first day when Longstreet shouted that he had "another Bull Run on them." But a Union musket ball disabled Longstreet, throwing his advance into disorder. Although Lee hastened forward to take command in person, the steam had disappeared from the Confederate drive. Darkness ended the fighting without a decision.

Grant had tested Lee and found him a mettlesome opponent. It was not yet clear whether Grant had met his match, but a witness to the struggle said: "I never saw a man so agitated in my life." Yet Grant, for all that he tossed on his cot that night, came to the right decision. The logical move was to try to get behind and beyond Lee's right flank on the way to Richmond. Thus Grant began his famous "sidling" by the left flank, moving toward Hanover by way of Spot-

sylvania Court House, on the edge of the Wilderness, five miles to the southwest.

On May 12 at a salient in Lee's line, called the "Bloody Angle," Spotsylvania produced the most savage hand-to-hand fighting of the war. Here, testified an aide to Grant, "rank after rank was riddled by shot and shell and bayonet-thrusts, and finally sank, a mass of torn and mutilated corpses; then fresh troops rushed madly forward to replace the dead, and so the murderous work went on. Guns were run up close to the parapet, and double charges of canister played their part in the bloody work. The fence-rails and logs in the breastworks were shattered into splinters, and trees over a foot and a half in diameter were cut in two...."

In an eloquent phrase, the aide added: "We had not only shot down an army, but also a forest." Often guns were fired with muzzle pressed against muzzle.

The Battle of the Wilderness was fought in an almost impenetrable forest. Troops under Major General James S. Wadsworth, saw their commander killed here (left). Fire, breaking out, added to the natural terrors of the Wilderness, especially for those charged with carrying out the wounded (above). Lincoln told a member of Congress: "Grant has gone to the Wilderness, crawled in, drawn up the ladder, and pulled in the hole after him, and I guess we'll have to wait till he comes out before we know just what he's up to." What Grant was "up to" was the hardest fight of his life. But instead of retreating, he sought a new battlefield—at Spotsylvania.

The Bloody Angle at Spotsylvania, fought May 12, 1864, where "skulls were crushed with clubbed muskets, and men stabbed to death with swords and bayonets thrust between the logs in the parapet which separated the combatants. Wild cheers, savage yells, and frantic shrieks rose above the sighing of the wind and the pattering of the rain."

"Grant turning Lee's left" was the caption Harper's Weekly *gave this cartoon (left). Following the battle of Spotsylvania, Grant again "sidled" to the left toward Richmond. Across the North Anna (below), Federal engineers lay pontoon bridges for a crossing by the Army of the Potomac.*

After Spotsylvania, Grant swung once more to the left and then, crossing the North Anna, his army was hung half on one side of the river and half on the other. Truly, here was a golden opportunity for Lee, except at that moment Lee lay in his tent, stricken with a violent intestinal illness and clenching his fists in pain. The army was immobilized, awaiting his recovery. So Grant slipped through his fingers, and when Dr. Gwathmey came in to attend Lee, the

Virginian muttered tightly: "If I can get one more pull at him, I will defeat him."

Grant shied off from meeting Lee between the North and South Anna but moved on to the south side of the Pamunkey, where in a burst of overconfidence he informed Washington: "Lee's army is really whipped." How wrong Grant was he would learn soon enough, for he came now to Cold Harbor where veterans under Lee recalled how soundly they had beaten McClellan

Union General William W. Stewart talks with Confederate General Edward Johnson, captured during the brutal fight at the "Bloody Angle." Popularly known as "Allegheny," Johnson was exchanged a short time thereafter, only to be captured once again in the fighting before Nashville, Tennessee.

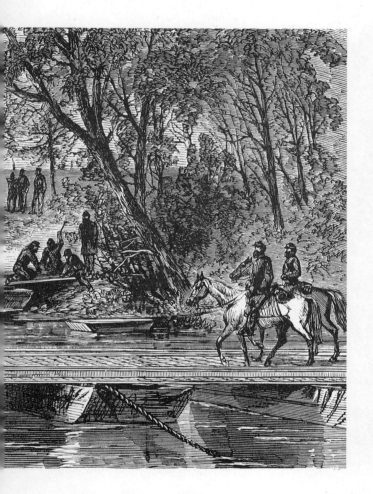

here two years before. On this familiar ground, every ridge, every stream, every foot of swamp could be used by Lee.

Determined to continue his "smash-'em-up" policy, Grant made two wrong guesses—first, he underestimated Lee, who was a brave, skillful, and determined general; second, he misjudged the fighting quality of the Rebels, who were not as half-starved as he believed. The Yankees who were to do the fighting at Cold Harbor were not

so easily misled and, awaiting the battle, they could be seen "calmly writing their names and home addresses on slips of paper and pinning them on the back of their coats, so that their dead bodies might be recognized and their fates made known to their families at home."

For a great many the precaution was wisely taken. Grant was face to face with the worst slaughter of the war. Over five acres of flaming battleground, he was beaten badly.

After Cold Harbor, fought from June 1 to June 3, 1864, Grant was called "the butcher." Of the final charge, a Confederate participant said: "Along the line of our salient, our infantry and our artillery fired at short range into a mass of men twenty-eight deep, who could neither advance nor retreat." Few Federals could even fire.

Tragic news suddenly swept the South. In early June, Sheridan had taken his cavalry toward Richmond to draw Jeb Stuart's horsemen off Grant's flank. Yellow Tavern, six miles north of Richmond, had brought a violent collision of the rival forces on June 8. A pistol shot had ripped into Stuart's abdomen, and comrades had carried him away to Richmond to die.

In a month of fighting against Lee, Grant's losses had been substantial. He had entered the Battle of the Wilderness, May 5-7, with 101,895 effectives and had counted 2,246 killed, 12,037 wounded, and 3,383 missing. (The Confederates, with 61,025 effectives, had an estimated 7,500 killed and wounded.) At Spotsylvania, May 12, he had 6,020 killed and 800 missing. (Confederate losses, though unknown, were approximately one-third as many.) And at Cold Harbor, June 1-3, Grant lost about 12,000 in killed and

abouts of 100,000 men while shifting them to launch a new campaign? Grant thought he could —and did—and suddenly he had moved south across the James River. Now he had the jump on Lee, an all-important edge in the developing race for Petersburg.

Situated on the south bank of the Appomattox River, Petersburg was the hub of five railroads —the Richmond and Petersburg running north, the Weldon running south into North Carolina, the Norfolk and Petersburg running southwest, the Petersburg and City Point running to the confluence of the James and Appomattox rivers eight miles distant, and the Richmond and Danville running north twenty-three miles to the Confederate capital. Thus Petersburg (census figures in 1860 placed its population at 18,266) was of vast strategic importance to both armies. Should it fall, Richmond likewise would be impossible to defend.

Lee, arriving at Petersburg on June 18, knew that he must hold Grant in check here at almost any cost. In Richmond the Confederate Congress was anxious to make Lee a military dictator (which was not altogether a compliment to Jefferson Davis, whom Lee had once served as an "orderly sergeant") and soldiers and civilians alike looked upon Lee as a saint, a savior who stood apart from other mortals. The spirit in which the South now accepted Lee was well expressed by a Rebel in the ranks, clinching an argument upon the subject of atheism: "Well, boys, the rest of us may have developed from monkeys; but I tell you none less than a God could have made such a man as Marse Robert!"

No offer of military dictatorship could sway Lee from what he considered his simple, holy duty—the defense of Virginia. Grant would discover how tenacious Lee could be as the siege of Petersburg stretched from hot summer to balmy autumn to chill winter.

Meanwhile, in Georgia, Sherman was on the move, striking hard in the knowledge that 1864 was the year when Lincoln must be re-elected.

wounded. (Confederate casualties unknown.)

Cold Harbor, Grant admitted, was a blunder: "I regret this assault more than any one I have ever ordered." Again, the croakers cried that Grant was throwing away an army, but the men in the ranks grew annoyed at this criticism of their commander and asked testily, "Who's shedding this blood, anyhow?" To all appearances Grant was entrenching at Cold Harbor, when in reality he was playing a very difficult game of war. Was it possible to screen the where-

FLIGHT TO ATLANTA

Was Sherman crazy?
Reporters believed he was, but
soldiers make him an idol

May–September, 1864

Red-bearded William Tecumseh Sherman, quick of mind, peppery of tongue, and with the disposition of a high-strung quarter horse, had no equal in either army. Sherman was, in his own right, a military institution who had served as a soldier in Charleston and as superintendent of a military academy in Louisiana, and who had loved ardently the land that he now intended to ravish. Once as a boy he had tried to dye his red hair only to have it become a hideous shade of green, and thereafter had been satisfied to live with himself as he was. And once as a boy he had hung a cat nine times to make certain it was dead, revealing a streak of nervous thoroughness that was his chief characteristic.

Despite a West Point training, Sherman had never been in a real battle until the opening fight at Manassas Junction, and that experience had completely unsettled him. He had begged Lincoln not to give him an independent command, but he had been shunted off to Kentucky nonetheless where his quarrels with reporters, his extravagant demands for reinforcements, and his hallucinations that he was about to be crushed by Confederate forces that didn't exist as a threat led to published reports that he was insane. Sherman seemed a dead goose in the army, but "Old Brains" Halleck, remembering that Sherman's brother was an influential senator, made a place for the general on his staff in St. Louis. Thus it was that Billy Sherman helped to plan and to supply the expedition that moved with such success against Forts Henry and Donelson, and which first brought Grant into the national limelight.

Never had Sherman admired anyone as much as Grant, and between them grew a warm, enduring friendship. After Shiloh, when the sting of unjust criticism led Grant to decide to quit the army, it was Sherman who strode into the tent where Grant already was packing to depart and talked him out of that rash decision. But in turn Sherman owed much to Grant, who had restored his confidence and taught him a style of war not found in the military textbooks and now, in the spring of 1864, gave him command over all the western armies. Said a soldier who served under both generals: "Grant was the creator of the western armies, but Billy Sherman was their idol."

THE REAR GUARD OF SHERMAN'S GREAT WESTERN ARMIES AS IT PLUNGED INTO GEORGIA TO CAPTURE ATLANTA.

Sherman spoke of his relations with Grant that spring: "There never was and never can be raised a question of rivalry or claim between us as to the relative merits of the manner in which we played our respective parts. We were as brothers—I the older man in years, he the higher in rank." Under Sherman's command now, by Grant's order, were the Army of the Cumberland, the Army of the Ohio, and the Army of the Tennessee—in round figures, a magnificent fighting force of 98,000 men and 250 guns. In an exuberant mood Sherman wrote: "With the month of May came the season for action." At the moment Sherman marched his armies from Chattanooga the Confederates were at Dalton, Georgia, but Sherman had no intention of giving battle in an arena where Joe Johnston had had months to entrench. Instead he planned to make a feint at Johnston's front, then swing on to Resaca, eighteen miles to the rear, where he would be across Johnston's lines of communication and supply.

The plan worked more easily than even Sherman had hoped, and on May 14—two days after Grant fought at Spotsylvania—Sherman's forces spent the day "creeping up among the bushes, rocks and ravines" to move upon Johnston's position at Resaca. Next morning a Union soldier came upon Sherman, sitting on a log with his back hunched against a tree, asleep.

"A pretty way we are commanded!" the soldier muttered.

Sherman blinked his eyes open, smiled and said: "Stop, my man. While you were sleeping last night, I was planning for you."

And Sherman returned to his nap.

The affair at Resaca, wrote a Confederate lieutenant, was a "death struggle with Sherman's well-clothed, well-fed and thoroughly rested veterans who moved against us in perfect step, with banners flying and bands playing, as though expecting to charm us." Three times Sherman's troops charged and were driven back —"a veritable picnic for the Confederates," the lieutenant added, "protected as we were by earthworks with clear and open ground in front." Too late, the lieutenant realized that the fighting at Resaca had been no more than "a clever ruse of Sherman's." Again, the Federals moved on the rear of Johnston's army, aiming for a point that would threaten the railroad below Calhoun and above Kingston. To escape the trap, Johnston hurried his boys across the Oostenaula River and set fire to the bridges in an effort to gain time on the Union forces.

The Confederate general reflected his mood in the phrases he used. Thus he fought with "greatly inferior numbers" and must "reduce the odds against us by partial engagements," while hoping that Sherman's strength would be lessened "by the expiration of terms of service of the regiments that had not reenlisted." Clearly, Johnston's nature had not changed from the days when he had driven Lee to distraction by refusing to stand firm against McClellan on the Peninsula or from a year ago in Mississippi when he had shied off from contesting with Grant in the defense of Jackson. General John Bell Hood, a favorite with Jefferson Davis, who had served with distinction under Lee and had now been transferred to Johnston, made no effort to disguise his displeasure with his new commander's methods. By depending too much on entrenchments, Hood insisted, waving the old school tie of the conservative West Pointer, Johnston deprived his troops of a "spirit of devil-me-care independence."

Johnston's answer, of course, was that he managed to keep his army intact, and he wouldn't accept Hood's philosophy that retreat and defeat were synonymous. With Sherman pressing him hard, Old Joe paused in Adairsville only long enough to decide that the valley of Oothcaloga Creek offered a poor battleground and pushed on to Cassville. Here a ridge south of town with a broad, open valley in front gave Johnston a position that he described as "the best I saw during the war."

A division under General John W. Geary assaulting Dug Gap, Georgia, where many who climbed the distant crests actually were hurled down by angry Confederates (above). Sherman's troops (below) form lines of battle at Resaca, where after a bruising day of creeping up rocks and ravines the Rebels were found.

*Sherman's relentless pressure on John-
ston found him falling steadily backward—
from Pine Mountain without a fight, and
from Lost Mountain after little more than
token resistance (right)—for to cover Marietta he had to shorten his line. Prisoners
fell to the Federals like a windfall, including the entire 14th Alabama Regiment.*

A Confederate private, Sam Watkins, was as
delighted with Cassville as Johnston. Never, said
Sam, had he seen troops "more certain of success," and the prospect of battle seemed "like
going to a frolic or a wedding." Sam's extravagant mood expanded: "The soldiers were
jubilant. Gladness was depicted on every countenance. I believe a sort of fanaticism had entered our souls. It seemed that whoever was
killed would be carried to the seventh heaven."
Then along the Rebel lines ran heart-chilling
orders:

"Halt! Retreat!"

Asked Sam, sick with perplexity: "What is
the matter?"

Johnston's answer was that after consulting
with his generals he had been led to serious
second thoughts about fighting at Cassville
where his troops would be exposed, and so he
had decided (as he maintained Generals Polk
and Hood urged him) "to abandon the ground
immediately and cross the Etowah." Old Sam
French, a New Jersey Quaker who had thrown
in with the Rebels, said that Hood and Polk
wouldn't be right if they declared that Christmas came in December. General Hardee, whose
Infantry and Rifle Tactics remained a basic text
in both armies, growled that they were all wrong.
The ground at Cassville could be held.

Sherman, who could know nothing of this

bickering within the Confederate command, pushed closer to Atlanta, and a youthful memory aided the red-headed Union leader: "In early days (1844), when a lieutenant of the Third Artillery, I had been sent from Charleston, South Carolina, to Marietta, Georgia, to assist Inspector-General Churchill to take testimony concerning certain losses of horses and accoutrements during the Florida War; and after completing the work at Marietta we transferred our party to Bellefonte, Alabama. I had ridden the distance on horseback, and had noted well the topography of the country, especially that about Kenesaw, Allatoona, and the Etowah River.... I therefore knew that the Allatoona Pass was

very strong, would be hard to force, and resolved not even to attempt it, but to turn the position, by moving from Kingston to Marietta *via* Dallas...."

Plainly, Sherman had the initiative. From May 25 through May 28 there was bloody fighting at New Hope Church, and the Yankees renamed the place "Hell-Hole." But Sherman's columns pushed on, an irresistible military steam roller in effect, forcing Johnston and his quarreling subordinates to fall back through a chain of isolated hills—Pine Mountain, Lost Mountain, Kenesaw Mountain. Grant might be stalemated before Lee at Petersburg, but apparently Sherman was roaring into Atlanta.

Or so Sherman hoped. When through torrents of rain on June 17 and 18 he approached Marietta, he found Johnston dug in on the slopes of Kenesaw Mountain. Sherman, suddenly slowed down, reacted in a depressed spirit. Johnston's position, he had to admit, was "as dangerous to assault as a permanent fort." Yet Sherman, in a reversal of his fast flanking movements that had carried him so far, decided to dig in and make a fight of it. Days dragged by as field piece was rolled up to contest with Rebel field piece. To keep up morale, Sherman sent quartermasters into the lines to distribute new pants and shoes to the men behind the breastworks.

Sherman began to have "general trouble"—specifically with "Fighting Joe" Hooker, who could not forget that he had once commanded the Army of the Potomac, and who seemed inclined to look down his nose at western generals like Schofield and McPherson, and Virginia-born Thomas. No one could safely talk down western armies to Sherman, and when Hooker complained that he was being asked to hold off three Confederate corps, Sherman exploded.

Johnston's whole damned army consisted of three corps! Schofield pitched into Hooker. The party was growing rough.

In the midst of these blistering tempers, the battle erupted at Kenesaw, and old Sam French on the Confederate side searched his Quaker soul and decided, as he wrote his wife, that "Sherman has no respect for the Fourth Commandment." But if French disliked fighting on the Sabbath, he was nonetheless pleased with what he saw as the wind, blowing gaps in the clouds of battle smoke, revealed "a pageantry on a grand scale."

How badly Sherman had blundered in accepting a fight at Kenesaw, on Johnston's terms, no one understood better than Ted Upson, who fought with the Indiana 100th: "We were in a bad fix. We could not go ahead and we could not get back." As Sherman's dead piled up on the mountainside, Ted crouched under a rock: "The Johnnys might have killed every one of us as we hugged its base, but they only yelled and threw stones at us."

Night seemed a long time coming.

The Federals shelled Pine Mountain, and Sherman, detecting a group of Confederate officers, ordered his gunners to "throw three volleys up that hillside" (above). Among the Rebel generals, who had been observing Sherman as coolly as he had scanned them, was the corpulent Leonidas Polk. When the Federal shells began to fall, the other generals (Johnston and Hardee) hustled to safety, but Polk, a stately walker, was hit in the breast by a fragment from an exploding shell. He died almost instantly. A division of "Fighting Joe" Hooker's Corps drives the Confederates through woods and over mountains (left) toward Marietta. "If the present system is continued," the outspoken Hardee wrote Jefferson Davis gloomily, "we may find ourselves at Atlanta before a serious battle is fought."

A VIEW OF KENESAW MOUNTAIN, SCENE OF SHERMAN'S FATAL ASSAULT.

That night, under a flag of truce, details from both armies went out to bury the dead. Pieces of boards from hardtack boxes marked the graves. Yankee digging beside Rebel carried on a quiet conversation:

"I hope to miss you, Yank, if I happen to shoot in your direction."

"May I never hit you, Johnny, if we fight again."

Johnston placed the Federal loss in killed

MORE OF SHERMAN'S BEST SOLDIERS LAY DEAD AND WOUNDED ON THE SLOPES OF KENESAW, DECLARED JOHNSTON.

and wounded at Kenesaw at 6,000, but Sherman cut his loss to 2,500. And Sherman had learned his lesson: he was finished abandoning his flanking movements for a frontal assault. He would leave the railroad, swing over near the Chattahoochee River and force Johnston to move down from Kenesaw to defend both river and railroad simultaneously. Then by left flank, Sherman intended to reach the railroad below Marietta and await developments.

Johnston responded as Sherman expected, quitting Kenesaw in a race to beat Sherman across the Chattahoochee. On July 4, Yankee pickets roamed the crest of the mountain and wondered why they had wasted a fight for this dirt-heap. Both generals now were committed: Sherman to attack, Johnston to defend, Atlanta. Johnston set Negroes building entrenchments at a furious pace, knowing Sherman must come at him along the Augusta and Marietta roads.

HAN THE NUMBER OF BRITISH VETERANS THAT FELL IN JACKSON'S VICTORY AT NEW ORLEANS.

Sherman's troops, marching into Marietta, encountered a new "old" problem, if one could trust the testimony of Ted Upson of the 100th Indiana: "...We have some 400 young women in the old Seminary Building near town. They have been working in a factory at Rossvill[e] making cloth for the Confederate government. The factories were destroyed and the girls are to be sent South or North whichever way they want to go. Some of them are tough and it's a hard job to keep them straight and to keep the men away from them. General Sherman says he would rather try to guard the whole Confederate Army, and I guess he is right about it."

Theodore R. Davis, who sketched the occupation of Marietta for *Harper's Weekly,* described that event in much more circumspect terms: "The town of Marietta, having a population of no more than two thousand souls, yet ranks as the sixth town of Georgia in regard to size. It was settled before Atlanta. Prior to the war Marietta College was one of the two or three prosperous institutions of the South. It exists now only in name. The town is almost entirely deserted by its inhabitants."

Sherman's concern was not for the factory girls from Rossville who lingered, or for the residents of the town who did not. His problem was to get at Johnston inside Atlanta. But the Confederacy had been badly shaken by Johnston's retreats, and Braxton Bragg had been sent to Georgia by Jefferson Davis to gauge the situation. Bragg reported that "position, num-

bers, and morale" now favored the Federals, and although Bragg could not call Hood "a man of genius, or a great general," he was "far better in the present emergency than anyone we have available." So, unexpectedly, the defenders of Atlanta learned on July 17 that Johnston had been replaced in command by Hood. Private Sam Watkins, staggering under the blow of Johnston's removal, confessed: "I saw, I will say, thousands of men cry like babies—regular, old-fashioned *boohoo, boohoo, boohoo.*" Sherman was delighted. Hood had stood No. 44 in his class at West Point. As a general, he was no great shakes.

Five days after Hood took command, Sherman opened the battle for Atlanta at a point approximately halfway between the present center of the city and the town square of Decatur, five miles to the east. The fighting on July 22, though it cost the Federals a severe loss in the death of General McPherson, really demonstrated, as Major James A. Connolly of the Illinois 123rd commented, "We are like the big boy, 'too big to be whipped'," adding: "I don't care how often they assault; we are here to *fight* them and *destroy* them, not to *chase* them, and if they have found their 'last ditch' all right, Sherman will soon put them in it, and the oftener they attack the sooner he'll have them in it."

Hooker, resigning his command, spoke in Cincinnati. Sherman had "run up against a rock at Atlanta." The country must expect a "disaster."

Sherman's troops occupy the public square in Marietta, Georgia (left) following Johnston's retreat from Kenesaw Mountain. Sherman wrote home: "I know the country swarms with thousands who would shoot me and thank their God they had slain a monster, and yet I have been more kindly disposed to the people of the South than any general of the whole army." A man who knew where he was going—and how to get there—Sherman meets with his staff (below) after occupying Atlanta. He looked upon Hood as easier than Johnston to defeat.

Sherman, writing Washington, admitted his own shortcomings: "I am too impatient for a siege, and don't know but this is as good a place as any to fight it out on, as farther inland. One thing is certain, whether we get inside of Atlanta or not, it will be a used-up community when we are done with it."

By late August, Sherman was convinced that Hood intended to hold onto Atlanta even though the Federal guns knocked down every house. So Sherman decided to move. On August 29, astride the West Point railroad at Fairburn, he not only was enjoying the sight of his troops ripping up rails and burning ties, but was also setting the stage for his final thrust at Hood. Sherman feinted, outwitting Hood completely, so that when the Federals converged on Jonesboro with six corps only a single Rebel corps under Hardee opposed them. The end had come that first of

September and Hood knew it. He evacuated the city, "not so much pained by the fall of Atlanta as by the *recurrence* of retreat, which I full well knew would further demoralize the Army and renew desertions."

Over the wires sped the message to the nation: "Atlanta is ours, and fairly won!" Within the Federal armies the joy was epitomized by General Thomas who, by Sherman's testimony, "snapped his fingers, whistled, and almost danced." More disconcerting to Atlantans than the occupation of their city by the Yankees was the decision Sherman quickly reached: "Hundreds of sutlers and traders were waiting at Nashville and Chattanooga, greedy to reach Atlanta with their wares and goods, with which to drive a profitable trade with the inhabitants. I gave positive orders that none of these traders, except three (one for each separate army), should

be permitted to come nearer than Chattanooga; and, moreover, I peremptorily required that all the citizens and families resident in Atlanta should go away, giving to each the option to go south or north, as their interests or feelings dictated. I was resolved to make Atlanta a pure military garrison or depot, with no civil population to influence military measures. I had seen Memphis, Vicksburg, Natchez, and New Orleans all captured from the enemy, and each at once was garrisoned by a full division of troops, if not more; so that success was actually crippling our armies in the field by detachments to guard and protect the interests of a hostile population."

While Hood and the Georgians generally howled at the "inhumanity" they were being forced to endure, Sherman settled himself comfortably in a house and listened to band concerts in the afternoon.

The Battle of Atlanta opened July 22, 1864, along Peachtree Creek. A painting by James E. Taylor (left) depicts a division in Cleburne's corps pushing back a Federal charge. Yet despite such brief triumphs, what Hood's army discovered was the fact that Sherman's force was "too big to be whipped." The "dead brook" at Ezra Church, where Union and Rebel troops fought on July 28 (above), was officially described as a "feeling" action designed to "compel Hood to come out from behind his fortified lines to attack us at a disadvantage." Which was hokum. Sherman hadn't expected a fight.

A cave in Atlanta (top, left) where citizens hid during the Federal shelling before Sherman broke through Hood's defenses at Jonesboro. The Yankee occupation of the city was quiet and orderly and Sherman set up his headquarters in the house of Judge Lyons (top, right), opposite one corner of Court House Square. His order, requiring citizens and families to leave Atlanta (opposite), he knew "would be strongly criticized," but in a philosophical mood he informed Washington: "I will answer that war is war, and not popularity-seeking." If southerners really wished "to die in the last ditch" he meant to give them that chance!

Sherman and Hood now put aside swords and took up pens to carry on their antagonisms. Hood ranted violently at Sherman's ordered evacuation of the city's civilians, calling it an "unprecedented" measure that "in studied and ingenious cruelty" transcended "all acts ever before brought to my attention in the dark history of war." Snappishly, Sherman advised Hood to "talk thus to the marines, but not to me." He proceeded—by his own light, at any rate—to give Hood a lesson in why he had no cause to complain:

"... You who, in the midst of peace and prosperity, have plunged a nation into war—dark and cruel war—who dared and badgered us into battle, insulted our flag, seized our arsenals and forts that were left in the honorable custody of peaceful ordnance-sergeants, seized and made 'prisoners of war' the very garrisons sent to protect your people against Negroes and Indians, long before any overt act was committed by the (to you) hated Lincoln Government; tried to force Kentucky and Missouri into rebellion, spite of themselves; falsified the vote of Louisiana; turned loose your privateers to plunder unarmed ships; expelled Union families by the thousands, burned their houses, and declared, by an act of Congress, the confiscation of all debts due Northern men ..."

Sherman loved a fight, verbal or otherwise.

ON LAND AND SEA

*Two naval victories
3,000 miles apart aid Lincoln's
bid for a second term*

March–November, 1864

In early 1864, Federal forces under General Nathaniel P. Banks invaded northwestern Louisiana and nearby Arkansas and Texas in the hope of seizing stores of cotton, encouraging reconstruction movements, and warning the French in Mexico that the day would yet come when the United States would be in a position to enforce the Monroe Doctrine. Admiral Porter brought his gunboats up the Red River to aid the expedition which had set the occupation of Shreveport as its final objective. By March 14, when Porter's flotilla reached Alexandria, Louisiana, a Federal disaster was in the making, for only piecemeal military support arrived and Confederate forces in the region were capably commanded by General Richard Taylor, son of the former President, "Old Rough and Ready."

Victory in early April was certainly all on the side of the Confederates. Banks, convinced that he would never fight his way into Shreve-port, ordered a retreat. Then at Pleasant Hill the Federals handled Taylor's force rather roughly and Banks again took heart, only to be dissuaded from continuing the campaign by his subordinates. Meanwhile, the Red River, already at an unprecedented low level and still falling, confronted Porter with the prodigious problem of saving his gunboats. Thousands of soldiers labored at Alexandria building a series of dams across the rocks at the falls, thus raising the water level to a point where the flotilla could pass over (below).

Neighboring steam mills were torn down for materials. Regiments of men from Maine who knew how to swing an axe felled trees. Flatboats were built to bring brick and stone down river. When, finally, the gunboats floated over the rocks and swept to safety in deep water, Porter wrote, "thirty thousand voices rose in one deafening cheer."

Special excursion trains from Paris carried the curious to Cherbourg to witness the duel between the Union's Kearsage *and the Rebel raider* Alabama *(listing, at left). In late 1862, the* Alabama *had sighted and sunk her first victim off Fayal—the* Ocmulgee, *out of Edgartown, Massachusetts— and since then had sent at least sixty other merchantmen to watery graves in every ocean of the world. This represented a financial loss to Yankee shipping of $6,574,609.86. Raphael Semmes, master of the* Alabama *(right), had put into the harbor of Cherbourg for repairs when the sloop* Kearsage *hove to on June 14, 1864.*

Since leaving Cape Town, where news had reached Raphael Semmes of Confederate reversals at Gettysburg, Vicksburg, and Missionary Ridge, the commander of the most feared of all Rebel raiders, the *Alabama,* had been in a depressed mood. Sailing north he managed to catch and sink only two vessels, and in the privacy of his journal he faced the truth: "The poor old *Alabama* was not what she had been. She was like the weary foxhound, limping back after a long chase, footsore and longing for quiet and repose." On June 11 the "weary foxhound" sought its quiet and repose in the French port of Cherbourg.

It was to find neither, for the Federal sloop *Kearsage*—New Hampshire-built and carrying 163 officers and men under a North Carolinian, John A. Winslow—was at that moment lying at anchor in the River Scheldt, near Flushing in the Netherlands. William L. Dayton, United States Minister to France, at once telegraphed Winslow of the *Alabama's* presence in Cherbourg, and three days later the *Kearsage* was waiting off the breakwater at Cherbourg, making clear to Semmes that his famous raider could not escape to the open sea without a battle.

In the five days Semmes gave to conditioning the *Alabama,* hucksters reaped rich profits hawking campstools and spyglasses to the growing crowds that lined the sea cliffs. On Sunday, June 19—a fair, bright day—Winslow was conducting religious services aboard the *Kearsage* when a lookout raised the shout:

"She's coming out, and heading straight for us!"

Winslow's men put aside their hymnals and rushed to their battle stations. Winslow drew off until some seven miles northwest of Cherbourg. Then the *Kearsage* wheeled around. The battle that followed was fought in a series of seven overlapping circles, for Winslow was determined that if he wounded the *Alabama* he was not going to give her a chance to run for port. As each vessel passed the other she threw a broadside from her battery, and the Yankees at once disclosed vastly superior marksmanship. Winslow's gunners aimed deliberately, hitting for the *Alabama's* waterline and pounding her hull until she was listing badly to starboard. For Semmes the jig was up. He surrendered.

Farragut's fleet, passing the forts and obstructions at the entrance of Mobile Bay, August 4, 1864, was about to deal another crushing blow to the Confederacy. The Rebel flag at the left flies over Fort Morgan, with which Federal monitors are duelling. Farragut's flagship Hartford leads the way into the bay followed by the Brooklyn, Richmond, Lackawanna, Monongahela, and Ossipee. Waiting for dawn on this historic day, Farragut wrote his son: "Take care of your mother, if I should go, and may God bless and preserve you." With "hearts of oak in wooden hulls" he expected that day to knock out two forts and the pride of Rebel ironclads. An aide, finding Farragut reading his Bible, suggested a glass of grog to warm the men to the morning's work. "No, sir!" Farragut snapped. "I never found that I needed rum to enable me to do my duty. I will order two cups of good coffee to each man at two o'clock, and at eight o'clock I will pipe all hands to breakfast in Mobile Bay." Moreover, he kept his word!

The U.S.S. Richmond *battles the Rebel ram* Tennessee *(above) at the time when the battle for Mobile Bay rose to its blazing climax. The ram, costing $883,880, measured 209 feet, her beam was forty-eight feet. Eight-inch iron plates covered two-thirds of the ship. A snarling fight all the way, Farragut's great triumph came when the* Tennessee, *surrounded on all sides (right), was captured. A flying fragment had smashed the leg of her commander.*

August, 1864, was called "the darkest month of the war" for Abraham Lincoln. Grant seemed bogged down before Petersburg, and Sherman had not yet smashed through to victory at Atlanta. At a meeting of the Cabinet on August 23 the President asked each member to sign the back of a paper, saying that at an appropriate time he would reveal what he had written. The memorandum read:

Executive Mansion
Washington, Aug. 23, 1864.
This morning, as for some days past, it seems exceedingly probable that this Administration will not be re-elected. Then it will be my duty to so co-operate with the President elect, as to save the Union between the election and the inauguration; as he will have secured his elec-
tion on such grounds that he can not possibly save it afterwards. A. Lincoln

The cry of the Democrats was that the war was a failure, and peace at any price was far to be preferred to continuing the senseless struggle. Lincoln needed military success badly to support his policies, yet he could not complain that the Union navy was failing him, for on the heels of the capture of the *Alabama* off Cherbourg came Farragut's success in Mobile Bay on August 5. At five forty-five that morning, with the fog lifting and a bright, clear summer day in prospect, Farragut told his fleet chief: "Well, Dayton, we might as well get under way."

One hour and two minutes later the Federal monitor *Tecumseh*, coming within range of Fort Morgan, opened the battle with a blast from her

fifteen-inch gun. Farragut, climbing into the shrouds above the poop deck of the Flagship *Hartford* to watch the action through a telescope, saw the ironclad *Tecumseh* reel to one side, then plunge bow foremost with her screw revolving in the air. Torn by a mine, the *Tecumseh,* with ninety-three of her company of 114, sank in a twinkling. The Federal fleet, blocked by the *Brooklyn,* which had been following the sunken monitor, floundered under the punishment of the guns of the Rebel forts. Tradition insists that Farragut cried: "Damn the torpedoes—go ahead!" But in any case, the *Hartford* took the lead under full steam, and at eight-thirty, dropping anchor three miles up the bay from the fort, the admiral made good a pre-dawn promise. He piped all hands to breakfast.

The Rebel ironclad *Tennessee,* under Admiral Franklin Buchanan, appeared to interrupt that repast. Straight for the *Hartford* headed the *Tennessee,* then, veering at the last moment, grazed her side. Farragut poured a broadside into the ironclad and wasted the shots against her plates. The Federal fleet was snarled by the *Lackawanna,* which rammed her own flagship. Farragut said to his signal officer: "Say to the *Lackawanna,* 'For God's sake, get out of the way and anchor!'" The Federal monitor *Chickasaw,* coming up onto the *Tennessee,* hung on "like a dog." A shell knocked off the ironclad's stack and the shutters jammed on her port guns. Then the *Chickasaw* shot away her rudder chain and a flying fragment smashed Buchanan's leg. The *Tennessee* ran up a white flag.

Meanwhile, Lee was playing an old game—sending a corps of infantry and two battalions of artillery under Jubal A. Early up the Shenandoah Valley toward Harpers Ferry. By mid-July, Early and his Confederates, reaching the outskirts of Washington, threw the capital into a state of alarm. But Early considered the fortifications around the city too strong to move against "blindly," adding peevishly: "If we had any friends in Washington, none of them came out to give us information, and this satisfied me that the place was not undefended." Tradition declares that Lincoln was a visitor to Fort Stevens during these troubled days, and that the President was peering over a parapet when Captain Oliver Wendell Holmes, failing to recognize Lincoln, cried: "Get down, you damn fool, before you get shot!" Secretary of

the Navy Welles, inspecting the fortifications, believed that the capital was out of danger, but only because the Rebels threw away a "remarkable" opportunity to benefit from the "neglect, ignorance, folly [and] imbecility" of the Federal military planners. "The Rebels," Welles wrote in his diary, "are making a show of fight while they are stealing horses, cattle, etc. through Maryland. They might easily have captured Washington. Stanton, Halleck and Grant are asleep or dumb."

After arriving "in sight of the dome of the capitol" and giving "the Federal authorities a terrible fright," Early decided to withdraw. So ended Lee's first effort at unbalancing the Federals, but Grant was no more successful at a novel approach to breaking through Rebel lines before Petersburg. Lieutenant Colonel Henry

GENERAL GRANT, STALEMATED BEFORE PETERSBURG, HOLDS A COUNCIL OF WAR AT MASSAPONAX CHURCH, VIRGINIA.

IN BOTH EAST AND WEST, REBEL DESERTERS COMING INTO UNION LINES WERE A VALUABLE SOURCE OF INFORMATION.

Pleasants of the Pennsylvania 48th, observing "a little cup of a ravine near to the enemy's works," conceived the notion of mining under it. In late June Pleasants and his boys began tunneling toward their objective. A main gallery 511 feet long, with left and right lateral galleries thirty-seven and thirty-eight feet long, were completed by carrying out the dirt in old cracker boxes. At the ends of the lateral galleries 8,000 pounds of powder were placed.

The time for blowing the mine was set for three-thirty on the morning of July 30. The plan was for Burnside to take the Ninth Corps through the breach made by the mine, advancing to an elevation some 400 yards distant (Cemetery Hill). The Fifth and Eighteenth Corps, following, were to fan out and establish a position leading to the fall of Petersburg and Richmond. Burnside, in a gesture of the overdramatic, arranged for a division of Negro troops to lead

the charge, but the night before, Meade changed the order and told General James H. Ledlie to take the lead with his all-white First Division.

A fuse died out at a splice and the explosion was delayed an hour. But then, said a witness, there was "a magnificent spectacle" as "the mass of earth" went up, hurling "men, guns, carriages and timbers" in a mushrooming cloud that appeared to be descending on the Federal lines. Men scattered and had to be reformed for the attack. Somewhat disordered, the charge began, but, commented a member of Ledlie's staff, "little did these men anticipate what they would see upon arriving there: an enormous hole in the ground about thirty feet deep, sixty feet wide, and 170 feet long, filled with dust, great blocks of clay, guns, broken carriages, projecting timbers, and men buried in various ways." A wave of nausea swept the Federal column at the sight of this human wreckage.

Fierce fighting from mid-June into late February, 1865, kept the Petersburg front in the headlines. Above, Federal infantry storms a Confederate fort — with inconclusive results. Meanwhile, Pleasants' Pennsylvanians (right) were busy tunneling under a Rebel fort. July brought the explosion and the bitter Battle of the Crater, a failure.

The best that could be said for the Battle of the Crater was that it became one of the war's more tragic fiascos. Burnside not once displayed any true grasp of the situation, and Ledlie not only shared a bomb-proof with Brigadier General Edward Ferraro, in command of the division of Negro troops, but this pair confined their attack that day to the bottle of medical rum they brought with them.

At first the Confederates fled, leaving a gap through which, had the Federal assault been vigorously pressed, Burnside might easily have gained Cemetery Hill. Instead the Yankees, plunging into the debris of the crater, bogged down in pits and cut-up trenches, utterly confused. The Rebels, holding their fire, came back, waiting for the Yankees to emerge from their self-made hole. George S. Bernard of the Virginia 12th witnessed a scene that made his "blood run cold":

"...Just about the outer end of the ditch by which I had entered stood a Negro soldier... begging for his life from two Confederate soldiers, who stood by him, one of them striking the poor wretch with a steel ramrod, the other holding a gun in his hand with which he seemed to be getting a shot at the Negro. The man with the gun fired it at the Negro, but did not seem to seriously injure him... The man with the ramrod continued to strike the Negro therewith, whilst the fellow with the gun deliberately reloaded it, and, placing its muzzle close against the stomach of the poor Negro, fired, at which the latter fell limp."

Preparing the Petersburg mine: carrying powder into the mine (above, left), and Colonel Pleasants of the Pennsylvania 48th superintending the arrival of the 8,000 pounds of powder (above, right) that was placed in the two lateral galleries. For weeks Pleasants and his men worked on their tunnel (below), and the colonel grumbled: "I found it impossible to get assistance from anybody; I had to do all the work myself. I had to remove all the earth in old boxes."

The Virginian turned away from this "brutal, horrible act." Other Confederates, equally repelled, cried: "That is too bad! It is shocking!" And yet, Bernard confessed, there were many such incidents, for the southerners "seemed infuriated at the idea of having to fight Negroes." Within ten minutes so many dead Negroes filled the place "that it was difficult to make one's way along the trench without stepping on them." For hours men huddled in the crater, agonized by their wounds and begging for water. By midafternoon the Confederates cleared the crater and captured those who remained. The Union's casualties had been high, its achievement noth-

ing. Burnside was removed from command and Ledlie permitted to resign.

In September, as Sherman pounded his way into Atlanta, the war news in the east was once more dominated by action in the Shenandoah Valley. At Winchester, Early's Confederate troops clashed with Union forces under Little Phil Sheridan. An early success for the jubilant Rebels found the graycoats declaring they would "get more grub and guns and things than our poor old quartermaster mules can pull," but at Fisher's Hill on September 22, Sheridan outflanked his adversaries and Confederate General John B. Gordon did not dispute the "hope-

lessness" of the situation for Early's troops: "The retreat (it is always so) was at first stubborn and slow, then rapid, then—a rout."

Sheridan now was free to carry out the program Grant had set for him in the Shenandoah Valley: "to eat out Virginia clear and clean . . . so that crows flying over it for the balance of this season will have to carry their provender with them." Reporting to Grant early in October, Sheridan would quote figures to prove he had followed orders: 2,000 barns filled with wheat, hay and farming equipment destroyed; seventy flour mills wrecked; 4,000 head of stock taken; 3,000 sheep killed and issued to the troops.

Looking toward the Rebel lines at four-thirty in the morning when the Petersburg mine was exploded and an earthen mass shot upward, mixed with flames, with lightning flashes, with torn timbers and bits of human bodies. The Federal troops, reaching the edge of the Crater, were sickened by what they saw — some men buried up to their necks, others to their waists, and some with only their feet and legs protruding from the soil.

Sheridan's campaign in the Shenandoah Valley that turned Early's first success into an ignominious rout. The Federals sweep toward the Rebel lines in the Battle of Middletown (top, left). Sheridan's cavalrymen, sabers in hand, break through the defenses in the Battle of Winchester (bottom, left). With Early beaten, the Valley was opened to Federal foraging parties (above). These were under orders to bring Virginia a "scorched earth" policy that would make it necessary for a crow, flying over the countryside, to carry its own provender. By early October the policy was a fact.

"A campaign of arson, rapine and starvation," cried Virginians as they described Sheridan's acts in the Valley. Sheridan simply shrugged. Like Sherman, ordering civilians out of Atlanta, he wasn't seeking popularity. When his engineer officer was murdered near Dayton, Sheridan repaid "this atrocious act" by burning the houses within five miles. He was achieving exactly what he wished: "The people here are getting sick of the war" where heretofore "they have had no reason to complain, because they have been living in great abundance . . ."

Confederate accounts of Sheridan in the Valley described the red glare of bonfires, the little children turned "voiceless and tearless in their pitiable terror," and a clergyman's daughter "tearing the yellow tresses from her head, taking up and repeating the oaths of passing skirmishers and shrieking with wild laughter, for the horrors of the night had driven her mad."

In mid-October, Early struck once more at Winchester, catching Sheridan's troops completely by surprise. Yet when urged to press his advantage, Early grew suddenly lethargic, declaring, "This is glory enough for one day." Sheridan, who was returning from a quick visit to Washington, found the roads blocked with his disordered troops. He rode among them, shouting: "If I had been with you this morning this disaster would not have happened. We must face the other way; we will go back and recover our camp." By nightfall, the battle had been reversed, and Sheridan's men cooked supper over fires they had abandoned that morning. Confederate General Gordon rode through open fields, finding Confederates seeking to avoid capture—"and occasionally a solitary soldier as lonely, if not as sad and thoughtful, as I."

THE TENT IN CHICAGO WHERE THE DEMOCRATS NOMINATED GENERAL GEORGE B. McCLELLAN.

THOMAS NAST SATIRIZES FOR HARPER'S WEEKLY HOW COPPERHEADS ENLISTED VOTERS.

PENNSYLVANIA SOLDIERS IN THE ARMY OF THE JAMES CAST THEIR VOTES AT HEADQUARTERS.

In Boston, a banker offered to bet $10,000 that if Lincoln won re-election, the war would continue another ten years. On election night, however, the first reports from Boston were so heavily in the President's favor that an excited supporter maintained "the Almighty must have stuffed the ballot boxes." Toward midnight experienced politicians knew the trend, and for all that McClellan and the Democrats had ranted that Lincoln and his war were failures, the President would carry every state except Kentucky, Delaware, and New Jersey—a victory in the electoral vote of 212 to twenty-one.

Meeting afterward with his Cabinet, Lincoln opened the memorandum he had written on August 23, predicting that he would not be re-elected and promising in that event to co-operate with General McClellan in saving the Union.

"The general," declared Secretary Seward, "would say, 'Yes, Yes'; & so on forever, and would have done nothing at all."

"At least," Lincoln said, "I would have done my duty and have stood clear before my own conscience...."

Seward smiled.

Harper's Weekly *taunted the Copperheads who rallied behind General McClellan and the Peace Democrats in an effort to defeat Lincoln's bid for re-election in 1864. The President, however, swept to an overwhelming electoral-vote victory.*

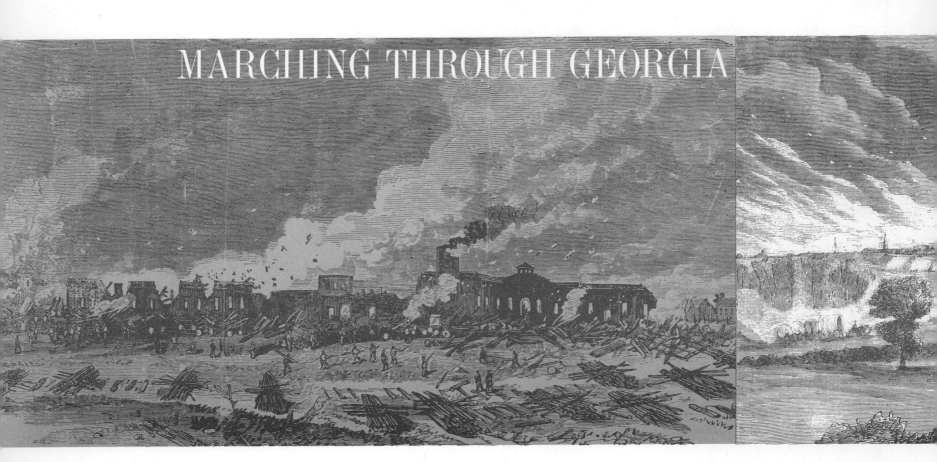

MARCHING THROUGH GEORGIA

*With Atlanta afire,
Sherman and his bummers prove
that war can be hellish*

COLUMNS OF SMOKE RISE FROM WITHIN ATLANTA AS SHERMAN STARTS HIS FAMOUS MARCH TO FAME AND INFAMY.

November–December, 1864

"I can make this march, and make all Georgia howl," Sherman had written Grant in early October. And although Sherman admitted that if he failed his plan would be called "the wild adventure of a crazy fool," he at last won Grant's approval of the scheme. So Sherman divided his army, sending one force under Thomas to handle Hood (who had fallen back toward Nashville), while he led the remaining force across Georgia to the sea. On November 15, orders were given to destroy military installations in Atlanta and by mid-afternoon, a Federal witness admitted, "fires were but the beginning of a general conflagration which would sweep over the entire city and blot it out of existence." Drunken Yankees roamed the streets, looted dwellings and stores, sang "Rally Round the Flag, Boys," and, a Confederate testified, the "ornaments of graves, such as marble lambs, miniature statuary, souvenirs of departed little ones," and even silver plates and tippings on coffins were "broken and scattered abroad."

In three columns Sherman marched his troops out of Atlanta next morning. Black smoke still hung like a pall over the ruined city, but the Federals were in high spirits. A band struck up "John Brown's Body" and the soldiers joined in the chorus. Catching sight of Sherman, the men called out:

"Uncle Billy, I guess Grant is waiting for us at Richmond!"

That night, in camp near Lithonia, Sherman's "bummers" practiced a trade at which they became artists—tearing up railroads.

"Such a day, if I live to the age of Methuselah, may God spare me from ever seeing again!" wrote Dolly Lunt of Sherman's visit to her plantation. "Like demons they rush in! My yards are full. To my smokehouse, my dairy, pantry, kitchen and cellar, like famished wolves they come, breaking locks and whatever is in their way. Two thousand pounds of meat in my smokehouse is gone in a twinkling."

General Hazen's division storms Fort McAllister, key to the defenses of Savannah, on December 13, 1864 (top) and by the account in Harper's Weekly *thirteen locomotives, 150 guns, and 35,000 bales of cotton were captured. By Sherman's order, Rebel prisoners were brought from the provost guard, armed with picks and spades, and marched in close formation along the road "so as to explode their own torpedoes, or to discover and dig them up" (below). Wrote Sherman: "I could hardly help laughing at their stepping so gingerly along the road." Torpedoes had killed many Yankees.*

What was happening to Sherman, puzzled easterners asked Grant, who, with a twinkle, replied: "Sherman's army is now somewhat in the condition of a ground-mole when he disappears under a lawn. You can here and there trace his track, but you are not quite certain where he will come out till you see his head."

At best, the Georgian militia and the Rebel cavalry under Joseph A. Wheeler could offer but token resistance against Sherman's force. To the Federals, the march was more like a lark than war, and no one enjoyed it more immensely than Sherman, who would remember a Negro girl "in the very ecstasy of the Methodist 'shout,' hugging the banner of one of the regiments, and jumping up to the 'feet of Jesus.' " The General chuckled at the occasion in Milledgeville, capital of the state, when his soldiers took over the chambers of the legislature and repealed the ordinance of secession. "Forage liberally on the country," Sherman had instructed his troops on leaving Atlanta, and they obeyed his order so well that they wrote the word "bummer" into the American language as a synonym for a member of any raiding party who plundered promiscuously. For all that the Macon *Telegraph* on December 7, 1864, reported the widespread despoilation of southern womanhood as "the cesspools of Northern infamy and corruption have been dredged to their vilest dregs," later scholarship would not substantiate these propagandistic flights of fancy.

Sherman's boys were moving too fast to be anything much less than well behaved. At night the Negroes came down from the plantations to sing and dance — entertainment, recalled one Federal, "far more grotesque and mirth-provoking than the broadest caricatures of 'Christy's Minstrels.' " An officer in the Indiana 70th wrote his wife about "the vast numbers of colored women following after us with babies in their arms." Another swore that it would have been "vexatious to the Grand Turk or to Brigham Young" if either could have seen "how many of the dark houris were in the employment of officers' servants and teamsters," but such testimony was rare. Driving straight ahead, Sherman by December 8 had reached Pooler's Station, eight miles from Savannah.

Fort McAllister, key to the capture of this seaport, was stormed five days later. The Confederates fought stubbornly, but Hazen's division soon made "the fort seem alive with flame," and when at last the Federal flag was run up over the fort, Sherman was unable to repress his elation, telling the group around him that "this nigger will have no sleep this night!" He wired Washington: "I regard Savannah as already *gained*" and wasn't far wrong, for the city's Rebel defenders under Hardee knew they were no match for Sherman's army. On the night of December 20, they silently pulled out.

The Navy Yard in Savannah burns (above) as Sherman's troops enter the seaport (top, right) on December 21, 1864, fulfilling the general's promise to his troops that he would provide oysters for their dinners before Christmas. For many years to follow Negroes in Savannah would date all events from "de time when Tecumpsey was here." A "Union" barbershop, quickly established by Sherman, was proof that he foresaw all risks!

Among Sherman's first acts, upon occupying Savannah, was the dispatch of a telegram that was quickly known in every city and hamlet throughout the North:

> *Savannah, Georgia, December 22, 1864.*
> *To His Excellency President Lincoln,*
> *Washington, D. C.:*
> *I beg to present you as a Christmas-gift the city of Savannah, with one hundred and fifty heavy guns and plenty of ammunition, also about twenty-five thousand bales of cotton.*
> *W. T. Sherman, Major General.*

Lincoln answered warmly. He had been "anxious if not fearful" when the general had proposed his march to the sea, and now that the undertaking was a success he must say to Sherman: "The honor is all yours." As the fourth Christmas of the war approached, the President, like almost everyone in the North, began to sense that the end was near. Yet despite that happy prospect, Lincoln, in his annual message to Congress, refused to yield the moral purpose for which he had fought so bitterly:

"In presenting the abandonment of armed resistance to the national authority on the part of the insurgents, as the only indispensable condition to ending the war on the part of the government, I retract nothing heretofore said as to slavery. I repeat the declaration made a year ago that 'while I remain in my present position I shall not attempt to retract or modify the emancipation proclamation, nor shall I return to slavery any person who is free by the terms of the proclamation, or by any of the Acts of Congress.' If the people should, by whatever mode or means, make it an Executive duty to re-enslave such persons, another, and not I, must be their instrument to perform it."

But the President knew the people would stand by him, and as much as anyone he had Sherman to thank—"Crazy" Sherman, who had been all but washed out of the army in '61.

GENERAL SHERMAN OFFERS A TOAST TO HIS STAFF (BELOW) AT THE CHRISTMAS DINNER HE GIVES IN SAVANNAH.

Grant and Sherman both had chafed at the delay in Tennessee, where, both generals believed, Thomas should have disposed of Hood long ago. Early December was filled with carping criticism of "The Rock of Chickamauga," who was deeply stung by the want of confidence in him. Yet Thomas prepared carefully for battle and something of the problems he faced and could understand better than anyone in Washington, was reflected in his telegram to the War Department on December 14: "The ice having melted away today, the enemy will be attacked tomorrow morning."

Thomas fought next morning the battle he had promised and, in character, sent Washington an unvarnished account of the action before Nashville: "I attacked the enemy's left this morning and drove it from the river, below the city, very nearly to the Franklin pike, a distance about eight miles. Have captured General Chalmers' headquarters and train, and a second train of about 20 wagons, with between 800 and 1,000 prisoners and 16 pieces of artillery. The troops behaved splendidly, all taking their share in assaulting and carrying the enemy's breast-works. I shall attack the enemy again tomorrow, if he stands to fight, and, if he retreats during the night, will pursue him, throwing a heavy cavalry force in his rear, to destroy his trains...."

From Washington, Lincoln wired Thomas: "You made a magnificent beginning. A grand consummation is within your reach. Do not let it slip." Thomas had no intention of throwing away his opportunity. Before December 16 ended he had pounded the Rebels so hard that, one Tennessean admitted ruefully, Hood's army "degenerated into a mob." Thomas reported to Washington—and if he took satisfaction in the facts, considering the needling he had suffered, no one could blame him—that the number of Confederate casualties and prisoners "have made a large number." Adding: "The woods, fields, and entrenchments are strewn with the enemy's small-arms, abandoned in their retreat. In conclusion, I am happy to state that all this has been effected with but a very small loss to us. Our loss does not probably exceed 3,000; very few killed."

In brief, it had been a smashing victory. And so 1864—the Year of the Proclamation plus one—drew to an end with Lincoln returned to the White House for another four years, with Grant holding Lee at bay before Petersburg (where time was all on the side of the Union), with Thomas in Nashville and Sherman in Savannah. Winning the war suddenly was only half of the problem confronting Lincoln. Now he must also plan on how to win the peace.

Charge of the Federal First Corps at the Battle of Nashville on December 15, 1864 (left), where George H. Thomas smashed Hood and Rebels sang to "The Yellow Rose of Texas" new words of how "the gallant Hood of Texas sure raised hell in Tennessee." Federal prisoners, exchanged at Charleston and homeward bound aboard the Star of the South (below) dance with joy—another sign that the war neared its end.

WITH MALICE TOWARD NONE

With peace at last won,
a great faith in America's future
is destroyed by an assassin

A kind of desperation took hold of the Richmond government that was expressed in extravagant schemes to strike some astonishing blows at the North. Thus, on October 19, 1864, Rebel raiders under Lieutenant Bennett H. Young, operating from Canada, carried the war to a town fifteen miles south of the border—St. Albans, Vermont. The citizens of the town were herded into the square and one was wounded. The banks were robbed and the hotels fired. But after the some 5,000 inhabitants of St. Albans had been held at bay for perhaps three-quarters of an hour, Federal troops appeared, the invaders fled, and the grandiose gesture amounted to nothing. Equally ridiculous was the plan of eight Confederate conspirators to burn New York City. Nineteen hotels were fired in late November, and a blaze started in Barnum's Museum created a panic, with people "getting hurt running over each other in the stampede." But wars were not won with tricks.

Rather, wars were won by hard-grinding, persistent effort to destroy a people's capacity for making and sustaining a war—an effort such as in mid-January enabled a Federal force at long last to succeed in capturing the port of Wilmington, North Carolina. Well could Confederate Vice President Alexander H. Stephens call

this loss "one of the greatest disasters which had befallen our cause from the beginning of the war." When Fort Fisher (guardian of Wilmington) was taken, the South lost the only port from which it could still ship out cotton and "the closing of the port of Wilmington was the complete shutting out of the Confederate States from all intercourse by sea with Foreign Countries."

Perhaps what Lincoln had learned better than anyone—or, at least, well enough to act upon—was the subtle fact that to end a war some climactic change must be brought to the political situation that had permitted the war to begin. By 1865 the idea was scarcely new with Lincoln. The German military authority, Karl von Clausewitz, had said, "War is the continuation of politics—by other means." And, as Carl Sandburg has pointed out, Clausewitz had said a great deal more in his volume, which was in the Library of Congress: "The spark in the breast of the commander must rekindle hope in the hearts of his men, and so long as he is equal to his task he remains their commander."

In this spirit, Lincoln still remained the commander of the North, and in this spirit he called Charles A. Dana into conference, needing his help to end the war in the only way, Lincoln knew, that it could be ended.

Federal forces under General Alfred H. Terry in the final assault on Fort Fisher (left) deal a crippling blow to the Confederacy by sealing off at last the port of Wilmington, North Carolina. Admiral Porter's fleet (right) fills the night with rockets in celebration of a victory that Confederate Vice President Alexander Stephens called a greater disaster to the South than the capture of Vicksburg or Atlanta. Now no cotton could go out and no munitions could come in.

THE PEACE COMMISSION: "FLYING TO ABRAHAM'S BOSOM"

Confederate Peace Commissioners met with Lincoln and Secretary Seward under the guns of Fortress Monroe on February 3. Although at this point the negotiations collapsed, Hunter of Virginia told Lincoln with a smile: "We have concluded that we shall not be hanged as long as you are President — if we behave ourselves."

VICE PRESIDENT ALEXANDER H. STEPHENS

R. M. T. HUNTER OF VIRGINIA

Dana, who served now as Assistant Secretary of War, did not disguise his admiration for the President, who "understood politics because he understood human nature." Of Lincoln, Dana wrote:

"The great quality of his appearance was benevolence and benignity: the wish to do somebody some good if he could; and yet there was no flabby philanthropy about Abraham Lincoln. He was all solid, hard, keen intelligence combined with goodness. Indeed, the expression of his bearing which impressed one most, after his benevolence and benignity, was his intelligent understanding. You felt that here was a man who saw through things, who understood, and you respected him accordingly."

What Lincoln had seen through, when he talked to Dana in the spring of 1864, was the war, believing that if the Constitution should be amended to prohibit slavery the measure "would be equivalent to new armies in the field, that it would be worth at least a million men, that it would be an intellectual army that would tend to paralyze the enemy and break the continuity of his ideas." In this belief in March, 1864, the President had urged Dana's support in swinging votes for the admission of Nevada, knowing that he could count on the new state to support a Thirteenth Amendment abolishing slavery. Dana argued afterward: "I have sometimes heard people complain of Nevada as superfluous and petty, not big enough to be a State; but when I hear this complaint, I always hear Abraham Lincoln saying, 'It is easier to admit Nevada than to raise another million of soldiers.'"

Lincoln refused to be discouraged by the fact that in 1864 the Thirteenth Amendment had failed to secure in the House of Representatives the two-thirds vote necessary for passage. In January, 1865, he renewed the fight, proving, as Dana contended, that he was "a supreme politician." Ten days before the Amendment was scheduled to come again before the House, Lincoln talked to a fellow ex-Whig, James A. Rollins, a Representative from Missouri, asking him to push passage of the amendment among the Border States men. Lincoln said: "The passage of this amendment will clinch the whole subject; it will bring the war, I have no doubt, rapidly to a close."

On the last day of January, with Lincoln pushing hard behind the scenes for passage, the amendment was brought to its second vote in the House. Spectators jammed the galleries. The pro-slavery advocates—or so reported Nicolay and Hay, who were reliable eyewitnesses—believed "up to noon" that they could defeat the measure. The usual pleas for postponement and for permission to offer amendments or substitutes took time, but there was something in the air—a kind of collective heartbeat, a sense of impending triumph — that brought senators crowding around the door of the lower chamber when at four o'clock Schuyler Colfax, Speaker of the House, ordered the roll called.

The sentiment of the gallery was no secret. Whenever a Democrat answered the roll call with an "Aye!" shrill cheers rang out. Outside the halls of Congress a battery waited to fire a one-hundred-gun salute—if the vote were right. Reporters, who had given up their seats in the press gallery to the overflow crowd of ladies, began to pick out notables present: three members of the Cabinet (Fessenden, Dennison, Blair), four Associate Justices of the Supreme Court, Chief Justice Salmon P. Chase. The roll call reached "W," and the Wood brothers of New York City voted "Nay." Then "Y," and Yeaman of Kentucky voted "Aye." The clerk now leaned over to Colfax, whispering the result of the tally: Ayes, 119; Nays, 56. By three votes the amendment had passed, but Colfax, wishing to place himself firmly on the record, asked that his name be called.

"Colfax," the clerk responded.

In a firm voice the Speaker of the House said: "Aye!"

The clerk then announced the result.

The House of Representatives as the clerk announced vote on the Thirteenth Amendment. Congressme

...ed in the aisles, ladies wept, and outside the Capitol a battery thundered. Slavery was dead.

Lincoln retained a supreme faith in the future of a nation reunited, and although negotiations with Confederate Peace Commissioners at Fortress Monroe on February 3 failed—principally because the Confederates insisted on negotiations between two countries instead of healing the wounds of one—the President confessed that he believed the North had been equally responsible with the South for the existence of slavery. Moreover, Lincoln said, it was his judgment that if the secessionist states would cease fighting and voluntarily abolish slavery, the government should indemnify slave owners. In round figures, Lincoln was suggesting an expenditure that could run as high as $400,000,000. Two days after returning from Fortress Monroe, he proposed the appropriation — provided hostilities were ended by April 1. Unanimously the Cabinet disapproved the idea as a political impracticality, and, sadly, Lincoln muttered: "You are all opposed to me."

So, outside the Cabinet meeting the suggested appropriation—and gesture of magnanimity to a stricken South—was never mentioned. It was plain that in winning the peace, as in winning the war, occasions would arise when Lincoln and his advisors would be poles apart. Yet the President believed implicitly in the enormous future of the country and in its ability, financially, to afford a just reconstruction. The signs of national growth, of a tomorrow that challenged the imagination, were everywhere, in his opinion. An overland telegraph to join America and Europe by way of Bering Strait and Asiatic Russia was underway. Gold, silver, and cinnabar deposits in the Sierra Nevadas and the Rockies were proving far richer than anyone had dared to dream in 1860. The size of the vote cast in the recent election, in Lincoln's estimate, demonstrated that "we have *more* men *now* than we had when the war *began;* that we are not exhausted, nor in process of exhaustion; that we are *gaining* strength, and may, if need be, maintain the contest indefinitely."

Appeals to new homesteaders, new investors reflect the country's changing mood: the Illinois Central offers 900,000 acres of farmland for sale (above) and oil wells begin to produce in Pennsylvania (bottom, right) while the Great Eastern (top, right) lays down the Atlantic cable.

NEW YORK AND LIVERPOOL PETROLEUM COMPANY.

ORGANIZED UNDER THE MINING AND MANUFACTURING LAWS OF THE STATE OF NEW YORK.

CAPITAL, ONE MILLION DOLLARS,

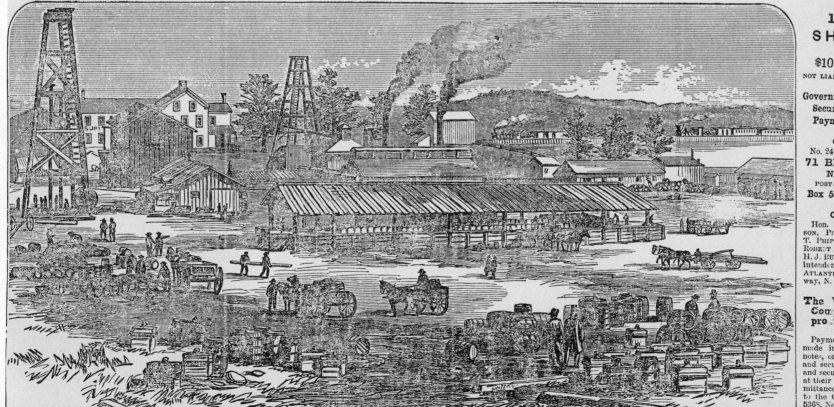

IN
100,000
SHARES,
AT
$10 per Share,
NOT LIABLE TO ASSESSMENT.

Government Bonds and
Securities taken in
Payment for Stock.

OFFICES:
No. 24 Empire Building,
71 BROADWAY,
NEW YORK.
POST-OFFICE ADDRESS,
Box 5368, New York.

OFFICERS:
Hon. Daniel S. Dickinson, President; William T. Phipps, Vice-President; Robert Bassett, Secretary; H. J. Burtis, Mining Superintendent, Titusville, Pa.; Atlantic Bank, 742 Broadway, N. Y., Treasury.

The Wells of this Company are now producing Oil.

Payment for stock may be made in drafts, registered notes, or government bonds and securities, which bonds and securities will be taken at their market value. Remittances may be addressed to the Company, P. O. Box 5368, New York City, or to Atlantic Bank,

AN UNFORGETTABLE TRAGEDY OF THE WAR—THE BURNING OF COLUMBIA, SOUTH CAROLINA, BY SHERMAN'S SOLDIERS.

In January, Sherman and his "Hellhounds" left Savannah and struck north through the Carolinas. The mood of the Federals was changed, and not for the better. Sherman's boast that he would "bring every Southern woman to the washtub" was suddenly no idle threat when Cavalry General Judson Kilpatrick openly bragged to the troops in the Minnesota 2nd: "There'll be damn little for you infantrymen to destroy after I've passed through that hellhole of secession." Like an avenging warrior, Sherman made straight for Columbia, South Carolina, where the convention had met in 1860 to draft the ordinance of secession that had divided the nation (and only a threatened outbreak of smallpox in Columbia had hastened the delegates on to Charleston to complete that fatal act). On February 17, 1865, his troops occupied the city. "These fiends," a southern girl called them, adding: "We cannot look at them with anything but horror and hatred, loathing and disgust."

Wild tales were told of the occupation of Columbia by Sherman's boys—of the soldier who told a housewife: "We hate your men like hell, but we love your women!"; of Yankees as "they surged down Main Street and through the State House," amusing themselves by taking pot shots at a portrait of Jefferson Davis; of soldiers reeling drunk from the wines found in Columbia cellars. Even to this day in Columbia a bronze tablet affixed to the statue of George Washington, standing before the State House, points an accusing finger at the North for those hours of desecration:

During the occupation of
Columbia by Sherman's army
February 17-19, 1865
soldiers brickbatted this
statue and broke off the
lower part of the
walking cane

Far more than Washington with half a cane

would make the citizens of Columbia remember the night that followed. By the testimony of a gifted southern historical novelist, William Gilmore Simms, the fires that destroyed Columbia broke out "in a filthy purlieu of low houses, of wood, on Gervais Street, occupied mostly as brothels." Simms told how the Federal soldiers spread the conflagration: "They carried with them, from house to house, pots and vessels containing combustible liquids, composed probably of phosphorous and other similar agents, turpentine, etc., and with balls of cotton saturated in this liquid, with which they also overspread the floors and walls; they conveyed the flames with wonderful rapidity from dwelling to dwelling. Each had his ready box of Lucifer matches, and, with a scrape upon the walls, the flames began to rage."

Seventeen-year-old Emma Florence LeConte recalled how, in the red glare of the burning city, she "could watch the wretches walking—generally staggering—back and forth from the camp to the town — shouting — hurrahing — cursing South Carolina — swearing — blaspheming — singing ribald songs and using such obscene language that we were forced to go indoors." From within the house, Emma looked back upon the city, aghast at what she beheld:

"... Imagine night turning into noonday, only with a blazing, scorching glare that was horrible—a copper colored sky across which swept columns of black rolling smoke glittering with sparks and flying embers, while all around us were falling thickly showers of burning flakes. . . ."

And another memory, of the common across from the college:

"... crowded with homeless women and children, a few wrapped in blankets and many shivering in the night air. Such a scene as this with the drunken fiendish soldiery in their dark uniforms, infuriated, cursing, screaming, exulting in their work, came nearer the material ideal of hell than anything I ever expect to see again."

Next morning residents of Columbia gazed in numbed disbelief at their smoldering, devastated city. By the mayor's estimate 366 acres had been destroyed, and 1,386 residences and stores burned. Stoically, on February 20, the army under Sherman pushed northward and two days later in Washington the lights were turned on the dome of the Capitol, at Lincoln's orders, in celebration of the Federal victories in Columbia, Wilmington, and Charleston. A British observer quipped that Sherman "had been flirting with Augusta, embracing Columbia, and now was making approaches to Charlotte."

With Sherman marching through the Carolinas, Charleston fell to the Federal troops. Citizens of the city, anxious to secure rations, flocked to the courthouse (below) to swear their allegiance.

LINCOLN TAKES THE OATH OF OFFICE AT HIS SECOND INAUGURATION, MARCH 4, 1865.

The gray, gloomy day began with a scandal when Vice President Andrew Johnson, fortifying himself with several drinks against the effects of a recent illness, somewhat tipsily took the oath of office. The President and his procession appeared on the inauguration platform—and "a tremendous shout, prolonged and loud, arose from the surging ocean of humanity around the Capitol building." Reporter Noah Brooks described Lincoln, "rising tall and gaunt among the groups around him." As he advanced, "a roar of applause shook the air, and, again and again repeated, finally died far away on the outer fringe of the throng, like a sweeping wave upon the shore." Then, as Lincoln began to speak, the sun burst through "in its unclouded meridian splendor, and flooded the spectacle with glory and with light."

In profound silence the great throng listened to the President's words—immortal words. The mystery of the war that had so long haunted him he now understood and he said:

"... If we shall suppose that African Slavery is one of those offenses which, in the providence of God, must needs come, but which, having continued through His appointed time, He now wills to remove, and that He gives to both North and South, this terrible war, as the woe to those by whom the offense came, shall we discern therein any departure from those divine attributes which the believers in a Living God always ascribe to him? Fondly do we hope—fervently do we pray—that this scourge of war may speedily pass away. Yet, if God wills that it continues, until all wealth piled by the bondman's two hundred and fifty years of unrequited toil shall be sunk, and until every drop of blood drawn with a lash, shall be paid by another drawn by the sword, as was said three thousand years ago, so still it must be said, 'The judgments of the Lord are true and righteous altogether.'"

The sun shining on the bronze statue of Freedom that now crowned the finished dome of the Capitol made it a beautiful symbol of the aims and aspirations of a Union nearing the end of war. And so, too, was this imperishable concluding paragraph of Lincoln's address:

"With malice toward none; with charity for all; with firmness in the right, as God gives us to see the right, let us strive on to finish the work we are in; to bind up the nation's wounds; to care for him who shall have borne the battle, and for his widow and his orphan—to do all which may achieve and cherish a just and lasting peace, among ourselves, and with all nations."

When Lincoln spoke these final words, wrote Noah Brooks, "there were many cheers and many tears." The President turned to Chief Justice Chase, took the oath of office and kissed the Bible. A salvo of artillery boomed on the air, the people cheered, and the President rode back to the White House accompanied "by a great procession."

On another gray, misty morning, later that month, a carriage brought Lincoln to Washington's Sixth Street Wharf. Looking worn out and breaking in health he boarded the steamer *River Queen* for the trip to City Point, Virginia, where he expected to meet with Grant and Sherman to discuss the possibilities that now lay ahead. "He wishes the war ended," Welles noted in his diary, "and to this end, that severe terms should not be exacted of the Rebels."

On March 27, at City Point, the three great architects of victory for the Union—Lincoln, Grant, and Sherman—met together for the first and only time. Grant explained to the President the military situation "and prospects," and Lincoln "asked if it would not be possible to end the matter without a pitched battle, with the attendant losses and suffering." Grant answered that this decision was "not within the control of our commanders, and must rest necessarily with the enemy." Lincoln, accepting the decision, spoke of the future, intimating that it "would relieve the situation" immeasurably if the political leaders of the Confederacy "would escape to a foreign country."

Leaving City Point on March 29, Grant told an aide: "I think we can send him [Lincoln] some good news in a day or two." Grant, possibly, wasted men—he did not waste words.

Lee knew the danger signals when Sheridan was speeded up the road leading northwest from Dinwiddie to Five Forks. Grant was having Sheridan menace the Confederate right while Grant jockeyed for the railroads essential to holding both Petersburg and Richmond. Lee hustled Pickett to Five Forks with five brigades, and again and again he gave warning: "Hold Five Forks at all hazards." Pickett and Fitzhugh Lee drove Sheridan back on March 30, but then General Tom Rosser arrived with some shad he had caught in the Nottoway River two days before. Neither Fitzhugh Lee nor Pickett could resist joining Rosser in a fish fry. They were picking the bones from their teeth on April 1 when Sheridan came charging back, hell-on-leather, and the result Pickett explained in a letter to his wife: "My darling, overpowered, defeated, cut in pieces, starving, captured, as we were, those that were left of us formed front north and south and met with sullen desperation their double onset." And having escaped with his own hide, Pickett advised philosophically: "The birds were hushed in the woods when I started to write, now one calls to its mate, 'Cheer up—cheer up!' Let's listen and obey the birds, my darling."

To Lee, losing Five Forks was a terrible blow. Officers, seeing Lee in full uniform next morning, wondered: Did he expect to be compelled to surrender that day? But Lee knew that now Petersburg must be abandoned, Richmond surrendered. As the Confederate columns withdrew under Grant's mounting pressure, General Gordon asked a boy why he was running. The reply: "Golly, I'm running 'cause I can't fly!"

Singing "John Brown's Body," the Massachusetts Colored 5th (left) marches into Charleston on February 21, 1865. A Federal cavalry charge at the Battle of Five Forks on April 1 (above), and (below) General Sheridan leading a charge.

On Sunday, April 2, Jefferson Davis and his Cabinet fled Richmond. That evening the capital was burned and looted by its own residents. Next day, singing "De Year Ob Jubilo," Yankee soldiers marched in, put out the fires, and restored order.

On the morning of April 4, Abraham Lincoln visited Richmond (above). Thirty-four guns announced the arrival of the President and, commented a cynical observer, "He flitted through the mass of human beings in Capitol Square, his carriage drawn by four horses, preceded by outriders, motioning the people, etc. out of the way, and followed by a mounted guard of thirty. The cortege passed rapidly, precisely as I have seen royal parties ride in Europe." Richmond womenfolk (right) snub Yankee occupation troops.

On a beautiful Sunday, Jefferson Davis was attending services in St. Paul's Church when a messenger brought word from Lee that Grant was overrunning Petersburg and Richmond was doomed. By nightfall Davis and his governmental aides were in flight to Danville, leaving behind a city in the throes of an hysterical self-destruction. Stores were looted, houses burned, vessels blown up in the James. Any vehicle that would travel—baggage wagons, carts, drays, ambulances — was enlisted by frenzied residents seeking to escape the crushing heels of the victorious "abolitionists." Next morning, quiet and orderly, the Federal troops marched into the confederate capital and, wrote an astonished inhabitant. "What we received from the enemy

that day was aid—protection—safety!"

Lincoln visited Richmond two days later, telling Admiral Porter: "Thank God that I have lived to see this! It seems to me that I have been dreaming a horrid dream for four years, and now the nightmare is gone." Hundreds of Negroes ran to see the President, throwing themselves at his feet (by Porter's reminiscences), and Lincoln said: "Don't kneel to me. That is not right. You must kneel to God only, and thank Him for the liberty you will hereafter enjoy." Everywhere crowds rushed to see the President but they only included, a southern woman maintained, "the low, lower, lowest of creation." Lincoln visited the home of Jefferson Davis, wandered through the dwelling, and

seated himself at Davis's desk, saying wistfully: "This must have been President Davis's chair." An observer said that Lincoln, crossing his long legs, "looked far off with a serious, dreamy expression." Later, meeting with a peace commission, Lincoln asserted good-humoredly that he "would save any repentant sinner from hanging." Charles Dana heard the advice that the President gave to General Godfrey Weitzel, in charge of the forces of occupation: "Let the people down easy."

That same April 4, Lee led his hungry, reeling army into Amelia Court House, where, foreseeing the possibility of the calamity that had now befallen him, he had instructed Richmond to store supplies so that he could fight on.

President Jefferson Davis, the members of the Confederate Cabinet, and their escort passing over the Georgia ridge (above), five days before their capture on May 5, 1865. The meeting between the two countrymen—Grant and Lee—at Appomattox Court House, Virginia, on Palm Sunday when surrender terms were arranged that virtually ended the brothers' war.

Someone in Richmond had blundered. There were no supplies in Amelia Court House.

For Lee an almost incredible week followed. Around him marched gaunt soldiers with bleeding gums from chewing on parched corn. Weary veterans threw muskets by the roadside, too exhausted to carry them any longer. Meanwhile, Federal cavalrymen were everywhere, sniping at the Confederate columns, burning their wagon trains. Stubborn, wanting still to fight, seeking a way to join his army with the forces under Joseph E. Johnston in North Carolina, Lee fell back doggedly. At Saylor's Creek on April 7 he fought a brave, but uneven contest that ended with Sheridan hacking Ewell's corps unmercifully, capturing Ewell, destroying 400 wagons and seizing sixteen artillery pieces. Irresistibly the dreadful truth was revealed to Lee and he said: "There is nothing left but to go and see General Grant, and I had rather die a thousand deaths." General E. Porter Alexander urged Lee to let the men take to the woods. "We would be like rabbits and partridges in the bushes and they could not scatter to follow us." But Lee shook his head, told Alexander to think of his country already "demoralized by four years of war," and added that if his army were to degenerate into "mere bands of marauders," they would bring on a situation from which the country might not recover for years. "You young fellows might go to bushwhacking," Lee said, "but the only dignified course for me would be to go to General Grant and surrender myself and take the consequences of my acts."

On April 9—Palm Sunday—Lee put on full uniform, embroidered belt and dress sword, tall hat and buff gauntlets. Officers watched, tears streaming down their cheeks, as he rode off to keep a rendezvous with Grant at Appomattox Court House. Lee was waiting when Grant and his staff strode up to the McLean farmhouse and dismounted.

"What General Lee's feelings were I do not know," Grant said afterward. "As he was a man of much dignity, it was impossible to say whether he felt inwardly glad, or felt sad and was too manly to show it. My own feelings, which had been quite jubilant on receipt of his letter [agreeing to this meeting], were sad and depressed."

The spirit of the occasion was that of two generals who were reuniting as countrymen. With a touch of self-consciousness, Grant apologized for coming straight from the field in a dusty, loose fatigue coat. He wore no side arms. The terms of surrender were discussed, written down on field notepaper, and signed. The ceremonies were brief and simple, then Lee shook hands with Grant, bowed to the other officers, and walked out onto the porch where, waiting for an aide to bring his horse, Lee three times struck the palm of his left hand with his right fist.

Grant stepped down from the porch and, moving toward Lee, raised his hat in salute. The other Union officers took off their hats and Lee returned the gesture of respect. Then, slowly, Lee rode off into the valley where the men in his army rushed to the roadside. They crowded around, shaking his hand, crying, "God help you, General." Lee struggled to speak and at last said: "Men, we have fought through this war together. I have done the best I could for you. My heart is too full to say more."

Five days later in Charleston Harbor the flag of the Union was raised once more above Fort Sumter by General Robert Anderson, who said:

"After four long, long years of war, I restore to its proper place this dear flag, which floated here during peace before the first act of this cruel rebellion. I thank God that I have lived to see this day, and to be here, to perform this, perhaps last act of my life, of duty to my country. My heart is filled with gratitude to that God who has so signally blessed us, who has given us blessings beyond measure. May all the nations bless and praise the name of the Lord, and all the world proclaim, 'Glory to God in the highest, and on earth peace, good-will toward men.'"

Lincoln, attending a Cabinet meeting on the morning of April 14, discussed Reconstruction: "We can't undertake to run State governments in all these Southern States. Their people must do that — though I reckon that at first some of them may do it badly." In the afternoon the President went for a drive with Mrs. Lincoln and spoke of the future: "Mary, we have had a hard time of it since we came to Washington, but the war is over, and with God's blessing we may hope for four years of peace and happiness, and then we will go back to Illinois and pass the rest of our lives in quiet." That evening Lincoln and his wife went to Ford's Theater to see Laura Keene in "Our American Cousin." A few minutes after ten, the door to the President's box was opened by an actor sorely sick in mind, John Wilkes Booth. He held a knife in one hand, a pistol in the other. He fired once. Lincoln slumped forward.

on the mortally wounded man, thought that his features were calm and striking. Next morning, at twenty-two minutes past seven, Abraham Lincoln died. In the silence of that startled room a voice whispered: "Now he belongs to the ages." Wrote Walt Whitman: "O Captain! my Captain! our fearful trip is done..."

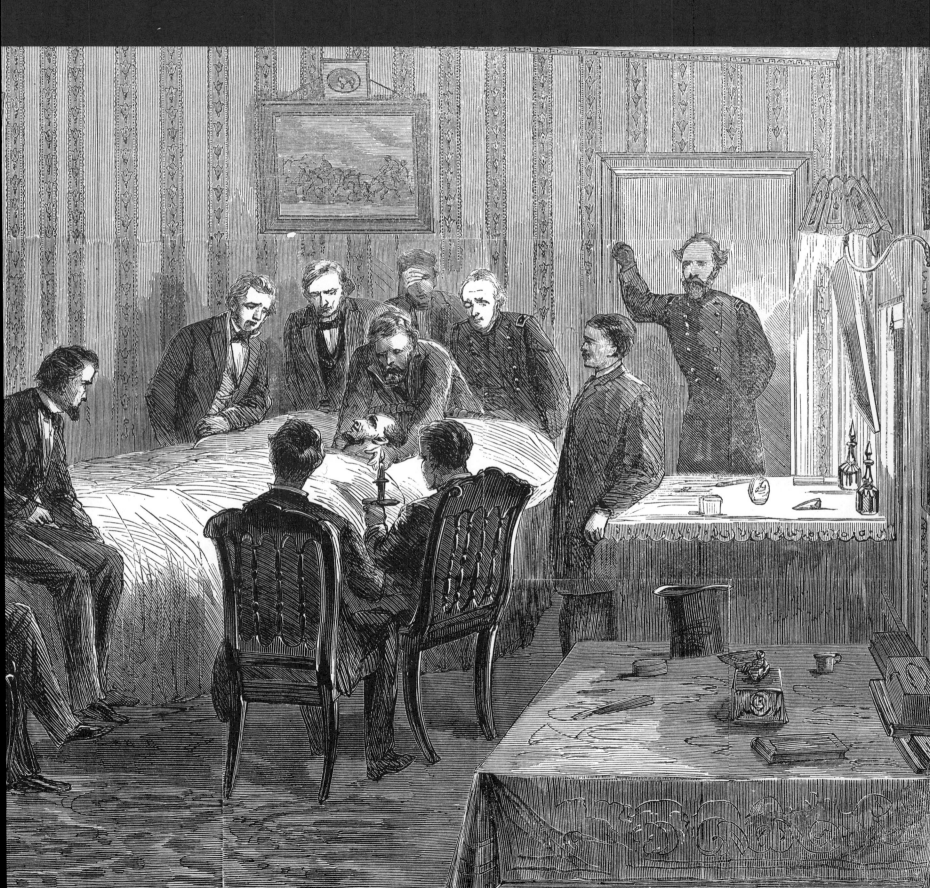

On May 23, 1865, 150,000 veterans of the Grand Army of the Republic marched triumphantly up Pennsylvania Avenue, Washington, D.C. before disbanding. Grant and Sherman shared the reviewing stand with President Johnson.

"*Under the sod and the dew, waiting the judgment-day; under the one, the Blue, under the other, the Gray*"—so sang Francis Miles Finch, inspired by a news item of how women in Columbus, Mississippi, had been impartial in their memory of the dead: "*They strewed flowers alike on the graves of the Confederate and of the National soldiers.*"